T0076689

Essentials of Compilation

Essentials of Compilation
An Incremental Approach in Python

Jeremy G. Siek

The MIT Press
Cambridge, Massachusetts
London, England

© 2023 Jeremy G. Siek

This work is subject to a Creative Commons CC-BY-ND-NC license.

Subject to such license, all rights are reserved.

The MIT Press would like to thank the anonymous peer reviewers who provided comments on drafts of this book. The generous work of academic experts is essential for establishing the authority and quality of our publications. We acknowledge with gratitude the contributions of these otherwise uncredited readers.

This book was set in Times LT Std Roman by the author. Printed and bound in the United States of America.

Library of Congress Cataloging-in-Publication Data

Names: Siek, Jeremy, author.
Title: Essentials of compilation : an incremental approach in Python / Jeremy G. Siek.
Description: Cambridge, Massachusetts : The MIT Press, [2023] | Includes bibliographical references and index.
Identifiers: LCCN 2022043053 (print) | LCCN 2022043054 (ebook) | ISBN 9780262048248 | ISBN 9780262375542 (epub) | ISBN 9780262375559 (pdf)
Subjects: LCSH: Compilers (Computer programs) | Python (Computer program language) | Programming languages (Electronic computers) | Computer programming.
Classification: LCC QA76.76.C65 S54 2023 (print) | LCC QA76.76.C65 (ebook) | DDC 005.4/53–dc23/eng/20221117
LC record available at https://lccn.loc.gov/2022043053
LC ebook record available at https://lccn.loc.gov/2022043054

10 9 8 7 6 5 4 3 2 1

This book is dedicated to Katie, my partner in everything, my children, who grew up during the writing of this book, and the programming language students at Indiana University, whose thoughtful questions made this a better book.

Contents

Preface

There is a magical moment when a programmer presses the *run* button and the software begins to execute. Somehow a program written in a high-level language is running on a computer that is capable only of shuffling bits. Here we reveal the wizardry that makes that moment possible. Beginning with the groundbreaking work of Backus and colleagues in the 1950s, computer scientists developed techniques for constructing programs called *compilers* that automatically translate high-level programs into machine code.

We take you on a journey through constructing your own compiler for a small but powerful language. Along the way we explain the essential concepts, algorithms, and data structures that underlie compilers. We develop your understanding of how programs are mapped onto computer hardware, which is helpful in reasoning about properties at the junction of hardware and software, such as execution time, software errors, and security vulnerabilities. For those interested in pursuing compiler construction as a career, our goal is to provide a stepping-stone to advanced topics such as just-in-time compilation, program analysis, and program optimization. For those interested in designing and implementing programming languages, we connect language design choices to their impact on the compiler and the generated code.

A compiler is typically organized as a sequence of stages that progressively translate a program to the code that runs on hardware. We take this approach to the extreme by partitioning our compiler into a large number of *nanopasses*, each of which performs a single task. This enables the testing of each pass in isolation and focuses our attention, making the compiler far easier to understand.

The most familiar approach to describing compilers is to dedicate each chapter to one pass. The problem with that approach is that it obfuscates how language features motivate design choices in a compiler. We instead take an *incremental* approach in which we build a complete compiler in each chapter, starting with a small input language that includes only arithmetic and variables. We add new language features in subsequent chapters, extending the compiler as necessary.

Our choice of language features is designed to elicit fundamental concepts and algorithms used in compilers.

- We begin with integer arithmetic and local variables in chapters 1 and 2, where we introduce the fundamental tools of compiler construction: *abstract syntax trees* and *recursive functions*.

- In chapter 3 we learn how to use the Lark parser framework to create a parser for the language of integer arithmetic and local variables. We learn about the parsing algorithms inside Lark, including Earley and LALR(1).
- In chapter 4 we apply *graph coloring* to assign variables to machine registers.
- Chapter 5 adds conditional expressions, which motivates an elegant recursive algorithm for translating them into conditional `goto` statements.
- Chapter 6 adds loops. This elicits the need for *dataflow analysis* in the register allocator.
- Chapter 7 adds heap-allocated tuples, motivating *garbage collection*.
- Chapter 8 adds functions as first-class values without lexical scoping, similar to functions in the C programming language (Kernighan and Ritchie 1988). The reader learns about the procedure call stack and *calling conventions* and how they interact with register allocation and garbage collection. The chapter also describes how to generate efficient tail calls.
- Chapter 9 adds anonymous functions with lexical scoping, that is, *lambda* expressions. The reader learns about *closure conversion*, in which lambdas are translated into a combination of functions and tuples.
- Chapter 10 adds *dynamic typing*. Prior to this point the input languages are statically typed. The reader extends the statically typed language with an **Any** type that serves as a target for compiling the dynamically typed language.
- Chapter 11 uses the **Any** type introduced in chapter 10 to implement a *gradually typed language* in which different regions of a program may be static or dynamically typed. The reader implements runtime support for *proxies* that allow values to safely move between regions.
- Chapter 12 adds *generics* with autoboxing, leveraging the **Any** type and type casts developed in chapters 10 and 11.

There are many language features that we do not include. Our choices balance the incidental complexity of a feature versus the fundamental concepts that it exposes. For example, we include tuples and not records because although they both elicit the study of heap allocation and garbage collection, records come with more incidental complexity.

Since 2009, drafts of this book have served as the textbook for sixteen-week compiler courses for upper-level undergraduates and first-year graduate students at the University of Colorado and Indiana University. Students come into the course having learned the basics of programming, data structures and algorithms, and discrete mathematics. At the beginning of the course, students form groups of two to four people. The groups complete approximately one chapter every two weeks, starting with chapter 2 and including chapters according to the students interests while respecting the dependencies between chapters shown in figure 0.1. Chapter 8 (functions) depends on chapter 7 (tuples) only in the implementation of efficient tail calls. The last two weeks of the course involve a final project in which students design and implement a compiler extension of their choosing. The last few chapters can be used in support of these projects. Many chapters include a challenge problem that we assign to the graduate students.

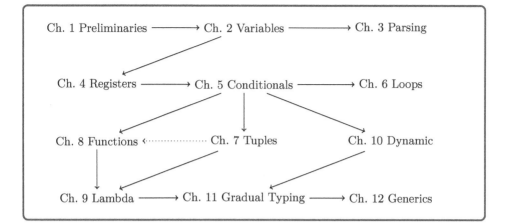

Figure 0.1
Diagram of chapter dependencies.

For compiler courses at universities on the quarter system (about ten weeks in length), we recommend completing the course through chapter 7 or chapter 8 and providing some scaffolding code to the students for each compiler pass. The course can be adapted to emphasize functional languages by skipping chapter 6 (loops) and including chapter 9 (lambda). The course can be adapted to dynamically typed languages by including chapter 10.

This book has been used in compiler courses at California Polytechnic State University, Portland State University, Rose–Hulman Institute of Technology, University of Freiburg, University of Massachusetts Lowell, and the University of Vermont.

This edition of the book uses Python both for the implementation of the compiler and for the input language, so the reader should be proficient with Python. There are many excellent resources for learning Python (Lutz 2013; Barry 2016; Sweigart 2019; Matthes 2019).The support code for this book is in the GitHub repository at the following location:

https://github.com/IUCompilerCourse/

The compiler targets x86 assembly language (Intel 2015), so it is helpful but not necessary for the reader to have taken a computer systems course (Bryant and O'Hallaron 2010). We introduce the parts of x86-64 assembly language that are needed in the compiler. We follow the System V calling conventions (Bryant and O'Hallaron 2005; Matz et al. 2013), so the assembly code that we generate works with the runtime system (written in C) when it is compiled using the GNU C compiler (`gcc`) on Linux and MacOS operating systems on Intel hardware. On the Windows operating system, `gcc` uses the Microsoft x64 calling convention (Microsoft 2018, 2020). So the assembly code that we generate does *not* work with the runtime system on Windows. One workaround is to use a virtual machine with Linux as the guest operating system.

Acknowledgments

The tradition of compiler construction at Indiana University goes back to research and courses on programming languages by Daniel Friedman in the 1970s and 1980s. One of his students, Kent Dybvig, implemented Chez Scheme (Dybvig 2006), an efficient, production-quality compiler for Scheme. Throughout the 1990s and 2000s, Dybvig taught the compiler course and continued the development of Chez Scheme. The compiler course evolved to incorporate novel pedagogical ideas while also including elements of real-world compilers. One of Friedman's ideas was to split the compiler into many small passes. Another idea, called "the game," was to test the code generated by each pass using interpreters.

Dybvig, with help from his students Dipanwita Sarkar and Andrew Keep, developed infrastructure to support this approach and evolved the course to use even smaller nanopasses (Sarkar, Waddell, and Dybvig 2004; Keep 2012). Many of the compiler design decisions in this book are inspired by the assignment descriptions of Dybvig and Keep (2010). In the mid 2000s, a student of Dybvig named Abdulaziz Ghuloum observed that the front-to-back organization of the course made it difficult for students to understand the rationale for the compiler design. Ghuloum proposed the incremental approach (Ghuloum 2006) on which this book is based.

I thank the many students who served as teaching assistants for the compiler course at IU including Carl Factora, Ryan Scott, Cameron Swords, and Chris Wailes. I thank Andre Kuhlenschmidt for work on the garbage collector and x86 interpreter, Michael Vollmer for work on efficient tail calls, and Michael Vitousek for help with the first offering of the incremental compiler course at IU.

I thank professors Bor-Yuh Chang, John Clements, Jay McCarthy, Joseph Near, Ryan Newton, Nate Nystrom, Peter Thiemann, Andrew Tolmach, and Michael Wollowski for teaching courses based on drafts of this book and for their feedback. I thank the National Science Foundation for the grants that helped to support this work: Grant Numbers 1518844, 1763922, and 1814460.

I thank Ronald Garcia for helping me survive Dybvig's compiler course in the early 2000s and especially for finding the bug that sent our garbage collector on a wild goose chase!

Jeremy G. Siek
Bloomington, Indiana

1 Preliminaries

In this chapter we introduce the basic tools needed to implement a compiler. Programs are typically input by a programmer as text, that is, a sequence of characters. The program-as-text representation is called *concrete syntax*. We use concrete syntax to concisely write down and talk about programs. Inside the compiler, we use *abstract syntax trees* (ASTs) to represent programs in a way that efficiently supports the operations that the compiler needs to perform. The process of translating concrete syntax to abstract syntax is called *parsing* and is studied in chapter 3. For now we use the **parse** function in Python's **ast** module to translate from concrete to abstract syntax.

ASTs can be represented inside the compiler in many different ways, depending on the programming language used to write the compiler. We use Python classes and objects to represent ASTs, especially the classes defined in the standard **ast** module for the Python source language. We use grammars to define the abstract syntax of programming languages (section 1.2) and pattern matching to inspect individual nodes in an AST (section 1.3). We use recursive functions to construct and deconstruct ASTs (section 1.4). This chapter provides a brief introduction to these components.

1.1 Abstract Syntax Trees

Compilers use abstract syntax trees to represent programs because they often need to ask questions such as, for a given part of a program, what kind of language feature is it? What are its subparts? Consider the program on the left and the diagram of its AST on the right (1.1). This program is an addition operation that has two subparts, a input operation and a negation. The negation has another subpart, the integer constant 8. By using a tree to represent the program, we can easily follow the links to go from one part of a program to its subparts.

$$\texttt{input\_int() + -8} \qquad\qquad (1.1)$$

We use the standard terminology for trees to describe ASTs: each rectangle above is called a *node*. The arrows connect a node to its *children*, which are also nodes. The top-most node is the *root*. Every node except for the root has a *parent* (the node of which it is the child). If a node has no children, it is a *leaf* node; otherwise it is an *internal* node.

We use a Python `class` for each kind of node. The following is the class definition for constants (aka literals) from the Python `ast` module.

```
class Constant:
  def __init__(self, value):
    self.value = value
```

An integer constant node includes just one thing: the integer value. To create an AST node for the integer 8, we write `Constant(8)`.

```
eight = Constant(8)
```

We say that the value created by `Constant(8)` is an *instance* of the `Constant` class. The following is the class definition for unary operators.

```
class UnaryOp:
  def __init__(self, op, operand):
    self.op = op
    self.operand = operand
```

The specific operation is specified by the `op` parameter. For example, the class `USub` is for unary subtraction. (More unary operators are introduced in later chapters.) To create an AST that negates the number 8, we write the following.

```
neg_eight = UnaryOp(USub(), eight)
```

The call to the `input_int` function is represented by the `Call` and `Name` classes.

```
class Call:
  def __init__(self, func, args):
    self.func = func
    self.args = args

class Name:
  def __init__(self, id):
    self.id = id
```

To create an AST node that calls `input_int`, we write

```
read = Call(Name('input_int'), [])
```

Finally, to represent the addition in (1.1), we use the `BinOp` class for binary operators.

```
class BinOp:
  def __init__(self, left, op, right):
    self.op = op
    self.left = left
    self.right = right
```

Similar to `UnaryOp`, the specific operation is specified by the `op` parameter, which for now is just an instance of the `Add` class. So to create the AST node that adds negative eight to some user input, we write the following.

```
ast1_1 = BinOp(read, Add(), neg_eight)
```

To compile a program such as (1.1), we need to know that the operation associated with the root node is addition and we need to be able to access its two children. Python provides pattern matching to support these kinds of queries, as we see in section 1.3.

We often write down the concrete syntax of a program even when we actually have in mind the AST, because the concrete syntax is more concise. We recommend that you always think of programs as abstract syntax trees.

1.2 Grammars

A programming language can be thought of as a *set* of programs. The set is infinite (that is, one can always create larger programs), so one cannot simply describe a language by listing all the programs in the language. Instead we write down a set of rules, a *context-free grammar*, for building programs. Grammars are often used to define the concrete syntax of a language, but they can also be used to describe the abstract syntax. We write our rules in a variant of Backus-Naur form (BNF) (Backus et al. 1960; Knuth 1964). As an example, we describe a small language, named $\mathcal{L}_{\mathsf{Int}}$, that consists of integers and arithmetic operations.

The first grammar rule for the abstract syntax of $\mathcal{L}_{\mathsf{Int}}$ says that an instance of the `Constant` class is an expression:

$$exp ::= \mathtt{Constant}\,(int) \tag{1.2}$$

Each rule has a left-hand side and a right-hand side. If you have an AST node that matches the right-hand side, then you can categorize it according to the left-hand side. Symbols in typewriter font, such as `Constant`, are *terminal* symbols and must literally appear in the program for the rule to be applicable. Our grammars do not mention *white space*, that is, delimiter characters like spaces, tabs, and new lines. White space may be inserted between symbols for disambiguation and to improve readability. A name such as *exp* that is defined by the grammar rules is a *nonterminal*. The name *int* is also a nonterminal, but instead of defining it with a grammar rule, we define it with the following explanation. An *int* is a sequence of decimals (0 to 9), possibly starting with – (for negative integers), such that the sequence of decimals represents an integer in the range -2^{63} to $2^{63} - 1$. This enables the representation of integers using 64 bits, which simplifies several aspects of compilation. In contrast, integers in Python have unlimited precision, but the techniques needed to handle unlimited precision fall outside the scope of this book.

The second grammar rule is the `input_int` operation, which receives an input integer from the user of the program.

$$exp ::= \mathtt{Call(Name('input\_int'),[])} \tag{1.3}$$

The third rule categorizes the negation of an *exp* node as an *exp*.

$$exp ::= \text{UnaryOp(USub(),} exp)\qquad\qquad(1.4)$$

We can apply these rules to categorize the ASTs that are in the $\mathcal{L}_{\text{Int}}$ language. For example, by rule (1.2), Constant(8) is an *exp*, and then by rule (1.4) the following AST is an *exp*.

UnaryOp(USub(), Constant(8))

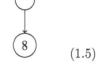

$$(1.5)$$

The next two grammar rules are for addition and subtraction expressions:

$$exp ::= \text{BinOp(}exp\text{,Add(),}exp)\qquad\qquad(1.6)$$

$$exp ::= \text{BinOp(}exp\text{,Sub(),}exp)\qquad\qquad(1.7)$$

We can now justify that the AST (1.1) is an *exp* in $\mathcal{L}_{\text{Int}}$. We know that $\text{Call(Name('input\_int'),[])}$ is an *exp* by rule (1.3), and we have already categorized $\text{UnaryOp(USub(), Constant(8))}$ as an *exp*, so we apply rule (1.6) to show that

$\text{BinOp(Call(Name('input\_int'),[]),Add(),UnaryOp(USub(),Constant(8)))}$

is an *exp* in the $\mathcal{L}_{\text{Int}}$ language.

If you have an AST for which these rules do not apply, then the AST is not in $\mathcal{L}_{\text{Int}}$. For example, the program input_int() * 8 is not in $\mathcal{L}_{\text{Int}}$ because there is no rule for the $*$ operator. Whenever we define a language with a grammar, the language includes only those programs that are justified by the grammar rules.

The language $\mathcal{L}_{\text{Int}}$ includes a second nonterminal *stmt* for statements. There is a statement for printing the value of an expression

$$stmt ::= \text{Expr(Call(Name('print'),[}exp\text{]))}$$

and a statement that evaluates an expression but ignores the result.

$$stmt ::= \text{Expr(}exp)$$

The last grammar rule for $\mathcal{L}_{\text{Int}}$ states that there is a Module node to mark the top of the whole program:

$$\mathcal{L}_{\text{Int}} ::= \text{Module(}stmt^*)$$

The asterisk $*$ indicates a list of the preceding grammar item, in this case a list of statements. The Module class is defined as follows:

```
class Module:
    def __init__(self, body):
        self.body = body
```

where body is a list of statements.

$$
\begin{aligned}
exp &\; ::= \; int \mid \texttt{input\_int()} \mid -exp \mid exp + exp \mid exp - exp \mid (exp) \\
stmt &\; ::= \; \texttt{print}(exp) \mid exp \\
\mathcal{L}_{\mathsf{Int}} &\; ::= \; stmt^*
\end{aligned}
$$

Figure 1.1
The concrete syntax of $\mathcal{L}_{\mathsf{Int}}$.

$$
\begin{aligned}
exp &\; ::= \; \texttt{Constant}(int) \mid \texttt{Call(Name('input\_int'),[])} \\
    &\quad\mid\; \texttt{UnaryOp(USub(),}exp\texttt{)} \mid \texttt{BinOp(}exp\texttt{,Add(),}exp\texttt{)} \\
    &\quad\mid\; \texttt{BinOp(}exp\texttt{,Sub(),}exp\texttt{)} \\
stmt &\; ::= \; \texttt{Expr(Call(Name('print'),[}exp\texttt{]))} \mid \texttt{Expr(}exp\texttt{)} \\
\mathcal{L}_{\mathsf{Int}} &\; ::= \; \texttt{Module(}stmt^*\texttt{)}
\end{aligned}
$$

Figure 1.2
The abstract syntax of $\mathcal{L}_{\mathsf{Int}}$.

It is common to have many grammar rules with the same left-hand side but different right-hand sides, such as the rules for *exp* in the grammar of $\mathcal{L}_{\mathsf{Int}}$. As shorthand, a vertical bar can be used to combine several right-hand sides into a single rule.

The concrete syntax for $\mathcal{L}_{\mathsf{Int}}$ is shown in figure 1.1 and the abstract syntax for $\mathcal{L}_{\mathsf{Int}}$ is shown in figure 1.2. We recommend using the **parse** function in Python's **ast** module to convert the concrete syntax into an abstract syntax tree.

1.3   Pattern Matching

As mentioned in section 1.1, compilers often need to access the parts of an AST node. As of version 3.10, Python provides the **match** feature to access the parts of a value. Consider the following example:

```
match ast1_1:
  case BinOp(child1, op, child2):
    print(op)
```

In the example above, the **match** form checks whether the AST (1.1) is a binary operator and binds its parts to the three pattern variables (**child1**, **op**, and **child2**). In general, each **case** consists of a *pattern* and a *body*. Patterns are recursively defined to be one of the following: a pattern variable, a class name followed by a pattern for each of its constructor's arguments, or other literals such as strings or lists. The body of each **case** may contain arbitrary Python code. The pattern variables can be used in the body, such as **op** in **print(op)**.

A `match` form may contain several clauses, as in the following function `leaf` that recognizes when an $\mathcal{L}_{\mathsf{Int}}$ node is a leaf in the AST. The `match` proceeds through the clauses in order, checking whether the pattern can match the input AST. The body of the first clause that matches is executed. The output of `leaf` for several ASTs is shown on the right side of the following:

```
def leaf(arith):
    match arith:
        case Constant(n):
            return True
        case Call(Name('input_int'), []):
            return True
        case UnaryOp(USub(), e1):
            return False
        case BinOp(e1, Add(), e2):
            return False
        case BinOp(e1, Sub(), e2):
            return False

print(leaf(Call(Name('input_int'), [])))          True
print(leaf(UnaryOp(USub(), eight)))               False
print(leaf(Constant(8)))                          True
```

When constructing a `match` expression, we refer to the grammar definition to identify which nonterminal we are expecting to match against, and then we make sure that (1) we have one case for each alternative of that nonterminal and (2) the pattern in each case corresponds to the corresponding right-hand side of a grammar rule. For the `match` in the `leaf` function, we refer to the grammar for $\mathcal{L}_{\mathsf{Int}}$ shown in figure 1.2. The *exp* nonterminal has five alternatives, so the `match` has five cases. The pattern in each case corresponds to the right-hand side of a grammar rule. For example, the pattern `BinOp(e1,Add(),e2)` corresponds to the right-hand side `BinOp(`*exp*`,Add(),`*exp*`)`. When translating from grammars to patterns, replace nonterminals such as *exp* with pattern variables of your choice (such as `e1` and `e2`).

1.4 Recursive Functions

Programs are inherently recursive. For example, an expression is often made of smaller expressions. Thus, the natural way to process an entire program is to use a recursive function. As a first example of such a recursive function, we define the function `is_exp` as shown in figure 1.3, to take an arbitrary value and determine whether or not it is an expression in $\mathcal{L}_{\mathsf{Int}}$. We say that a function is defined by *structural recursion* if it is defined using a sequence of match cases that correspond to a grammar and the body of each case makes a recursive call on each child node.[1] We define a second function, named `is_stmt`, that recognizes whether a value is

---

1. This principle of structuring code according to the data definition is advocated in the book *How to Design Programs* by Felleisen et al. (2001).

```
def is_exp(e):
  match e:
    case Constant(n):
      return True
    case Call(Name('input_int'), []):
      return True
    case UnaryOp(USub(), e1):
      return is_exp(e1)
    case BinOp(e1, Add(), e2):
      return is_exp(e1) and is_exp(e2)
    case BinOp(e1, Sub(), e2):
      return is_exp(e1) and is_exp(e2)
    case _:
      return False

def is_stmt(s):
  match s:
    case Expr(Call(Name('print'), [e])):
      return is_exp(e)
    case Expr(e):
      return is_exp(e)
    case _:
      return False

def is_Lint(p):
  match p:
    case Module(body):
      return all([is_stmt(s) for s in body])
    case _:
      return False

print(is_Lint(Module([Expr(ast1_1)])))
print(is_Lint(Module([Expr(BinOp(read, Sub(),
             UnaryOp(Add(), Constant(8))))])))
```

Figure 1.3
Example of recursive functions for $\mathcal{L}_{\mathsf{Int}}$. These functions recognize whether an AST is in $\mathcal{L}_{\mathsf{Int}}$.

a $\mathcal{L}_{\mathsf{Int}}$ statement. Finally, figure 1.3 contains the definition of is_Lint, which determines whether an AST is a program in $\mathcal{L}_{\mathsf{Int}}$. In general, we can write one recursive function to handle each nonterminal in a grammar. Of the two examples at the bottom of the figure, the first is in $\mathcal{L}_{\mathsf{Int}}$ and the second is not.

1.5 Interpreters

The behavior of a program is defined by the specification of the programming language. For example, the Python language is defined in the Python language reference (Python Software Foundation 2021b) and the CPython interpreter (Python Software Foundation 2021a). In this book we use interpreters to specify each language that we consider. An interpreter that is designated as the definition of a language is called a *definitional interpreter* (Reynolds 1972). We warm up by creating a definitional interpreter for the $\mathcal{L}_{\mathsf{Int}}$ language. This interpreter serves as a second example of structural recursion. The definition of the `interp_Lint` function is shown in figure 1.4. The body of the function matches on the `Module` AST node and then invokes `interp_stmt` on each statement in the module. The `interp_stmt` function includes a case for each grammar rule of the *stmt* nonterminal, and it calls `interp_exp` on each subexpression. The `interp_exp` function includes a case for each grammar rule of the *exp* nonterminal. We use several auxiliary functions such as `add64` and `input_int` that are defined in the support code for this book.

Let us consider the result of interpreting a few $\mathcal{L}_{\mathsf{Int}}$ programs. The following program adds two integers:

```
print(10 + 32)
```

The result is 42, the answer to life, the universe, and everything: 42![2] We wrote this program in concrete syntax, whereas the parsed abstract syntax is

```
Module([Expr(Call(Name('print'),
                  [BinOp(Constant(10), Add(), Constant(32))]))])
```

The following program demonstrates that expressions may be nested within each other, in this case nesting several additions and negations.

```
print(10 + -(12 + 20))
```

What is the result of this program?

The last feature of the $\mathcal{L}_{\mathsf{Int}}$ language, the `input_int` operation, prompts the user of the program for an integer. Recall that program (1.1) requests an integer input and then subtracts 8. So, if we run

```
interp_Lint(Module([Expr(Call(Name('print'), [ast1_1]))]))
```

and if the input is 50, the result is 42.

We include the `input_int` operation in $\mathcal{L}_{\mathsf{Int}}$ so that a clever student cannot implement a compiler for $\mathcal{L}_{\mathsf{Int}}$ that simply runs the interpreter during compilation to obtain the output and then generates the trivial code to produce the output.[3]

The job of a compiler is to translate a program in one language into a program in another language so that the output program behaves the same way as the input program. This idea is depicted in the following diagram. Suppose we have

---

2. *The Hitchhiker's Guide to the Galaxy* by Douglas Adams.
3. Yes, a clever student did this in the first instance of this course!

```
def interp_exp(e):
    match e:
        case BinOp(left, Add(), right):
            l = interp_exp(left); r = interp_exp(right)
            return add64(l, r)
        case BinOp(left, Sub(), right):
            l = interp_exp(left); r = interp_exp(right)
            return sub64(l, r)
        case UnaryOp(USub(), v):
            return neg64(interp_exp(v))
        case Constant(value):
            return value
        case Call(Name('input_int'), []):
            return input_int()

def interp_stmt(s):
    match s:
        case Expr(Call(Name('print'), [arg])):
            print(interp_exp(arg))
        case Expr(value):
            interp_exp(value)

def interp_Lint(p):
    match p:
        case Module(body):
            for s in body:
                interp_stmt(s)
```

Figure 1.4
Interpreter for the $\mathcal{L}_{\mathsf{Int}}$ language.

two languages, $\mathcal{L}_1$ and $\mathcal{L}_2$, and a definitional interpreter for each language. Given a compiler that translates from language $\mathcal{L}_1$ to $\mathcal{L}_2$ and given any program P_1 in $\mathcal{L}_1$, the compiler must translate it into some program P_2 such that interpreting P_1 and P_2 on their respective interpreters with same input i yields the same output o.

$$
\begin{array}{ccc}
 & \xrightarrow{\text{compile}} & \\
P_1 & & P_2 \\
 & \text{interp\_}\mathcal{L}_1(i) \quad \Big\downarrow \text{interp\_}\mathcal{L}_2(i) & \\
 & o &
\end{array}
\tag{1.8}
$$

We establish the convention that if running the definitional interpreter on a program produces an error, then the meaning of that program is *unspecified* unless the exception raised is a `TrappedError`. A compiler for the language is under no

obligation regarding programs with unspecified behavior; it does not have to produce an executable, and if it does, that executable can do anything. On the other
hand, if the error is a `TrappedError`, then the compiler must produce an executable
and it is required to report that an error occurred. To signal an error, exit with a
return code of 255. The interpreters in chapters 10 and 11 and in section 7.9 use
`TrappedError`.

In the next section we see our first example of a compiler.

1.6 Example Compiler: A Partial Evaluator

In this section we consider a compiler that translates $\mathcal{L}_{Int}$ programs into $\mathcal{L}_{Int}$
programs that may be more efficient. The compiler eagerly computes the parts
of the program that do not depend on any inputs, a process known as *partial
evaluation* (Jones, Gomard, and Sestoft 1993). For example, given the following
program

```
print(input_int() + -(5 + 3) )
```

our compiler translates it into the program

```
print(input_int() + -8)
```

Figure 1.5 gives the code for a simple partial evaluator for the $\mathcal{L}_{Int}$ language. The
output of the partial evaluator is a program in $\mathcal{L}_{Int}$. In figure 1.5, the structural
recursion over *exp* is captured in the `pe_exp` function, whereas the code for partially
evaluating the negation and addition operations is factored into three auxiliary
functions: `pe_neg`, `pe_add` and `pe_sub`. The input to these functions is the output
of partially evaluating the children. The `pe_neg`, `pe_add` and `pe_sub` functions
check whether their arguments are integers and if they are, perform the appropriate
arithmetic. Otherwise, they create an AST node for the arithmetic operation.

To gain some confidence that the partial evaluator is correct, we can test whether
it produces programs that produce the same result as the input programs. That is,
we can test whether it satisfies the diagram of (1.8).

Exercise 1.1 Create three programs in the $\mathcal{L}_{Int}$ language and test whether partially
evaluating them with `pe_Lint` and then interpreting them with `interp_Lint` gives
the same result as directly interpreting them with `interp_Lint`.

```
def pe_neg(r):
  match r:
    case Constant(n):
      return Constant(neg64(n))
    case _:
      return UnaryOp(USub(), r)

def pe_add(r1, r2):
  match (r1, r2):
    case (Constant(n1), Constant(n2)):
      return Constant(add64(n1, n2))
    case _:
      return BinOp(r1, Add(), r2)

def pe_sub(r1, r2):
  match (r1, r2):
    case (Constant(n1), Constant(n2)):
      return Constant(sub64(n1, n2))
    case _:
      return BinOp(r1, Sub(), r2)

def pe_exp(e):
  match e:
    case BinOp(left, Add(), right):
      return pe_add(pe_exp(left), pe_exp(right))
    case BinOp(left, Sub(), right):
      return pe_sub(pe_exp(left), pe_exp(right))
    case UnaryOp(USub(), v):
      return pe_neg(pe_exp(v))
    case Constant(value):
      return e
    case Call(Name('input_int'), []):
      return e

def pe_stmt(s):
  match s:
    case Expr(Call(Name('print'), [arg])):
      return Expr(Call(Name('print'), [pe_exp(arg)]))
    case Expr(value):
      return Expr(pe_exp(value))

def pe_P_int(p):
  match p:
    case Module(body):
      new_body = [pe_stmt(s) for s in body]
      return Module(new_body)
```

Figure 1.5
A partial evaluator for $\mathcal{L}_{\mathsf{Int}}$.

2   Integers and Variables

This chapter covers compiling a subset of Python to x86-64 assembly code (Intel 2015). The subset, named $\mathcal{L}_{Var}$, includes integer arithmetic and local variables. We often refer to x86-64 simply as x86. The chapter first describes the $\mathcal{L}_{Var}$ language (section 2.1) and then introduces x86 assembly (section 2.2). Because x86 assembly language is large, we discuss only the instructions needed for compiling $\mathcal{L}_{Var}$. We introduce more x86 instructions in subsequent chapters. After introducing $\mathcal{L}_{Var}$ and x86, we reflect on their differences and create a plan to break down the translation from $\mathcal{L}_{Var}$ to x86 into a handful of steps (section 2.3). The rest of the chapter gives detailed hints regarding each step. We aim to give enough hints that the well-prepared reader, together with a few friends, can implement a compiler from $\mathcal{L}_{Var}$ to x86 in a short time. To suggest the scale of this first compiler, we note that the instructor solution for the $\mathcal{L}_{Var}$ compiler is approximately 300 lines of code.

2.1   The $\mathcal{L}_{Var}$ Language

The $\mathcal{L}_{Var}$ language extends the $\mathcal{L}_{Int}$ language with variables. The concrete syntax of the $\mathcal{L}_{Var}$ language is defined by the grammar presented in figure 2.1, and the abstract syntax is presented in figure 2.2. The nonterminal *var* may be any Python identifier. As in $\mathcal{L}_{Int}$, input_int is a nullary operator, - is a unary operator, and + is a binary operator. Similarly to $\mathcal{L}_{Int}$, the abstract syntax of $\mathcal{L}_{Var}$ includes the Module instance to mark the top of the program. Despite the simplicity of the $\mathcal{L}_{Var}$ language, it is rich enough to exhibit several compilation techniques.

The $\mathcal{L}_{Var}$ language includes an assignment statement, which defines a variable for use in later statements and initializes the variable with the value of an expression. The abstract syntax for assignment is defined in figure 2.2. The concrete syntax for assignment is

   var = *exp*

For example, the following program initializes the variable x to 32 and then prints the result of 10 + x, producing 42.

```
x = 12 + 20
print(10 + x)
```

$$
\begin{array}{rcl}
exp & ::= & int \mid \mathtt{input\_int\,()} \mid -exp \mid exp + exp \mid exp - exp \mid (exp) \\
stmt & ::= & \mathtt{print}\,(exp) \mid exp \\
\hline
exp & ::= & var \\
stmt & ::= & var = exp \\
\mathcal{L}_{\mathsf{Var}} & ::= & stmt^*
\end{array}
$$

Figure 2.1
The concrete syntax of $\mathcal{L}_{\mathsf{Var}}$.

$$
\begin{array}{rcl}
exp & ::= & \mathtt{Constant}\,(int) \mid \mathtt{Call(Name('input\_int'),[])} \\
 & \mid & \mathtt{UnaryOp(USub()}, exp) \mid \mathtt{BinOp}(exp, \mathtt{Add()}, exp) \\
 & \mid & \mathtt{BinOp}(exp, \mathtt{Sub()}, exp) \\
stmt & ::= & \mathtt{Expr(Call(Name('print'),[}exp\mathtt{]))} \mid \mathtt{Expr}(exp) \\
\hline
exp & ::= & \mathtt{Name}(var) \\
stmt & ::= & \mathtt{Assign([Name}(var)\mathtt{]},\ exp) \\
\mathcal{L}_{\mathsf{Var}} & ::= & \mathtt{Module}(stmt^*)
\end{array}
$$

Figure 2.2
The abstract syntax of $\mathcal{L}_{\mathsf{Var}}$.

2.1.1 Extensible Interpreters via Method Overriding

To prepare for discussing the interpreter of $\mathcal{L}_{\mathsf{Var}}$, we explain why we implement it in an object-oriented style. Throughout this book we define many interpreters, one for each language that we study. Because each language builds on the prior one, there is a lot of commonality between these interpreters. We want to write down the common parts just once instead of many times. A naive interpreter for $\mathcal{L}_{\mathsf{Var}}$ would handle the case for variables but dispatch to an interpreter for $\mathcal{L}_{\mathsf{Int}}$ in the rest of the cases. The following code sketches this idea. (We explain the `env` parameter in section 2.1.2.)

```
def interp_Lint(e, env):           def interp_Lvar(e, env):
  match e:                           match e:
    case UnaryOp(USub(), e1):          case Name(id):
      return - interp_Lint(e1, env)      return env[id]
    ...                                case _:
                                         return interp_Lint(e, env)
```

The problem with this naive approach is that it does not handle situations in which an $\mathcal{L}_{\mathsf{Var}}$ feature, such as a variable, is nested inside an $\mathcal{L}_{\mathsf{Int}}$ feature, such as the − operator, as in the following program.

```
y = 10
print(-y)
```

If we invoke `interp_Lvar` on this program, it dispatches to `interp_Lint` to handle
the - operator, but then it recursively calls `interp_Lint` again on its argument.
Because there is no case for `Name` in `interp_Lint`, we get an error!

To make our interpreters extensible we need something called *open recursion*, in
which the tying of the recursive knot is delayed until the functions are composed.
Object-oriented languages provide open recursion via method overriding. The fol-
lowing code uses method overriding to interpret $\mathcal{L}_{Int}$ and $\mathcal{L}_{Var}$ using Python `class`
definitions. We define one class for each language and define a method for inter-
preting expressions inside each class. The class for $\mathcal{L}_{Var}$ inherits from the class for
$\mathcal{L}_{Int}$, and the method `interp_exp` in $\mathcal{L}_{Var}$ overrides the `interp_exp` in $\mathcal{L}_{Int}$. Note
that the default case of `interp_exp` in $\mathcal{L}_{Var}$ uses `super` to invoke `interp_exp`, and
because $\mathcal{L}_{Var}$ inherits from $\mathcal{L}_{Int}$, that dispatches to the `interp_exp` in $\mathcal{L}_{Int}$.

```
class InterpLint:                     def InterpLvar(InterpLint):
  def interp_exp(e):                    def interp_exp(e):
    match e:                              match e:
      case UnaryOp(USub(), e1):             case Name(id):
        return neg64(self.interp_exp(e1))     return env[id]
        ...                                 case _:
    ...                                       return super().interp_exp(e)
                                          ...
```

We return to the troublesome example, repeated here:

```
y = 10
print(-y)
```

We can invoke the `interp_exp` method for $\mathcal{L}_{Var}$ on the -y expression, which we call
e0, by creating an object of the $\mathcal{L}_{Var}$ class and calling the `interp_exp` method

```
InterpLvar().interp_exp(e0)
```

To process the - operator, the default case of `interp_exp` in $\mathcal{L}_{Var}$ dispatches to the
`interp_exp` method in $\mathcal{L}_{Int}$. But then for the recursive method call, it dispatches
to `interp_exp` in $\mathcal{L}_{Var}$, where the `Name` node is handled correctly. Thus, method
overriding gives us the open recursion that we need to implement our interpreters
in an extensible way.

2.1.2 Definitional Interpreter for $\mathcal{L}_{Var}$

Having justified the use of classes and methods to implement interpreters, we revisit
the definitional interpreter for $\mathcal{L}_{Int}$ shown in figure 2.3 and then extend it to create
an interpreter for $\mathcal{L}_{Var}$, shown in figure 2.4. We change the `interp_stmt` method in
the interpreter for $\mathcal{L}_{Int}$ to take two extra parameters named `env`, which we discuss
in the next paragraph, and `cont` for *continuation*, which is the technical name for
what comes after a particular point in a program. The `cont` parameter is the list
of statements that follow the current statement. Note that `interp_stmts` invokes
`interp_stmt` on the first statement and passes the rest of the statements as the
argument for `cont`. This organization enables each statement to decide what if

anything should be evaluated after it, for example, allowing a **return** statement to exit early from a function (see Chapter 8).

The interpreter for $\mathcal{L}_{\mathsf{Var}}$ adds two new cases for variables and assignment. For assignment, we need a way to communicate the value bound to a variable to all the uses of the variable. To accomplish this, we maintain a mapping from variables to values called an *environment*. We use a Python dictionary to represent the environment. The **interp_exp** function takes the current environment, **env**, as an extra parameter. When the interpreter encounters a variable, it looks up the corresponding value in the environment. If the variable is not in the environment (because the variable was not defined) then the lookup will fail and the interpreter will halt with an error. Recall that the compiler is not obligated to compile such programs (Section 1.5).[1] When the interpreter encounters an assignment, it evaluates the initializing expression and then associates the resulting value with the variable in the environment.

The goal for this chapter is to implement a compiler that translates any program P_1 written in the $\mathcal{L}_{\mathsf{Var}}$ language into an x86 assembly program P_2 such that P_2 exhibits the same behavior when run on a computer as the P_1 program interpreted by **interp_Lvar**. That is, they output the same integer n. We depict this correctness criteria in the following diagram:

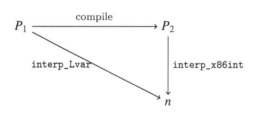

Next we introduce the x86$_{\mathsf{Int}}$ subset of x86 that suffices for compiling $\mathcal{L}_{\mathsf{Var}}$.

2.2 The x86$_{\mathsf{Int}}$ Assembly Language

Figure 2.5 defines the concrete syntax for x86$_{\mathsf{Int}}$. We use the AT&T syntax expected by the GNU assembler. A program begins with a **main** label followed by a sequence of instructions. The **globl** directive makes the **main** procedure externally visible so that the operating system can call it. An x86 program is stored in the computer's memory. For our purposes, the computer's memory is a mapping of 64-bit addresses to 64-bit values. The computer has a *program counter* (PC) stored in the **rip** register that points to the address of the next instruction to be executed. For most instructions, the program counter is incremented after the instruction is executed so that it points to the next instruction in memory. Most x86 instructions take two operands, each of which is an integer constant (called an *immediate value*), a *register*, or a memory location.

---

1. In Chapter 5 we introduce type checking rules that prohibit access to undefined variables.

```
class InterpLint:
  def interp_exp(self, e, env):
    match e:
      case BinOp(left, Add(), right):
        l = self.interp_exp(left, env)
        r = self.interp_exp(right, env)
        return add64(l, r)
      case BinOp(left, Sub(), right):
        l = self.interp_exp(left, env)
        r = self.interp_exp(right, env)
        return sub64(l, r)
      case UnaryOp(USub(), v):
        return neg64(self.interp_exp(v, env))
      case Constant(value):
        return value
      case Call(Name('input_int'), []):
        return int(input())

  def interp_stmt(self, s, env, cont):
    match s:
      case Expr(Call(Name('print'), [arg])):
        val = self.interp_exp(arg, env)
        print(val, end='')
        return self.interp_stmts(cont, env)
      case Expr(value):
        self.interp_exp(value, env)
        return self.interp_stmts(cont, env)
      case _:
        raise Exception('error in interp_stmt, unexpected ' + repr(s))

  def interp_stmts(self, ss, env):
    match ss:
      case []:
        return 0
      case [s, *ss]:
        return self.interp_stmt(s, env, ss)

  def interp(self, p):
    match p:
      case Module(body):
        self.interp_stmts(body, {})

def interp_Lint(p):
  return InterpLint().interp(p)
```

Figure 2.3
Interpreter for $\mathcal{L}_{\mathsf{Int}}$ as a class.

```
class InterpLvar(InterpLint):
  def interp_exp(self, e, env):
    match e:
      case Name(id):
        return env[id]
      case _:
        return super().interp_exp(e, env)

  def interp_stmt(self, s, env, cont):
    match s:
      case Assign([Name(id)], value):
        env[id] = self.interp_exp(value, env)
        return self.interp_stmts(cont, env)
      case _:
        return super().interp_stmt(s, env, cont)

def interp_Lvar(p):
  return InterpLvar().interp(p)
```

Figure 2.4
Interpreter for the $\mathcal{L}_{\mathsf{Var}}$ language.

$$
\begin{array}{lll}
reg & ::= & \text{rsp} \mid \text{rbp} \mid \text{rax} \mid \text{rbx} \mid \text{rcx} \mid \text{rdx} \mid \text{rsi} \mid \text{rdi} \mid \\
    &   & \text{r8} \mid \text{r9} \mid \text{r10} \mid \text{r11} \mid \text{r12} \mid \text{r13} \mid \text{r14} \mid \text{r15} \\
arg & ::= & \$int \mid \%reg \mid int(\%reg) \\
instr & ::= & \text{addq}\, arg, arg \mid \text{subq}\, arg, arg \mid \text{negq}\, arg \mid \text{movq}\, arg, arg \mid \\
      &   & \text{callq}\, label \mid \text{pushq}\, arg \mid \text{popq}\, arg \mid \text{retq} \\
\text{x86}_{\mathsf{Int}} & ::= & \text{.globl main} \\
      &   & \text{main}: instr^*
\end{array}
$$

Figure 2.5
The syntax of the x86$_{\mathsf{Int}}$ assembly language (AT&T syntax).

A register is a special kind of variable that holds a 64-bit value. There are 16 general-purpose registers in the computer; their names are given in figure 2.5. A register is written with a percent sign, %, followed by its name, for example, %rax.

An immediate value is written using the notation $\$n$ where n is an integer. An access to memory is specified using the syntax $n(\%r)$, which obtains the address stored in register r and then adds n bytes to the address. The resulting address is used to load or to store to memory depending on whether it occurs as a source or destination argument of an instruction.

An arithmetic instruction such as $\text{addq}\, s, d$ reads from the source s and destination d, applies the arithmetic operation, and then writes the result to the

```
      .globl main
  main:
      movq $10, %rax
      addq $32, %rax
      retq
```

Figure 2.6
An x86 program that computes 10 + 32.

destination d. The move instruction $movq\,s,d$ reads from s and stores the result in d. The callq *label* instruction jumps to the procedure specified by the label, and retq returns from a procedure to its caller. We discuss procedure calls in more detail further in this chapter and in chapter 8. The last letter q indicates that these instructions operate on quadwords, which are 64-bit values.

Appendix A.1 contains a reference for all the x86 instructions used in this book.

Figure 2.6 depicts an x86 program that computes 10 + 32. The instruction movq $10, %rax puts 10 into register rax, and then addq $32, %rax adds 32 to the 10 in rax and puts the result, 42, into rax. The last instruction retq finishes the main function by returning the integer in rax to the operating system. The operating system interprets this integer as the program's exit code. By convention, an exit code of 0 indicates that a program has completed successfully, and all other exit codes indicate various errors.

We exhibit the use of memory for storing intermediate results in the next example. Figure 2.7 lists an x86 program that computes 52 + -10. This program uses a region of memory called the *procedure call stack* (*stack* for short). The stack consists of a separate *frame* for each procedure call. The memory layout for an individual frame is shown in figure 2.8. The register rsp is called the *stack pointer* and contains the address of the item at the top of the stack. In general, we use the term *pointer* for something that contains an address. The stack grows downward in memory, so we increase the size of the stack by subtracting from the stack pointer. In the context of a procedure call, the *return address* is the location of the instruction that immediately follows the call instruction on the caller side. The function call instruction, callq, pushes the return address onto the stack prior to jumping to the procedure. The register rbp is the *base pointer* and is used to access variables that are stored in the frame of the current procedure call. The base pointer of the caller is stored immediately after the return address. Figure 2.8 shows the memory layout of a frame with storage for n variables, which are numbered from 1 to n. Variable 1 is stored at address –8(%rbp), variable 2 at –16(%rbp), and so on.

In the program shown in figure 2.7, consider how control is transferred from the operating system to the main function. The operating system issues a callq main instruction that pushes its return address on the stack and then jumps to main. In x86-64, the stack pointer rsp must be divisible by 16 bytes prior to the execution of any callq instruction, so that when control arrives at main, the rsp is 8 bytes

```
    .globl main
main:
    pushq      %rbp
    movq       %rsp, %rbp
    subq       $16, %rsp
    movq       $10, -8(%rbp)
    negq       -8(%rbp)
    movq       -8(%rbp), %rax
    addq       $52, %rax
    addq       $16, %rsp
    popq       %rbp
    retq
```

Figure 2.7
An x86 program that computes 52 + -10.

Position	Contents
8(%rbp)	return address
0(%rbp)	old rbp
–8(%rbp)	variable 1
–16(%rbp)	variable 2
...	...
0(%rsp)	variable n

Figure 2.8
Memory layout of a frame.

out of alignment (because the `callq` pushed the return address). The first three instructions are the typical *prelude* for a procedure. The instruction `pushq %rbp` first subtracts 8 from the stack pointer `rsp` and then saves the base pointer of the caller at address `rsp` on the stack. The next instruction `movq %rsp, %rbp` sets the base pointer to the current stack pointer, which is pointing to the location of the old base pointer. The instruction `subq $16, %rsp` moves the stack pointer down to make enough room for storing variables. This program needs one variable (8 bytes), but we round up to 16 bytes so that `rsp` is 16-byte-aligned, and then we are ready to make calls to other functions.

The first instruction after the prelude is `movq $10, -8(%rbp)`, which stores 10 in variable 1. The instruction `negq -8(%rbp)` changes the contents of variable 1 to –10. The next instruction moves the –10 from variable 1 into the `rax` register. Finally, `addq $52, %rax` adds 52 to the value in `rax`, updating its contents to 42.

The *conclusion* of the `main` function consists of the last three instructions. The first two restore the `rsp` and `rbp` registers to their states at the beginning of the procedure. In particular, `addq $16, %rsp` moves the stack pointer to point to the old base pointer. Then `popq %rbp` restores the old base pointer to `rbp` and adds 8

```
reg    ::=  'rsp' | 'rbp' | 'rax' | 'rbx' | 'rcx' | 'rdx' | 'rsi' | 'rdi' |
            'r8' | 'r9' | 'r10' | 'r11' | 'r12' | 'r13' | 'r14' | 'r15'
arg    ::=  Immediate(int) | Reg(reg) | Deref(reg,int)
instr  ::=  Instr('addq',[arg,arg]) | Instr('subq',[arg,arg])
        |   Instr('movq',[arg,arg]) | Instr('negq',[arg])
        |   Instr('pushq',[arg]) | Instr('popq',[arg])
        |   Callq(label,int) | Retq() | Jump(label)
x86Int ::=  X86Program(instr*)
```

Figure 2.9
The abstract syntax of x86$_{Int}$ assembly.

to the stack pointer. The last instruction, retq, jumps back to the procedure that called this one and adds 8 to the stack pointer.

Our compiler needs a convenient representation for manipulating x86 programs, so we define an abstract syntax for x86, shown in figure 2.9. We refer to this language as x86$_{Int}$. The main difference between this and the concrete syntax of x86$_{Int}$ (figure 2.5) is that labels, instruction names, and register names are explicitly represented by strings. Regarding the abstract syntax for callq, the Callq AST node includes an integer for representing the arity of the function, that is, the number of arguments, which is helpful to know during register allocation (chapter 4).

2.3 Planning the Trip to x86

To compile one language to another, it helps to focus on the differences between the two languages because the compiler will need to bridge those differences. What are the differences between $\mathcal{L}_{Var}$ and x86 assembly? Here are some of the most important ones:

1. x86 arithmetic instructions typically have two arguments and update the second argument in place. In contrast, $\mathcal{L}_{Var}$ arithmetic operations take two arguments and produce a new value. An x86 instruction may have at most one memory-accessing argument. Furthermore, some x86 instructions place special restrictions on their arguments.
2. An argument of an $\mathcal{L}_{Var}$ operator can be a deeply nested expression, whereas x86 instructions restrict their arguments to be integer constants, registers, and memory locations.
3. A program in $\mathcal{L}_{Var}$ can have any number of variables, whereas x86 has 16 registers and the procedure call stack.

We ease the challenge of compiling from $\mathcal{L}_{Var}$ to x86 by breaking down the problem into several steps, which deal with these differences one at a time. Each of these steps is called a *pass* of the compiler. This term indicates that each step passes over, or traverses, the AST of the program. Furthermore, we follow the nanopass approach, which means that we strive for each pass to accomplish one clear objective rather than two or three at the same time. We begin by sketching how we might implement each pass and give each pass a name. We then figure out an ordering of the passes and the input/output language for each pass. The very first pass has $\mathcal{L}_{\mathsf{Var}}$ as its input language, and the last pass has $\mathsf{x86}_{\mathsf{Int}}$ as its output language. In between these two passes, we can choose whichever language is most convenient for expressing the output of each pass, whether that be $\mathcal{L}_{\mathsf{Var}}$, $\mathsf{x86}_{\mathsf{Int}}$, or a new *intermediate language* of our own design. Finally, to implement each pass we write one recursive function per nonterminal in the grammar of the input language of the pass.

Our compiler for $\mathcal{L}_{\mathsf{Var}}$ consists of the following passes:

remove_complex_operands ensures that each subexpression of a primitive operation or function call is a variable or integer, that is, an *atomic* expression. We refer to nonatomic expressions as *complex*. This pass introduces temporary variables to hold the results of complex subexpressions.

select_instructions handles the difference between $\mathcal{L}_{\mathsf{Var}}$ operations and x86 instructions. This pass converts each $\mathcal{L}_{\mathsf{Var}}$ operation to a short sequence of instructions that accomplishes the same task.

assign_homes replaces variables with registers or stack locations.

The next question is, in what order should we apply these passes? This question can be challenging because it is difficult to know ahead of time which orderings will be better (that is, will be easier to implement, produce more efficient code, and so on), and therefore ordering often involves trial and error. Nevertheless, we can plan ahead and make educated choices regarding the ordering.

The **select_instructions** and **assign_homes** passes are intertwined. In chapter 8 we learn that in x86, registers are used for passing arguments to functions and that it is preferable to assign parameters to their corresponding registers. This suggests that it would be better to start with the **select_instructions** pass, which generates the instructions for argument passing, before performing register allocation. On the other hand, by selecting instructions first we may run into a dead end in **assign_homes**. Recall that only one argument of an x86 instruction may be a memory access, but **assign_homes** might be forced to assign both arguments to memory locations. A sophisticated approach is to repeat the two passes until a solution is found. However, to reduce implementation complexity we recommend placing **select_instructions** first, followed by the **assign_homes**, and then a third pass named **patch_instructions** that uses a reserved register to fix outstanding problems.

Figure 2.10 presents the ordering of the compiler passes and identifies the input and output language of each pass. The output of the **select_instructions** pass is the $\mathsf{x86}_{\mathsf{Var}}$ language, which extends $\mathsf{x86}_{\mathsf{Int}}$ with an unbounded number of program-scope variables and removes the restrictions regarding instruction arguments. The last pass, **prelude_and_conclusion**, places the program instructions inside a **main** function with instructions for the prelude and conclusion. The remainder of this chapter provides guidance on the implementation of each of the compiler passes represented in figure 2.10.

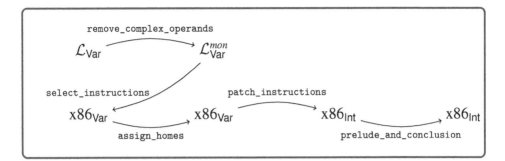

Figure 2.10
Diagram of the passes for compiling $\mathcal{L}_{\text{Var}}$.

$$
\begin{array}{rcl}
atm & ::= & \texttt{Constant}(int) \mid \texttt{Name}(var) \\
exp & ::= & atm \mid \texttt{Call}(\texttt{Name}('\texttt{input\_int}'),[]) \\
 & \mid & \texttt{UnaryOp}(\texttt{USub}(),atm) \mid \texttt{BinOp}(atm,\texttt{Add}(),atm) \\
 & \mid & \texttt{BinOp}(atm,\texttt{Sub}(),atm) \\
stmt & ::= & \texttt{Expr}(\texttt{Call}(\texttt{Name}('\texttt{print}'),[atm])) \mid \texttt{Expr}(exp) \\
 & \mid & \texttt{Assign}([\texttt{Name}(var)],\ exp) \\
\mathcal{L}_{\text{Var}}^{mon} & ::= & \texttt{Module}(stmt^*)
\end{array}
$$

Figure 2.11
$\mathcal{L}_{\text{Var}}^{mon}$ is $\mathcal{L}_{\text{Var}}$ with operands restricted to atomic expressions.

2.4 Remove Complex Operands

The `remove_complex_operands` pass compiles $\mathcal{L}_{\text{Var}}$ programs into a restricted form in which the arguments of operations are atomic expressions. Put another way, this pass removes complex operands, such as the expression `-10` in the following program. This is accomplished by introducing a new temporary variable, assigning the complex operand to the new variable, and then using the new variable in place of the complex operand, as shown in the output of `remove_complex_operands` on the right.

```
x = 42 + -10
print(x + 10)
```

$\Rightarrow$

```
tmp_0 = -10
x = 42 + tmp_0
tmp_1 = x + 10
print(tmp_1)
```

Figure 2.11 presents the grammar for the output of this pass, the language $\mathcal{L}_{\text{Var}}^{mon}$. The only difference is that operator arguments are restricted to be atomic expressions that are defined by the *atm* nonterminal. In particular, integer constants and variables are atomic.

The atomic expressions are pure (they do not cause or depend on side effects) whereas complex expressions may have side effects, such as

`Call(Name('input_int'),[])`. A language with this separation between pure expressions versus expressions with side effects is said to be in monadic normal form (Moggi 1991; Danvy 2003), which explains the *mon* in the name $\mathcal{L}_{\text{Var}}^{mon}$. An important invariant of the `remove_complex_operands` pass is that the relative ordering among complex expressions is not changed, but the relative ordering between atomic expressions and complex expressions can change and often does. These changes are behavior preserving because atomic expressions are pure.

We recommend implementing this pass with an auxiliary method named `rco_exp` with two parameters: an $\mathcal{L}_{\text{Var}}$ expression and a Boolean that specifies whether the expression needs to become atomic or not. The `rco_exp` method should return a pair consisting of the new expression and a list of pairs, associating new temporary variables with their initializing expressions.

Returning to the example program with the expression `42 + -10`, the subexpression `-10` should be processed using the `rco_exp` function with `True` as the second argument, because `-10` is an argument of the `+` operator and therefore needs to become atomic. The output of `rco_exp` applied to `-10` is as follows.

$$
\text{-10} \qquad\qquad \Rightarrow \qquad \begin{array}{l} \texttt{tmp\_1} \\ \texttt{[(tmp\_1, -10)]} \end{array}
$$

Take special care of programs, such as the following, that assign an atomic expression to a variable. You should leave such assignments unchanged, as shown in the program on the right:

```
a = 42                          a = 42
b = a                     ⇒     b = a
print(b)                        print(b)
```

A careless implementation might produce the following output with unnecessary temporary variables.

```
tmp_1 = 42
a = tmp_1
tmp_2 = a
b = tmp_2
print(b)
```

Exercise 2.1 Implement the `remove_complex_operands` pass in `compiler.py`, creating auxiliary functions for each nonterminal in the grammar, that is, `rco_exp` and `rco_stmt`. We recommend that you use the function `utils.generate_name()` to generate fresh names from a stub string.

Exercise 2.2 Create five $\mathcal{L}_{\text{Var}}$ programs that exercise the most interesting parts of the `remove_complex_operands` pass. The five programs should be placed in the subdirectory `tests/var`, and the file names should end with the file extension `.py`.

Run the `run-tests.py` script in the support code to check whether the output programs produce the same result as the input programs.

2.5 Select Instructions

In the `select_instructions` pass we begin the work of translating to $x86_{Var}$. The target language of this pass is a variant of x86 that still uses variables, so we add an AST node of the form `Name(var)` to the *arg* nonterminal of the $x86_{Int}$ abstract syntax (figure 2.9). We recommend implementing an auxiliary function named `select_stmt` for the *stmt* nonterminal.

Next consider the cases for the *stmt* nonterminal, starting with arithmetic operations. For example, consider the following addition operation, on the left side. (Let arg_1 and arg_2 be the translations of atm_1 and atm_2, respectively.) There is an `addq` instruction in x86, but it performs an in-place update. So, we could move arg_1 into the `rax` register, then add arg_2 to `rax`, and then finally move `rax` into *var*.

$$var = atm_1 + atm_2 \qquad \Rightarrow \qquad \begin{array}{l} \texttt{movq } arg_1, \texttt{ \%rax} \\ \texttt{addq } arg_2, \texttt{ \%rax} \\ \texttt{movq \%rax, } var \end{array}$$

However, with some care we can generate shorter sequences of instructions. Suppose that one or more of the arguments of the addition is the same variable as the left-hand side of the assignment. Then the assignment statement can be translated into a single `addq` instruction, as follows.

$$var = atm_1 + var \qquad \Rightarrow \qquad \texttt{addq } arg_1, \texttt{ } var$$

On the other hand, if atm_2 is not the same variable as the left-hand side, then we can move arg_1 into the left-hand *var* and then add arg_2 to *var*.

$$var = atm_1 + atm_2 \qquad \Rightarrow \qquad \begin{array}{l} \texttt{movq } arg_1, \texttt{ } var \\ \texttt{addq } arg_2, \texttt{ } var \end{array}$$

The `input_int` operation does not have a direct counterpart in x86 assembly, so we provide this functionality with the function `read_int` in the file `runtime.c`, written in C (Kernighan and Ritchie 1988). In general, we refer to all the functionality in this file as the *runtime system*, or simply the *runtime* for short. When compiling your generated x86 assembly code, you need to compile `runtime.c` to `runtime.o` (an *object file*, using `gcc` with option `-c`) and link it into the executable. For our purposes of code generation, all you need to do is translate an assignment of `input_int` into a call to the `read_int` function followed by a move from `rax` to the left-hand side variable. (The return value of a function is placed in `rax`.)

$$var = \texttt{input\_int()}; \qquad \Rightarrow \qquad \begin{array}{l} \texttt{callq read\_int} \\ \texttt{movq \%rax, } var \end{array}$$

Similarly, we translate the **print** operation, shown below, into a call to the
print_int function defined in **runtime.c**. In x86, the first six arguments to functions are passed in registers, with the first argument passed in register **rdi**. So we
move the *arg* into **rdi** and then call **print_int** using the **callq** instruction.

$$\text{print}(atm) \quad \Rightarrow \quad \begin{array}{l}\texttt{movq } arg\texttt{, \%rdi} \\ \texttt{callq print\_int}\end{array}$$

We recommend that you use the function **utils.label_name** to transform strings
into labels, for example, in the target of the **callq** instruction. This practice makes
your compiler portable across Linux and Mac OS X, which requires an underscore
prefixed to all labels.

Exercise 2.3 Implement the **select_instructions** pass in **compiler.py**. Create
three new example programs that are designed to exercise all the interesting cases
in this pass. Run the **run-tests.py** script to check whether the output programs
produce the same result as the input programs.

2.6 Assign Homes

The **assign_homes** pass compiles x86$_{Var}$ programs to x86$_{Var}$ programs that no longer
use program variables. Thus, the **assign_homes** pass is responsible for placing all
the program variables in registers or on the stack. For runtime efficiency, it is better
to place variables in registers, but because there are only sixteen registers, some
programs must necessarily resort to placing some variables on the stack. In this
chapter we focus on the mechanics of placing variables on the stack. We study an
algorithm for placing variables in registers in chapter 4.

Consider again the following $\mathcal{L}_{Var}$ program from section 2.4:

```
a = 42
b = a
print(b)
```

The output of **select_instructions** is shown next, on the left, and the output
of **assign_homes** is on the right. In this example, we assign variable **a** to stack
location -8(%rbp) and variable **b** to location -16(%rbp).

```
movq $42, a                    movq $42, -8(%rbp)
movq a, b        ⇒             movq -8(%rbp), -16(%rbp)
movq b, %rax                   movq -16(%rbp), %rax
```

The **assign_homes** pass should replace all uses of variables with stack locations.
In the process of assigning variables to stack locations, it is convenient for you to
compute and store the size of the frame (in bytes) in the field **stack_space** of
the **X86Program** node, which is needed later to generate the conclusion of the **main**
procedure. The x86-64 standard requires the frame size to be a multiple of 16 bytes.

Exercise 2.4 Implement the `assign_homes` pass in `compiler.py`, defining auxiliary functions for each of the nonterminals in the x86$_{\text{Var}}$ grammar. We recommend that the auxiliary functions take an extra parameter that maps variable names to homes (stack locations for now). Run the `run-tests.py` script to check whether the output programs produce the same result as the input programs.

2.7 Patch Instructions

The `patch_instructions` pass compiles from x86$_{\text{Var}}$ to x86$_{\text{Int}}$ by making sure that each instruction adheres to the restriction that at most one argument of an instruction may be a memory reference.

We return to the following example.

```
a = 42
b = a
print(b)
```

The `assign_homes` pass produces the following translation.

```
movq $42, -8(%rbp)
movq -8(%rbp), -16(%rbp)
movq -16(%rbp), %rdi
callq print_int
```

The second `movq` instruction is problematic because both arguments are stack locations. We suggest fixing this problem by moving from the source location to the register `rax` and then from `rax` to the destination location, as follows.

```
movq -8(%rbp), %rax
movq %rax, -16(%rbp)
```

There is a similar corner case that also needs to be dealt with. If one argument is an immediate integer larger than 2^{16} and the other is a memory reference, then the instruction is invalid. One can fix this, for example, by first moving the immediate integer into `rax` and then using `rax` in place of the integer.

Exercise 2.5 Implement the `patch_instructions` pass in `compiler.py`. Create three new example programs that are designed to exercise all the interesting cases in this pass. Run the `run-tests.py` script to check whether the output programs produce the same result as the input programs.

2.8 Generate Prelude and Conclusion

The last step of the compiler from $\mathcal{L}_{\text{Var}}$ to x86 is to generate the `main` function with a prelude and conclusion wrapped around the rest of the program, as shown in figure 2.7 and discussed in section 2.2.

When running on Mac OS X, your compiler should prefix an underscore to all labels (for example, changing `main` to `_main`). The Python `platform.system` function returns `'Linux'`, `'Windows'`, or `'Darwin'` (for Mac).

Exercise 2.6 Implement the `prelude_and_conclusion` pass in `compiler.py`. Run the `run-tests.py` script to check whether the output programs produce the same result as the input programs. That script translates the x86 AST that you produce into a string by invoking the `repr` method that is implemented by the x86 AST classes in `x86_ast.py`.

2.9 Challenge: Partial Evaluator for $\mathcal{L}_{Var}$

This section describes two optional challenge exercises that involve adapting and improving the partial evaluator for $\mathcal{L}_{Int}$ that was introduced in section 1.6.

Exercise 2.7 Adapt the partial evaluator from section 1.6 (figure 1.5) so that it applies to $\mathcal{L}_{Var}$ programs instead of $\mathcal{L}_{Int}$ programs. Recall that $\mathcal{L}_{Var}$ adds variables and assignment to the $\mathcal{L}_{Int}$ language, so you will need to add cases for them in the `pe_exp` and `pe_stmt` functions. Once complete, add the partial evaluation pass to the front of your compiler, and check that your compiler still passes all the tests.

Exercise 2.8 Improve on the partial evaluator by replacing the `pe_neg` and `pe_add` auxiliary functions with functions that know more about arithmetic. For example, your partial evaluator should translate

$$1 + (\text{input\_int}() + 1) \quad \text{into} \quad 2 + \text{input\_int}()$$

To accomplish this, the `pe_exp` function should produce output in the form of the *residual* nonterminal of the following grammar. The idea is that when processing an addition expression, we can always produce one of the following: (1) an integer constant, (2) an addition expression with an integer constant on the left-hand side but not the right-hand side, or (3) an addition expression in which neither subexpression is a constant.

$$
\begin{aligned}
\textit{inert} \quad &::= \quad \textit{var} \mid \text{input\_int}() \mid \textit{-var} \mid \text{-input\_int}() \mid \textit{inert} + \textit{inert} \\
\textit{residual} \quad &::= \quad \textit{int} \mid \textit{int} + \textit{inert} \mid \textit{inert}
\end{aligned}
$$

The `pe_add` and `pe_neg` functions may assume that their inputs are *residual* expressions and they should return *residual* expressions. Once the improvements are complete, make sure that your compiler still passes all the tests. After all, fast code is useless if it produces incorrect results!

3   Parsing

In this chapter we learn how to use the Lark parser framework (Shinan 2020) to translate the concrete syntax of $\mathcal{L}_{\text{Int}}$ (a sequence of characters) into an abstract syntax tree. You are then asked to create a parser for $\mathcal{L}_{\text{Var}}$ using Lark. We also describe the parsing algorithms used inside Lark, studying the Earley (1970) and LALR(1) algorithms (DeRemer 1969; Anderson, Eve, and Horning 1973).

A parser framework such as Lark takes in a specification of the concrete syntax and an input program and produces a parse tree. Even though a parser framework does most of the work for us, using one properly requires some knowledge. In particular, we must learn about its specification languages and we must learn how to deal with ambiguity in our language specifications. Also, some algorithms, such as LALR(1), place restrictions on the grammars they can handle, in which case knowing the algorithm helps with trying to decipher the error messages.

The process of parsing is traditionally subdivided into two phases: *lexical analysis* (also called scanning) and *syntax analysis* (also called parsing). The lexical analysis phase translates the sequence of characters into a sequence of *tokens*, that is, words consisting of several characters. The parsing phase organizes the tokens into a *parse tree* that captures how the tokens were matched by rules in the grammar of the language. The reason for the subdivision into two phases is to enable the use of a faster but less powerful algorithm for lexical analysis and the use of a slower but more powerful algorithm for parsing. The Lark parser framework that we use in this chapter includes both lexical analyzers and parsers. The next section discusses lexical analysis, and the remainder of the chapter discusses parsing.

3.1   Lexical Analysis and Regular Expressions

The lexical analyzers produced by Lark turn a sequence of characters (a string) into a sequence of token objects. For example, a Lark generated lexer for $\mathcal{L}_{\text{Int}}$ converts the string

```
'print(1 + 3)'
```

into the following sequence of token objects:

```
Token('PRINT', 'print')
Token('LPAR', '(')
Token('INT', '1')
Token('PLUS', '+')
Token('INT', '3')
Token('RPAR', ')')
Token('NEWLINE', '\n')
```

Each token includes a field for its `type`, such as `'INT'`, and a field for its `value`, such as `'1'`.

Following in the tradition of `lex` (Lesk and Schmidt 1975), the specification language for Lark's lexer is one regular expression for each type of token. The term *regular* comes from the term *regular languages*, which are the languages that can be recognized by a finite state machine. A *regular expression* is a pattern formed of the following core elements:[1]

- A single character c is a regular expression, and it matches only itself. For example, the regular expression a matches only the string `'a'`.
- Two regular expressions separated by a vertical bar $R_1 | R_2$ form a regular expression that matches any string that matches R_1 or R_2. For example, the regular expression a|c matches the string `'a'` and the string `'c'`.
- Two regular expressions in sequence $R_1 R_2$ form a regular expression that matches any string that can be formed by concatenating two strings, where the first string matches R_1 and the second string matches R_2. For example, the regular expression (a|c)b matches the strings `'ab'` and `'cb'`. (Parentheses can be used to control the grouping of operators within a regular expression.)
- A regular expression followed by an asterisks $R*$ (called Kleene closure) is a regular expression that matches any string that can be formed by concatenating zero or more strings that each match the regular expression R. For example, the regular expression ((a|c)b)* matches the string `'abcbab'` but not `'abc'`.

For our convenience, Lark also accepts the following extended set of regular expressions that are automatically translated into the core regular expressions.

- A set of characters enclosed in square brackets $[c_1 c_2 \ldots c_n]$ is a regular expression that matches any one of the characters. So, $[c_1 c_2 \ldots c_n]$ is equivalent to the regular expression $c_1 | c_2 | \ldots | c_n$.
- A range of characters enclosed in square brackets $[c_1 - c_2]$ is a regular expression that matches any character between c_1 and c_2, inclusive. For example, [a-z] matches any lowercase letter in the alphabet.
- A regular expression followed by the plus symbol $R+$ is a regular expression that matches any string that can be formed by concatenating one or more strings that

---

1. Regular expressions traditionally include the empty regular expression that matches any zero-length part of a string, but Lark does not support the empty regular expression.

each match R. So $R+$ is equivalent to $R(R*)$. For example, $[a-z]+$ matches `'b'` and `'bzca'`.

- A regular expression followed by a question mark $R?$ is a regular expression that matches any string that either matches R or is the empty string. For example, `a?b` matches both `'ab'` and `'b'`.

In a Lark grammar file, each kind of token is specified by a *terminal*, which is defined by a rule that consists of the name of the terminal followed by a colon followed by a sequence of literals. The literals include strings such as `"abc"`, regular expressions surrounded by / characters, terminal names, and literals composed using the regular expression operators (+, *, etc.). For example, the `DIGIT`, `INT`, and `NEWLINE` terminals are specified as follows:

```
DIGIT: /[0-9]/
INT: "-"? DIGIT+
NEWLINE: (/\r/? /\n/)+
```

3.2   Grammars and Parse Trees

In section 1.2 we learned how to use grammar rules to specify the abstract syntax of a language. We now take a closer look at using grammar rules to specify the concrete syntax. Recall that each rule has a left-hand side and a right-hand side, where the left-hand side is a nonterminal and the right-hand side is a pattern that defines what can be parsed as that nonterminal. For concrete syntax, each right-hand side expresses a pattern for a string instead of a pattern for an abstract syntax tree. In particular, each right-hand side is a sequence of *symbols*, where a symbol is either a terminal or a nonterminal. The nonterminals play the same role as in the abstract syntax, defining categories of syntax. The nonterminals of a grammar include the tokens defined in the lexer and all the nonterminals defined by the grammar rules.

As an example, let us take a closer look at the concrete syntax of the $\mathcal{L}_{\mathsf{Int}}$ language, repeated here.

$$
\begin{array}{rcl}
exp & ::= & int \mid \texttt{input\_int()} \mid - exp \mid exp + exp \mid exp - exp \mid (exp) \\
stmt & ::= & \texttt{print}(exp) \mid exp \\
\mathcal{L}_{\mathsf{Int}} & ::= & stmt^*
\end{array}
$$

The Lark syntax for grammar rules differs slightly from the variant of BNF that we use in this book. In particular, the notation ::= is replaced by a single colon, and the use of typewriter font for string literals is replaced by quotation marks. The following grammar serves as a first draft of a Lark grammar for $\mathcal{L}_{\mathsf{Int}}$.

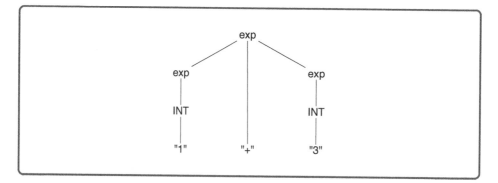

Figure 3.1
The parse tree for '1+3'.

```
exp: INT
   | "input_int" "(" ")"
   | "-" exp
   | exp "+" exp
   | exp "-" exp
   | "(" exp ")"

stmt_list:
   | stmt NEWLINE stmt_list

lang_int: stmt_list
```

Let us begin by discussing the rule **exp: INT**, which says that if the lexer matches a string to **INT**, then the parser also categorizes the string as an **exp**. Recall that in section 1.2 we defined the corresponding *int* nonterminal with a sentence in English. Here we specify **INT** more formally using a type of token **INT** and its regular expression **"-"? DIGIT+**.

The rule **exp: exp "+" exp** says that any string that matches **exp**, followed by the + character, followed by another string that matches **exp**, is itself an **exp**. For example, the string '1+3' is an **exp** because '1' and '3' are both **exp** by the rule **exp: INT**, and then the rule for addition applies to categorize '1+3' as an **exp**. We can visualize the application of grammar rules to parse a string using a *parse tree*. Each internal node in the tree is an application of a grammar rule and is labeled with its left-hand side nonterminal. Each leaf node is a substring of the input program. The parse tree for '1+3' is shown in figure 3.1.

The result of parsing '1+3' with this Lark grammar is the following parse tree as represented by **Tree** and **Token** objects.

```
Tree('lang_int',
    [Tree('stmt', [Tree('exp', [Tree('exp', [Token('INT', '1')]),
                                 Tree('exp', [Token('INT', '3')])])]),
     Token('NEWLINE', '\n')])
```

The nodes that come from the lexer are `Token` objects, whereas the nodes from the parser are `Tree` objects. Each `Tree` object has a `data` field containing the name of the nonterminal for the grammar rule that was applied. Each `Tree` object also has a `children` field that is a list containing trees and/or tokens. Note that Lark does not produce nodes for string literals in the grammar. For example, the `Tree` node for the addition expression has only two children for the two integers but is missing its middle child for the `"+"` terminal. This would be problematic except that Lark provides a mechanism for customizing the `data` field of each `Tree` node on the basis of which rule was applied. Next to each alternative in a grammar rule, write `->` followed by a string that you want to appear in the `data` field. The following is a second draft of a Lark grammar for $\mathcal{L}_{\mathsf{Int}}$, this time with more specific labels on the `Tree` nodes.

```
exp: INT                      -> int
   | "input_int" "(" ")"      -> input_int
   | "-" exp                  -> usub
   | exp "+" exp              -> add
   | exp "-" exp              -> sub
   | "(" exp ")"              -> paren

stmt: "print" "(" exp ")" -> print
    | exp                     -> expr

stmt_list:                    -> empty_stmt
    | stmt NEWLINE stmt_list -> add_stmt

lang_int: stmt_list           -> module
```

Here is the resulting parse tree.

```
Tree('module',
  [Tree('expr', [Tree('add', [Tree('int', [Token('INT', '1')]),
                              Tree('int', [Token('INT', '3')])])]),
   Token('NEWLINE', '\n')])
```

3.3 Ambiguous Grammars

A grammar is *ambiguous* when a string can be parsed in more than one way. For example, consider the string `'1-2+3'`. This string can be parsed in two different ways using our draft grammar, resulting in the two parse trees shown in figure 3.2. This example is problematic because interpreting the second parse tree would yield −4 even through the correct answer is 2.

To deal with this problem we can change the grammar by categorizing the syntax in a more fine-grained fashion. In this case we want to disallow the application of the rule `exp: exp "-" exp` when the child on the right is an addition. To do this we can replace the `exp` after `"-"` with a nonterminal that categorizes all the expressions except for addition, as in the following.

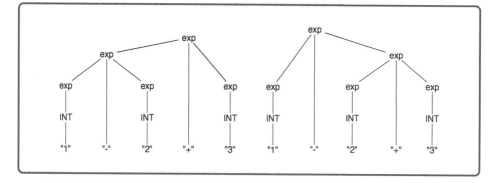

Figure 3.2
The two parse trees for `'1-2+3'`.

```
exp: exp "-" exp_no_add  -> sub
   | exp "+" exp          -> add
   | exp_no_add

exp_no_add: INT                 -> int
   | "input_int" "(" ")"  -> input_int
   | "-" exp                    -> usub
   | exp "-" exp_no_add   -> sub
   | "(" exp ")"                -> paren
```

However, there remains some ambiguity in the grammar. For example, the string `'1-2-3'` can still be parsed in two different ways, as `'(1-2)-3'` (correct) or `'1-(2-3)'` (incorrect). That is, subtraction is left associative. Likewise, addition in Python is left associative. We also need to consider the interaction of unary subtraction with both addition and subtraction. How should we parse `'-1+2'`? Unary subtraction has higher *precedence* than addition and subtraction, so `'-1+2'` should parse the same as `'(-1)+2'` and not `'-(1+2)'`. The grammar in figure 3.3 handles the associativity of addition and subtraction by using the nonterminal `exp_hi` for all the other expressions, and it uses `exp_hi` for the second child in the rules for addition and subtraction. Furthermore, unary subtraction uses `exp_hi` for its child.

For languages with more operators and more precedence levels, one must refine the `exp` nonterminal into several nonterminals, one for each precedence level.

3.4   From Parse Trees to Abstract Syntax Trees

As we have seen, the output of a Lark parser is a parse tree, that is, a tree consisting of `Tree` and `Token` nodes. So, the next step is to convert the parse tree to an abstract syntax tree. This can be accomplished with a recursive function that inspects the `data` field of each node and then constructs the corresponding AST node, using recursion to handle its children. The following is an excerpt from the `parse_tree_to_ast` function for $\mathcal{L}_{\mathsf{Int}}$.

```
exp: exp "+" exp_hi       -> add
   | exp "-" exp_hi       -> sub
   | exp_hi

exp_hi: INT                    -> int
      | "input_int" "(" ")" -> input_int
      | "-" exp_hi          -> usub
      | "(" exp ")"         -> paren

stmt: "print" "(" exp ")" -> print
    | exp                 -> expr

stmt_list:                     -> empty_stmt
      | stmt NEWLINE stmt_list -> add_stmt

lang_int: stmt_list       -> module
```

Figure 3.3
An unambiguous Lark grammar for $\mathcal{L}_{\text{Int}}$.

```
def parse_tree_to_ast(e):
  if e.data == 'int':
    return Constant(int(e.children[0].value))
  elif e.data == 'input_int':
    return Call(Name('input_int'), [])
  elif e.data == 'add':
    e1, e2 = e.children
    return BinOp(parse_tree_to_ast(e1), Add(), parse_tree_to_ast(e2))
  ...
  else:
    raise Exception('unhandled parse tree', e)
```

Exercise 3.1 Use Lark to create a lexer and parser for $\mathcal{L}_{\text{Var}}$. Use Lark's default parsing algorithm (Earley) with the **ambiguity** option set to `'explicit'` so that if your grammar is ambiguous, the output will include multiple parse trees that will indicate to you that there is a problem with your grammar. Your parser should ignore white space, so we recommend using Lark's **%ignore** directive as follows.

```
WS: /[ \t\f\r\n]/+
%ignore WS
```

Change your compiler from chapter 2 to use your Lark parser instead of using the **parse** function from the **ast** module. Test your compiler on all the $\mathcal{L}_{\text{Var}}$ programs that you have created, and create four additional programs that test for ambiguities in your grammar.

3.5 Earley's Algorithm

In this section we discuss the parsing algorithm of Earley (1970), the default algorithm used by Lark. The algorithm is powerful in that it can handle any context-free grammar, which makes it easy to use, but it is not a particularly efficient parsing algorithm. Earley's algorithm is $O(n^3)$ for ambiguous grammars and $O(n^2)$ for unambiguous grammars, where n is the number of tokens in the input string (Hopcroft, Motwani, and Ullman 2006). In section 3.6 we learn about the LALR(1) algorithm, which is more efficient but cannot handle all context-free grammars.

Earley's algorithm can be viewed as an interpreter; it treats the grammar as the program being interpreted, and it treats the concrete syntax of the program-to-be-parsed as its input. Earley's algorithm uses a data structure called a *chart* to keep track of its progress and to store its results. The chart is an array with one slot for each position in the input string, where position 0 is before the first character and position n is immediately after the last character. So, the array has length $n + 1$ for an input string of length n. Each slot in the chart contains a set of *dotted rules*. A dotted rule is simply a grammar rule with a period indicating how much of its right-hand side has already been parsed. For example, the dotted rule

```
exp: exp "+" . exp_hi
```

represents a partial parse that has matched an `exp` followed by + but has not yet parsed an `exp` to the right of +. Earley's algorithm starts with an initialization phase and then repeats three actions—prediction, scanning, and completion—for as long as opportunities arise. We demonstrate Earley's algorithm on a running example, parsing the following program:

```
print(1 + 3)
```

The algorithm's initialization phase creates dotted rules for all the grammar rules whose left-hand side is the start symbol and places them in slot 0 of the chart. We also record the starting position of the dotted rule in parentheses on the right. For example, given the grammar in figure 3.3, we place

```
lang_int: . stmt_list      (0)
```

in slot 0 of the chart. The algorithm then proceeds with *prediction* actions in which it adds more dotted rules to the chart based on the nonterminals that come immediately after a period. In the dotted rule above, the nonterminal `stmt_list` appears after a period, so we add all the rules for `stmt_list` to slot 0, with a period at the beginning of their right-hand sides, as follows:

```
stmt_list: .                      (0)
stmt_list: . stmt NEWLINE stmt_list (0)
```

We continue to perform prediction actions as more opportunities arise. For example, the `stmt` nonterminal now appears after a period, so we add all the rules for `stmt`.

```
stmt: . "print" "(" exp ")" (0)
stmt: . exp                 (0)
```

This reveals yet more opportunities for prediction, so we add the grammar rules for `exp` and `exp_hi` to slot 0.

```
exp: . exp "+" exp_hi          (0)
exp: . exp "-" exp_hi          (0)
exp: . exp_hi                  (0)
exp_hi: . INT                  (0)
exp_hi: . "input_int" "(" ")"  (0)
exp_hi: . "-" exp_hi           (0)
exp_hi: . "(" exp ")"          (0)
```

We have exhausted the opportunities for prediction, so the algorithm proceeds to *scanning*, in which we inspect the next input token and look for a dotted rule at the current position that has a matching terminal immediately following the period. In our running example, the first input token is `"print"`, so we identify the rule in slot 0 of the chart where `"print"` follows the period:

```
stmt: . "print" "(" exp ")"      (0)
```

We advance the period past `"print"` and add the resulting rule to slot 1:

```
stmt: "print" . "(" exp ")"      (0)
```

If the new dotted rule had a nonterminal after the period, we would need to carry out a prediction action, adding more dotted rules to slot 1. That is not the case, so we continue scanning. The next input token is `"("`, so we add the following to slot 2 of the chart.

```
stmt: "print" "(" . exp ")"      (0)
```

Now we have a nonterminal after the period, so we carry out several prediction actions, adding dotted rules for `exp` and `exp_hi` to slot 2 with a period at the beginning and with starting position 2.

```
exp: . exp "+" exp_hi          (2)
exp: . exp "-" exp_hi          (2)
exp: . exp_hi                  (2)
exp_hi: . INT                  (2)
exp_hi: . "input_int" "(" ")"  (2)
exp_hi: . "-" exp_hi           (2)
exp_hi: . "(" exp ")"          (2)
```

With this prediction complete, we return to scanning, noting that the next input token is `"1"`, which the lexer parses as an `INT`. There is a matching rule in slot 2:

```
exp_hi: . INT          (2)
```

so we advance the period and put the following rule into slot 3.

```
exp_hi: INT .          (2)
```

This brings us to *completion* actions. When the period reaches the end of a dotted rule, we recognize that the substring has matched the nonterminal on the left-hand side of the rule, in this case `exp_hi`. We therefore need to advance the periods in any dotted rules into slot 2 (the starting position for the finished rule) if the period is immediately followed by `exp_hi`. So we identify

```
exp: . exp_hi              (2)
```

and add the following dotted rule to slot 3

```
exp: exp_hi .              (2)
```

This triggers another completion step for the nonterminal `exp`, adding two more dotted rules to slot 3.

```
exp: exp . "+" exp_hi      (2)
exp: exp . "-" exp_hi      (2)
```

Returning to scanning, the next input token is `"+"`, so we add the following to slot 4.

```
exp: exp "+" . exp_hi      (2)
```

The period precedes the nonterminal `exp_hi`, so prediction adds the following dotted rules to slot 4 of the chart.

```
exp_hi: . INT                      (4)
exp_hi: . "input_int" "(" ")" (4)
exp_hi: . "-" exp_hi               (4)
exp_hi: . "(" exp ")"              (4)
```

The next input token is `"3"` which the lexer categorized as an `INT`, so we advance the period past `INT` for the rules in slot 4, of which there is just one, and put the following into slot 5.

```
exp_hi: INT .              (4)
```

The period at the end of the rule triggers a completion action for the rules in slot 4, one of which has a period before `exp_hi`. So we advance the period and put the following into slot 5.

```
exp: exp "+" exp_hi .      (2)
```

This triggers another completion action for the rules in slot 2 that have a period before `exp`.

```
stmt: "print" "(" exp . ")" (0)
exp: exp . "+" exp_hi       (2)
exp: exp . "-" exp_hi       (2)
```

We scan the next input token `")"`, placing the following dotted rule into slot 6.

```
stmt: "print" "(" exp ")" . (0)
```

This triggers the completion of `stmt` in slot 0

```
stmt_list: stmt . NEWLINE stmt_list (0)
```

The last input token is a `NEWLINE`, so we advance the period and place the new dotted rule into slot 7.

```
stmt_list: stmt NEWLINE . stmt_list (0)
```

We are close to the end of parsing the input! The period is before the `stmt_list` nonterminal, so we apply prediction for `stmt_list` and then `stmt`.

```
stmt_list: .                           (7)
stmt_list: . stmt NEWLINE stmt_list    (7)
stmt: . "print" "(" exp ")"            (7)
stmt: . exp                            (7)
```

There is immediately an opportunity for completion of `stmt_list`, so we add the following to slot 7.

```
stmt_list: stmt NEWLINE stmt_list . (0)
```

This triggers another completion action for `stmt_list` in slot 0

```
lang_int: stmt_list .             (0)
```

which in turn completes `lang_int`, the start symbol of the grammar, so the parsing of the input is complete.

For reference, we give a general description of Earley's algorithm.

1. The algorithm begins by initializing slot 0 of the chart with the grammar rule for the start symbol, placing a period at the beginning of the right-hand side, and recording its starting position as 0.
2. The algorithm repeatedly applies the following three kinds of actions for as long as there are opportunities to do so.
   - Prediction: If there is a rule in slot k whose period comes before a nonterminal, add the rules for that nonterminal into slot k, placing a period at the beginning of their right-hand sides and recording their starting position as k.
   - Scanning: If the token at position k of the input string matches the symbol after the period in a dotted rule in slot k of the chart, advance the period in the dotted rule, adding the result to slot $k + 1$.
   - Completion: If a dotted rule in slot k has a period at the end, inspect the rules in the slot corresponding to the starting position of the completed rule. If any of those rules have a nonterminal following their period that matches the left-hand side of the completed rule, then advance their period, placing the new dotted rule in slot k.

   While repeating these three actions, take care never to add duplicate dotted rules to the chart.

We have described how Earley's algorithm recognizes that an input string matches a grammar, but we have not described how it builds a parse tree. The basic idea is simple, but building parse trees in an efficient way is more complex, requiring a data structure called a shared packed parse forest (Tomita 1985). The simple idea is to attach a partial parse tree to every dotted rule in the chart. Initially, the node associated with a dotted rule has no children. As the period moves to the right, the nodes from the subparses are added as children to the node.

As mentioned at the beginning of this section, Earley's algorithm is $O(n^2)$ for unambiguous grammars, which means that it can parse input files that contain thousands of tokens in a reasonable amount of time, but not millions. In the next section we discuss the LALR(1) parsing algorithm, which is efficient enough to use with even the largest of input files.

3.6   The LALR(1) Algorithm

The LALR(1) algorithm (DeRemer 1969; Anderson, Eve, and Horning 1973) can be viewed as a two-phase approach in which it first compiles the grammar into a state machine and then runs the state machine to parse an input string. The second phase has time complexity $O(n)$ where n is the number of tokens in the input, so LALR(1) is the best one could hope for with respect to efficiency. A particularly influential implementation of LALR(1) is the yacc parser generator by Johnson (1979); yacc stands for "yet another compiler compiler." The LALR(1) state machine uses a stack to record its progress in parsing the input string. Each element of the stack is a pair: a state number and a grammar symbol (a terminal or a nonterminal). The symbol characterizes the input that has been parsed so far, and the state number is used to remember how to proceed once the next symbol's worth of input has been parsed. Each state in the machine represents where the parser stands in the parsing process with respect to certain grammar rules. In particular, each state is associated with a set of dotted rules.

Figure 3.4 shows an example LALR(1) state machine (also called parse table) for the following simple but ambiguous grammar:

```
exp: INT
   | exp "+" exp
stmt: "print" exp
start: stmt
```

Consider state 1 in figure 3.4. The parser has just read in a "print" token, so the top of the stack is (1,"print"). The parser is part of the way through parsing the input according to grammar rule 1, which is signified by showing rule 1 with a period after the "print" token and before the exp nonterminal. There are two rules that could apply next, rules 2 and 3, so state 1 also shows those rules with a period at the beginning of their right-hand sides. The edges between states indicate which transitions the machine should make depending on the next input token. So, for example, if the next input token is INT then the parser will push INT and the target state 4 on the stack and transition to state 4. Suppose that we are now at the end of the input. State 4 says that we should reduce by rule 3, so we pop from the stack the same number of items as the number of symbols in the right-hand side of the rule, in this case just one. We then momentarily jump to the state at the top of the stack (state 1) and then follow the goto edge that corresponds to the left-hand side of the rule we just reduced by, in this case exp, so we arrive at state 3. (A slightly longer example parse is shown in figure 3.4.)

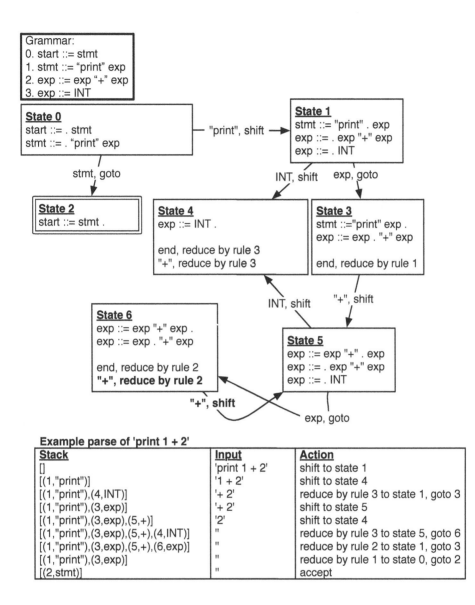

Figure 3.4
An LALR(1) parse table and a trace of an example run.

In general, the algorithm works as follows. First, set the current state to state 0. Then repeat the following, looking at the next input token.

- If there there is a shift edge for the input token in the current state, push the edge's target state and the input token onto the stack and proceed to the edge's target state.
- If there is a reduce action for the input token in the current state, pop k elements from the stack, where k is the number of symbols in the right-hand side of the

rule being reduced. Jump to the state at the top of the stack and then follow the goto edge for the nonterminal that matches the left-hand side of the rule that we are reducing by. Push the edge's target state and the nonterminal on the stack.

Notice that in state 6 of figure 3.4 there is both a shift and a reduce action for the token PLUS, so the algorithm does not know which action to take in this case. When a state has both a shift and a reduce action for the same token, we say there is a *shift/reduce conflict*. In this case, the conflict will arise, for example, in trying to parse the input print 1 + 2 + 3. After having consumed print 1 + 2, the parser will be in state 6 and will not know whether to reduce to form an exp of 1 + 2 or to proceed by shifting the next + from the input.

A similar kind of problem, known as a *reduce/reduce* conflict, arises when there are two reduce actions in a state for the same token. To understand which grammars give rise to shift/reduce and reduce/reduce conflicts, it helps to know how the parse table is generated from the grammar, which we discuss next.

The parse table is generated one state at a time. State 0 represents the start of the parser. We add the grammar rule for the start symbol to this state with a period at the beginning of the right-hand side, similarly to the initialization phase of the Earley parser. If the period appears immediately before another nonterminal, we add all the rules with that nonterminal on the left-hand side. Again, we place a period at the beginning of the right-hand side of each new rule. This process, called *state closure*, is continued until there are no more rules to add (similarly to the prediction actions of an Earley parser). We then examine each dotted rule in the current state I. Suppose that a dotted rule has the form $A ::= s_1 . X s_2$, where A and X are symbols and s_1 and s_2 are sequences of symbols. We create a new state and call it J. If X is a terminal, we create a shift edge from I to J (analogously to scanning in Earley), whereas if X is a nonterminal, we create a goto edge from I to J. We then need to add some dotted rules to state J. We start by adding all dotted rules from state I that have the form $B ::= s_1 . X s_2$ (where B is any nonterminal and s_1 and s_2 are arbitrary sequences of symbols), with the period moved past the X. (This is analogous to completion in Earley's algorithm.) We then perform state closure on J. This process repeats until there are no more states or edges to add.

We then mark states as accepting states if they have a dotted rule that is the start rule with a period at the end. Also, to add the reduce actions, we look for any state containing a dotted rule with a period at the end. Let n be the rule number for this dotted rule. We then put a reduce n action into that state for every token Y. For example, in figure 3.4 state 4 has a dotted rule with a period at the end. We therefore put a reduce by rule 3 action into state 4 for every token.

When inserting reduce actions, take care to spot any shift/reduce or reduce/reduce conflicts. If there are any, abort the construction of the parse table.

Exercise 3.2 Working on paper, walk through the parse table generation process for the grammar at the top of figure 3.4, and check your results against the parse table shown in figure 3.4.

Exercise 3.3 Change the parser in your compiler for $\mathcal{L}_{Var}$ to set the `parser` option of Lark to `'lalr'`. Test your compiler on all the $\mathcal{L}_{Var}$ programs that you have created. In doing so, Lark may signal an error due to shift/reduce or reduce/reduce conflicts in your grammar. If so, change your Lark grammar for $\mathcal{L}_{Var}$ to remove those conflicts.

3.7 Further Reading

In this chapter we have just scratched the surface of the field of parsing, with the study of a very general but less efficient algorithm (Earley) and with a more limited but highly efficient algorithm (LALR). There are many more algorithms and classes of grammars that fall between these two ends of the spectrum. We recommend to the reader Aho et al. (2006) for a thorough treatment of parsing.

Regarding lexical analysis, we have described the specification language, which are the regular expressions, but not the algorithms for recognizing them. In short, regular expressions can be translated to nondeterministic finite automata, which in turn are translated to finite automata. We refer the reader again to Aho et al. (2006) for all the details on lexical analysis.

4 Register Allocation

In chapter 2 we learned how to compile $\mathcal{L}_{\mathsf{Var}}$ to x86, storing variables on the procedure call stack. The CPU may require tens to hundreds of cycles to access a location on the stack, whereas accessing a register takes only a single cycle. In this chapter we improve the efficiency of our generated code by storing some variables in registers. The goal of register allocation is to fit as many variables into registers as possible. Some programs have more variables than registers, so we cannot always map each variable to a different register. Fortunately, it is common for different variables to be in use during different periods of time during program execution, and in those cases we can map multiple variables to the same register.

The program shown in figure 4.1 serves as a running example. The source program is on the left and the output of instruction selection is on the right. The program is almost completely in the x86 assembly language, but it still uses variables. Consider variables x and z. After the variable x has been moved to z, it is no longer in use. Variable z, on the other hand, is used only after this point, so x and z could share the same register.

```
                                   After instruction selection:

                                   movq $1, v
                                   movq $42, w
Example 𝓛_Var program:             movq v, x
                                   addq $7, x
v = 1                              movq x, y
w = 42                             movq x, z
x = v + 7                          addq w, z
y = x                              movq y, tmp_0
z = x + w                          negq tmp_0
print(z + (- y))                   movq z, tmp_1
                                   addq tmp_0, tmp_1
                                   movq tmp_1, %rdi
                                   callq print_int
```

Figure 4.1
A running example for register allocation.

The topic of section 4.2 is how to compute where a variable is in use. Once we have that information, we compute which variables are in use at the same time, that is, which ones *interfere* with each other, and represent this relation as an undirected graph whose vertices are variables and edges indicate when two variables interfere (section 4.3). We then model register allocation as a graph coloring problem (section 4.4).

If we run out of registers despite these efforts, we place the remaining variables on the stack, similarly to how we handled variables in chapter 2. It is common to use the verb *spill* for assigning a variable to a stack location. The decision to spill a variable is handled as part of the graph coloring process.

We make the simplifying assumption that each variable is assigned to one location (a register or stack address). A more sophisticated approach is to assign a variable to one or more locations in different regions of the program. For example, if a variable is used many times in short sequence and then used again only after many other instructions, it could be more efficient to assign the variable to a register during the initial sequence and then move it to the stack for the rest of its lifetime. We refer the interested reader to Cooper and Torczon (2011) (chapter 13) for more information about that approach.

4.1 Registers and Calling Conventions

As we perform register allocation, we must be aware of the *calling conventions* that govern how function calls are performed in x86. Even though $\mathcal{L}_{\mathsf{Var}}$ does not include programmer-defined functions, our generated code includes a `main` function that is called by the operating system and our generated code contains calls to the `read_int` function.

Function calls require coordination between two pieces of code that may be written by different programmers or generated by different compilers. Here we follow the System V calling conventions that are used by the GNU C compiler on Linux and MacOS (Bryant and O'Hallaron 2005; Matz et al. 2013). The calling conventions include rules about how functions share the use of registers. In particular, the caller is responsible for freeing some registers prior to the function call for use by the callee. These are called the *caller-saved registers* and they are

```
rax rcx rdx rsi rdi r8 r9 r10 r11
```

On the other hand, the callee is responsible for preserving the values of the *callee-saved registers*, which are

```
rsp rbp rbx r12 r13 r14 r15
```

We can think about this caller/callee convention from two points of view, the caller view and the callee view, as follows:

- The caller should assume that all the caller-saved registers get overwritten with arbitrary values by the callee. On the other hand, the caller can safely assume that all the callee-saved registers retain their original values.

- The callee can freely use any of the caller-saved registers. However, if the callee wants to use a callee-saved register, the callee must arrange to put the original value back in the register prior to returning to the caller. This can be accomplished by saving the value to the stack in the prelude of the function and restoring the value in the conclusion of the function.

In x86, registers are also used for passing arguments to a function and for the return value. In particular, the first six arguments of a function are passed in the following six registers, in this order.

```
rdi rsi rdx rcx r8 r9
```

We refer to these six registers are the argument-passing registers . If there are more than six arguments, the convention is to use space on the frame of the caller for the rest of the arguments. In chapter 8, we instead pass a tuple containing the sixth argument and the rest of the arguments, which simplifies the treatment of efficient tail calls. For now, the only functions we care about are `read_int` and `print_int`, which take zero and one argument, respectively. The register `rax` is used for the return value of a function.

The next question is how these calling conventions impact register allocation. Consider the $\mathcal{L}_{\mathsf{Var}}$ program presented in figure 4.2. We first analyze this example from the caller point of view and then from the callee point of view. We refer to a variable that is in use during a function call as a *call-live variable*.

The program makes two calls to `input_int`. The variable x is call-live because it is in use during the second call to `input_int`; we must ensure that the value in x does not get overwritten during the call to `input_int`. One obvious approach is to save all the values that reside in caller-saved registers to the stack prior to each function call and to restore them after each call. That way, if the register allocator chooses to assign x to a caller-saved register, its value will be preserved across the call to `input_int`. However, saving and restoring to the stack is relatively slow. If x is not used many times, it may be better to assign x to a stack location in the first place. Or better yet, if we can arrange for x to be placed in a callee-saved register, then it won't need to be saved and restored during function calls.

We recommend an approach that captures these issues in the interference graph, without complicating the graph coloring algorithm. During liveness analysis we know which variables are call-live because we compute which variables are in use at every instruction (section 4.2). When we build the interference graph (section 4.3), we can place an edge in the interference graph between each call-live variable and the caller-saved registers. This will prevent the graph coloring algorithm from assigning call-live variables to caller-saved registers.

On the other hand, for variables that are not call-live, we prefer placing them in caller-saved registers to leave more room for call-live variables in the callee-saved registers. This can also be implemented without complicating the graph coloring algorithm. We recommend that the graph coloring algorithm assign variables to natural numbers, choosing the lowest number for which there is no interference. After the coloring is complete, we map the numbers to registers and stack locations:

Generated x86 assembly:

```
                            .globl main
                    main:
                            pushq %rbp
                            movq %rsp, %rbp
                            pushq %rbx
                            subq $8, %rsp
                            callq read_int
Example ℒ_Var program:     movq %rax, %rbx
                            callq read_int
x = input_int()             movq %rax, %rcx
y = input_int()             movq %rbx, %rdx
print((x + y) + 42)         addq %rcx, %rdx
                            movq %rdx, %rcx
                            addq $42, %rcx
                            movq %rcx, %rdi
                            callq print_int
                            addq $8, %rsp
                            popq %rbx
                            popq %rbp
                            retq
```

Figure 4.2
An example with function calls.

mapping the lowest numbers to caller-saved registers, the next lowest to callee-saved registers, and the largest numbers to stack locations. This ordering gives preference to registers over stack locations and to caller-saved registers over callee-saved registers.

Returning to the example in figure 4.2, let us analyze the generated x86 code on the right-hand side. Variable x is assigned to rbx, a callee-saved register. Thus, it is already in a safe place during the second call to read_int. Next, variable y is assigned to rcx, a caller-saved register, because y is not a call-live variable.

We have completed the analysis from the caller point of view, so now we switch to the callee point of view, focusing on the prelude and conclusion of the main function. As usual, the prelude begins with saving the rbp register to the stack and setting the rbp to the current stack pointer. We now know why it is necessary to save the rbp: it is a callee-saved register. The prelude then pushes rbx to the stack because (1) rbx is a callee-saved register and (2) rbx is assigned to a variable (x). The other callee-saved registers are not saved in the prelude because they are not used. The prelude subtracts 8 bytes from the rsp to make it 16-byte aligned. Shifting attention to the conclusion, we see that rbx is restored from the stack with a popq instruction.

4.2 Liveness Analysis

The `uncover_live` function performs *liveness analysis*; that is, it discovers which variables are in use in different regions of a program. A variable or register is *live* at a program point if its current value is used at some later point in the program. We refer to variables, stack locations, and registers collectively as *locations*. Consider the following code fragment in which there are two writes to b. Are variables a and b both live at the same time?

```
1  movq $5, a
2  movq $30, b
3  movq a, c
4  movq $10, b
5  addq b, c
```

The answer is no, because a is live from line 1 to 3 and b is live from line 4 to 5. The integer written to b on line 2 is never used because it is overwritten (line 4) before the next read (line 5).

The live locations for each instruction can be computed by traversing the instruction sequence back to front (i.e., backward in execution order). Let $I_1, \ldots, I_n$ be the instruction sequence. We write $L_{\text{after}}(k)$ for the set of live locations after instruction I_k and write $L_{\text{before}}(k)$ for the set of live locations before instruction I_k. We recommend representing these sets with the Python `set` data structure.

The locations that are live after an instruction are its *live-after* set, and the locations that are live before an instruction are its *live-before* set. The live-after set of an instruction is always the same as the live-before set of the next instruction.

$$L_{\text{after}}(k) = L_{\text{before}}(k+1) \tag{4.1}$$

To start things off, there are no live locations after the last instruction, so

$$L_{\text{after}}(n) = \emptyset \tag{4.2}$$

We then apply the following rule repeatedly, traversing the instruction sequence back to front.

$$L_{\text{before}}(k) = (L_{\text{after}}(k) - W(k)) \cup R(k), \tag{4.3}$$

where $W(k)$ are the locations written to by instruction I_k, and $R(k)$ are the locations read by instruction I_k.

Let us walk through the previous example, applying these formulas starting with the instruction on line 5 of the code fragment. We collect the answers in figure 4.3. The L_{after} for the `addq b, c` instruction is $\emptyset$ because it is the last instruction (formula (4.2)). The L_{before} for this instruction is $\{b, c\}$ because it reads from variables b and c (formula (4.3)):

$$L_{\text{before}}(5) = (\emptyset - \{c\}) \cup \{b, c\} = \{b, c\}$$

```
1   movq $5, a
2   movq $30, b
3   movq a, c
4   movq $10, b
5   addq b, c
```

$$L_{\text{before}}(1) = \emptyset, L_{\text{after}}(1) = \{a\}$$

$$L_{\text{before}}(2) = \{a\}, L_{\text{after}}(2) = \{a\}$$

$$L_{\text{before}}(3) = \{a\}, L_{\text{after}}(2) = \{c\}$$

$$L_{\text{before}}(4) = \{c\}, L_{\text{after}}(4) = \{b, c\}$$

$$L_{\text{before}}(5) = \{b, c\}, L_{\text{after}}(5) = \emptyset$$

Figure 4.3
Example output of liveness analysis on a short example.

Moving on the the instruction `movq $10, b` at line 4, we copy the live-before set from line 5 to be the live-after set for this instruction (formula (4.1)).

$$L_{\text{after}}(4) = \{b, c\}$$

This move instruction writes to b and does not read from any variables, so we have the following live-before set (formula (4.3)).

$$L_{\text{before}}(4) = (\{b, c\} - \{b\}) \cup \emptyset = \{c\}$$

The live-before for instruction `movq a, c` is $\{a\}$ because it writes to $\{c\}$ and reads from $\{a\}$ (formula (4.3)). The live-before for `movq $30, b` is $\{a\}$ because it writes to a variable that is not live and does not read from a variable. Finally, the live-before for `movq $5, a` is $\emptyset$ because it writes to variable a.

Exercise 4.1 Perform liveness analysis by hand on the running example in figure 4.1, computing the live-before and live-after sets for each instruction. Compare your answers to the solution shown in figure 4.4.

Exercise 4.2 Implement the `uncover_live` function. Return a dictionary that maps each instruction to its live-after set. We recommend creating auxiliary functions to (1) compute the set of locations that appear in an *arg*, (2) compute the locations read by an instruction (the *R* function), and (3) the locations written by an instruction (the *W* function). The `callq` instruction should include all the caller-saved registers in its write set *W* because the calling convention says that those registers may be written to during the function call. Likewise, the `callq` instruction should include the appropriate argument-passing registers in its read set *R*, depending on the arity of the function being called. (This is why the abstract syntax for `callq` includes the arity.)

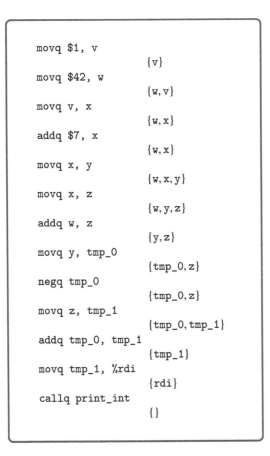

```
movq $1, v
                    {v}
movq $42, w
                    {w,v}
movq v, x
                    {w,x}
addq $7, x
                    {w,x}
movq x, y
                    {w,x,y}
movq x, z
                    {w,y,z}
addq w, z
                    {y,z}
movq y, tmp_0
                    {tmp_0,z}
negq tmp_0
                    {tmp_0,z}
movq z, tmp_1
                    {tmp_0,tmp_1}
addq tmp_0, tmp_1
                    {tmp_1}
movq tmp_1, %rdi
                    {rdi}
callq print_int
                    {}
```

Figure 4.4
The running example annotated with live-after sets.

4.3 Build the Interference Graph

On the basis of the liveness analysis, we know where each location is live. However, during register allocation, we need to answer questions of the specific form: are locations u and v live at the same time? (If so, they cannot be assigned to the same register.) To make this question more efficient to answer, we create an explicit data structure, an *interference graph*. An interference graph is an undirected graph that has a node for every variable and register and has an edge between two nodes if they are live at the same time, that is, if they interfere with each other. We provide implementations of directed and undirected graph data structures in the file `graph.py` of the support code.

A straightforward way to compute the interference graph is to look at the set of live locations between each instruction and add an edge to the graph for every pair of variables in the same set. This approach is less than ideal for two reasons. First, it can be expensive because it takes $O(n^2)$ time to consider every pair in a set of n live locations. Second, in the special case in which two locations hold the same value (because one was assigned to the other), they can be live at the same time without interfering with each other.

A better way to compute the interference graph is to focus on writes (Appel and Palsberg 2003). The writes performed by an instruction must not overwrite something in a live location. So for each instruction, we create an edge between the locations being written to and the live locations. (However, a location never interferes with itself.) For the `callq` instruction, we consider all the caller-saved registers to have been written to, so an edge is added between every live variable and every caller-saved register. Also, for `movq` there is the special case of two variables holding the same value. If a live variable v is the same as the source of the `movq`, then there is no need to add an edge between v and the destination, because they both hold the same value. Hence we have the following two rules:

1. If instruction I_k is a move instruction of the form `movq` s, d, then for every $v \in L_{\text{after}}(k)$, if $v \neq d$ and $v \neq s$, add the edge (d, v).
2. For any other instruction I_k, for every $d \in W(k)$ and every $v \in L_{\text{after}}(k)$, if $v \neq d$, add the edge (d, v).

Working from the top to bottom of figure 4.4, we apply these rules to each instruction. We highlight a few of the instructions. The first instruction is `movq $1`, v, and the live-after set is $\{v\}$. Rule 1 applies, but there is no interference because v is the destination of the move. The fourth instruction is `addq $7`, x, and the live-after set is $\{w, x\}$. Rule 2 applies, so x interferes with w. The next instruction is `movq x, y`, and the live-after set is $\{w, x, y\}$. Rule 1 applies, so y interferes with w but not x, because x is the source of the move and therefore x and y hold the same value. Figure 4.5 lists the interference results for all the instructions, and the resulting interference graph is shown in figure 4.6. We elide the register nodes from the interference graph in figure 4.6 because there were no interference edges involving registers and we did not wish to clutter the graph, but in general one needs to include all the registers in the interference graph.

Exercise 4.3 Implement a function named `build_interference` according to the algorithm suggested above that returns the interference graph.

4.4 Graph Coloring via Sudoku

We come to the main event discussed in this chapter, mapping variables to registers and stack locations. Variables that interfere with each other must be mapped to different locations. In terms of the interference graph, this means that adjacent vertices must be mapped to different locations. If we think of locations as colors, the register allocation problem becomes the graph coloring problem (Balakrishnan 1996; Rosen 2002).

The reader may be more familiar with the graph coloring problem than he or she realizes; the popular game of sudoku is an instance of the graph coloring problem. The following describes how to build a graph out of an initial sudoku board.

```
movq $1, v          no interference
movq $42, w         w interferes with v
movq v, x           x interferes with w
addq $7, x          x interferes with w
movq x, y           y interferes with w but not x
movq x, z           z interferes with w and y
addq w, z           z interferes with y
movq y, tmp_0       tmp_0 interferes with z
negq tmp_0          tmp_0 interferes with z
movq z, tmp_1       tmp_0 interferes with tmp_1
addq tmp_0, tmp_1   no interference
movq tmp_1, %rdi    no interference
callq print_int     no interference.
```

Figure 4.5
Interference results for the running example.

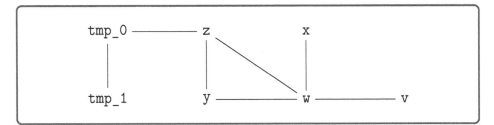

Figure 4.6
The interference graph of the example program.

- There is one vertex in the graph for each sudoku square.
- There is an edge between two vertices if the corresponding squares are in the same row, in the same column, or in the same 3×3 region.
- Choose nine colors to correspond to the numbers 1 to 9.
- On the basis of the initial assignment of numbers to squares on the sudoku board, assign the corresponding colors to the corresponding vertices in the graph.

If you can color the remaining vertices in the graph with the nine colors, then you have also solved the corresponding game of sudoku. Figure 4.7 shows an initial sudoku game board and the corresponding graph with colored vertices. Here we use a monochrome representation of colors, mapping the sudoku number 1 to black, 2 to white, and 3 to gray. We show edges for only a sampling of the vertices (the colored ones) because showing edges for all the vertices would make the graph unreadable.

Some techniques for playing sudoku correspond to heuristics used in graph coloring algorithms. For example, one of the basic techniques for sudoku is called Pencil Marks. The idea is to use a process of elimination to determine what numbers are no longer available for a square and to write those numbers in the square (writing very small). For example, if the number 1 is assigned to a square, then write the

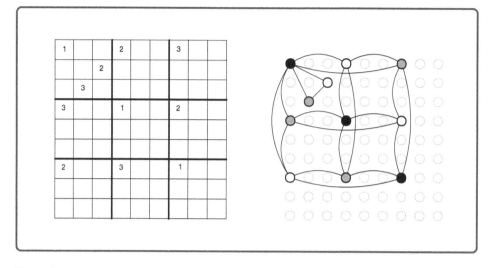

Figure 4.7
A sudoku game board and the corresponding colored graph.

pencil mark 1 in all the squares in the same row, column, and region to indicate that 1 is no longer an option for those other squares. The Pencil Marks technique corresponds to the notion of *saturation* due to Brélaz (1979). The saturation of a vertex, in sudoku terms, is the set of numbers that are no longer available. In graph terminology, we have the following definition:

$$\text{saturation}(u) = \{ c \mid \exists v. v \in \text{adjacent}(u) \text{ and color}(v) = c \}$$

where $\text{adjacent}(u)$ is the set of vertices that share an edge with u.

The Pencil Marks technique leads to a simple strategy for filling in numbers: if there is a square with only one possible number left, then choose that number! But what if there are no squares with only one possibility left? One brute-force approach is to try them all: choose the first one, and if that ultimately leads to a solution, great. If not, backtrack and choose the next possibility. One good thing about Pencil Marks is that it reduces the degree of branching in the search tree. Nevertheless, backtracking can be terribly time consuming. One way to reduce the amount of backtracking is to use the most-constrained-first heuristic (aka minimum remaining values) (Russell and Norvig 2003). That is, in choosing a square, always choose one with the fewest possibilities left (the vertex with the highest saturation). The idea is that choosing highly constrained squares earlier rather than later is better, because later on there may not be any possibilities left in the highly saturated squares.

However, register allocation is easier than sudoku, because the register allocator can fall back to assigning variables to stack locations when the registers run out. Thus, it makes sense to replace backtracking with greedy search: make the best choice at the time and keep going. We still wish to minimize the number of colors needed, so we use the most-constrained-first heuristic in the greedy search. Figure 4.8 gives the pseudocode for a simple greedy algorithm for register allocation

Algorithm: DSATUR
Input: A graph G
Output: An assignment color[v] for each vertex $v \in G$

$W \leftarrow$ vertices(G)
while $W \neq \emptyset$ **do**
    pick a vertex u from W with the highest saturation,
        breaking ties randomly
    find the lowest color c that is not in {color[v] : $v \in$ adjacent(u)}
    color[u] $\leftarrow c$
    $W \leftarrow W - \{u\}$

Figure 4.8
The saturation-based greedy graph coloring algorithm.

based on saturation and the most-constrained-first heuristic. It is roughly equivalent to the DSATUR graph coloring algorithm (Brélaz 1979). Just as in sudoku, the algorithm represents colors with integers. The integers 0 through $k-1$ correspond to the k registers that we use for register allocation. In particular, we recommend the following correspondence, with $k = 11$.

```
0: rcx, 1: rdx, 2: rsi, 3: rdi, 4: r8, 5: r9,
6: r10, 7: rbx, 8: r12, 9: r13, 10: r14
```

The integers k and larger correspond to stack locations. The registers that are not used for register allocation, such as rax, are assigned to negative integers. In particular, we recommend the following correspondence.

```
-1: rax, -2: rsp, -3: rbp, -4: r11, -5: r15
```

With the DSATUR algorithm in hand, let us return to the running example and consider how to color the interference graph shown in figure 4.6. We annotate each variable node with a dash to indicate that it has not yet been assigned a color. Each register node (not shown) should be assigned the number that the register corresponds to, for example, color rcx with the number 0 and rdx with 1. The saturation sets are also shown for each node; all of them start as the empty set.

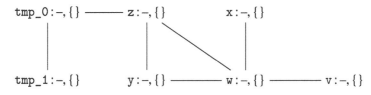

The algorithm says to select a maximally saturated vertex, but they are all equally saturated. So we flip a coin and pick tmp_0 and then we color it with the first available integer, which is 0. We mark 0 as no longer available for tmp_1 and z because they interfere with `tmp_0`.

$$\texttt{tmp\_0}:0,\{\} \longrightarrow \texttt{z}:-,\{0\} \qquad \texttt{x}:-,\{\}$$

$$\texttt{tmp\_1}:-,\{0\} \qquad \texttt{y}:-,\{\} \longrightarrow \texttt{w}:-,\{\} \longrightarrow \texttt{v}:-,\{\}$$

We repeat the process. The most saturated vertices are z and `tmp_1`, so we choose z and color it with the first available number, which is 1. We add 1 to the saturation for the neighboring vertices `tmp_0`, y, and w.

$$\texttt{tmp\_0}:0,\{1\} \longrightarrow \texttt{z}:1,\{0\} \qquad \texttt{x}:-,\{\}$$

$$\texttt{tmp\_1}:-,\{0\} \qquad \texttt{y}:-,\{1\} \longrightarrow \texttt{w}:-,\{1\} \longrightarrow \texttt{v}:-,\{\}$$

The most saturated vertices are now `tmp_1`, w, and y. We color w with the first available color, which is 0.

$$\texttt{tmp\_0}:0,\{1\} \longrightarrow \texttt{z}:1,\{0\} \qquad \texttt{x}:-,\{0\}$$

$$\texttt{tmp\_1}:-,\{0\} \qquad \texttt{y}:-,\{0,1\} \longrightarrow \texttt{w}:0,\{1\} \longrightarrow \texttt{v}:-,\{0\}$$

Now y is the most saturated, so we color it with 2.

$$\texttt{tmp\_0}:0,\{1\} \longrightarrow \texttt{z}:1,\{0,2\} \qquad \texttt{x}:-,\{0\}$$

$$\texttt{tmp\_1}:-,\{0\} \qquad \texttt{y}:2,\{0,1\} \longrightarrow \texttt{w}:0,\{1,2\} \longrightarrow \texttt{v}:-,\{0\}$$

The most saturated vertices are `tmp_1`, x, and v. We choose to color v with 1.

$$\texttt{tmp\_0}:0,\{1\} \longrightarrow \texttt{z}:1,\{0,2\} \qquad \texttt{x}:-,\{0\}$$

$$\texttt{tmp\_1}:-,\{0\} \qquad \texttt{y}:2,\{0,1\} \longrightarrow \texttt{w}:0,\{1,2\} \longrightarrow \texttt{v}:1,\{0\}$$

We color the remaining two variables, `tmp_1` and x, with 1.

$$\texttt{tmp\_0}:0,\{1\} \longrightarrow \texttt{z}:1,\{0,2\} \qquad \texttt{x}:1,\{0\}$$

$$\texttt{tmp\_1}:1,\{0\} \qquad \texttt{y}:2,\{0,1\} \longrightarrow \texttt{w}:0,\{1,2\} \longrightarrow \texttt{v}:1,\{0\}$$

So, we obtain the following coloring:

$$\{\texttt{tmp\_0} \mapsto 0, \texttt{tmp\_1} \mapsto 1, \texttt{z} \mapsto 1, \texttt{x} \mapsto 1, \texttt{y} \mapsto 2, \texttt{w} \mapsto 0, \texttt{v} \mapsto 1\}$$

We recommend creating an auxiliary function named `color_graph` that takes an interference graph and a list of all the variables in the program. This function should return a mapping of variables to their colors (represented as natural numbers). By creating this helper function, you will be able to reuse it in chapter 8 when we add support for functions.

To prioritize the processing of highly saturated nodes inside the `color_graph` function, we recommend using the priority queue data structure in the file `priority_queue.py` of the support code.

With the coloring complete, we finalize the assignment of variables to registers and stack locations. We map the first k colors to the k registers and the rest of the colors to stack locations. Suppose for the moment that we have just one register to use for register allocation, `rcx`. Then we have the following assignment.

$$\{0 \mapsto \texttt{\%rcx}, \ 1 \mapsto \texttt{-8(\%rbp)}, \ 2 \mapsto \texttt{-16(\%rbp)}\}$$

Composing this mapping with the coloring, we arrive at the following assignment of variables to locations.

$$\{\texttt{v} \mapsto \texttt{-8(\%rbp)}, \texttt{w} \mapsto \texttt{\%rcx}, \texttt{x} \mapsto \texttt{-8(\%rbp)}, \texttt{y} \mapsto \texttt{-16(\%rbp)},$$

$$\texttt{z} \mapsto \texttt{-8(\%rbp)}, \texttt{tmp\_0} \mapsto \texttt{\%rcx}, \texttt{tmp\_1} \mapsto \texttt{-8(\%rbp)}\}$$

Adapt the code from the **assign_homes** pass (section 2.6) to replace the variables with their assigned location. Applying this assignment to our running example shown next, on the left, yields the program on the right.

```
movq $1, v                        movq $1, -8(%rbp)
movq $42, w                       movq $42, %rcx
movq v, x                         movq -8(%rbp), -8(%rbp)
addq $7, x                        addq $7, -8(%rbp)
movq x, y                         movq -8(%rbp), -16(%rbp)
movq x, z                         movq -8(%rbp), -8(%rbp)
addq w, z            ⇒            addq %rcx, -8(%rbp)
movq y, tmp_0                     movq -16(%rbp), %rcx
negq tmp_0                        negq %rcx
movq z, tmp_1                     movq -8(%rbp), -8(%rbp)
addq tmp_0, tmp_1                 addq %rcx, -8(%rbp)
movq tmp_1, %rdi                  movq -8(%rbp), %rdi
callq print_int                   callq print_int
```

Exercise 4.4 Implement the **allocate_registers** pass. Create five programs that exercise all aspects of the register allocation algorithm, including spilling variables to the stack. Run the **run-tests.py** script to check whether the output programs produce the same result as the input programs.

4.5 Patch Instructions

The remaining step in the compilation to x86 is to ensure that the instructions have at most one argument that is a memory access. In the running example, the instruction movq -8(%rbp), -16(%rbp) is problematic. Recall from section 2.7 that the fix is to first move -8(%rbp) into rax and then move rax into -16(%rbp). The moves from -8(%rbp) to -8(%rbp) are also problematic, but they can simply be deleted. In general, we recommend deleting all the trivial moves whose source and destination are the same location. The following is the output of patch_instructions on the running example.

```
movq $1, -8(%rbp)
movq $42, %rcx
movq -8(%rbp), -8(%rbp)                movq $1, -8(%rbp)
addq $7, -8(%rbp)                      movq $42, %rcx
movq -8(%rbp), -16(%rbp)               addq $7, -8(%rbp)
movq -8(%rbp), -8(%rbp)                movq -8(%rbp), %rax
addq %rcx, -8(%rbp)         ⇒         movq %rax, -16(%rbp)
movq -16(%rbp), %rcx                   addq %rcx, -8(%rbp)
negq %rcx                              movq -16(%rbp), %rcx
movq -8(%rbp), -8(%rbp)                negq %rcx
addq %rcx, -8(%rbp)                    addq %rcx, -8(%rbp)
movq -8(%rbp), %rdi                    movq -8(%rbp), %rdi
callq print_int                       callq print_int
```

Exercise 4.5 Update the patch_instructions compiler pass to delete trivial moves. Run the script to test the patch_instructions pass.

4.6 Generate Prelude and Conclusion

Recall that this pass generates the prelude and conclusion instructions to satisfy the x86 calling conventions (section 4.1). With the addition of the register allocator, the callee-saved registers used by the register allocator must be saved in the prelude and restored in the conclusion. In the allocate_registers pass, add a field named used_callee to the X86Program AST node that stores the set of callee-saved registers that were assigned to variables. The prelude_and_conclusion pass can then access this information to decide which callee-saved registers need to be saved and restored. When calculating the amount to adjust the rsp in the prelude, make sure to take into account the space used for saving the callee-saved registers. Also, remember that the frame needs to be a multiple of 16 bytes! We recommend using the following equation for the amount A to subtract from the rsp. Let S be the number of stack locations used by spilled variables[1] and C be the number of callee-saved registers that were allocated to variables. The *align* function rounds a

---

1. Sometimes two or more spilled variables are assigned to the same stack location, so S can be less than the number of spilled variables.

number up to the nearest 16 bytes.

$$A = align(8S + 8C) - 8C$$

The reason we subtract $8C$ in this equation is that the prelude uses `pushq` to save each of the callee-saved registers, and `pushq` subtracts 8 from the `rsp`.

Figure 4.9 shows the x86 code generated for the running example (figure 4.1). To demonstrate both the use of registers and the stack, we limit the register allocator for this example to use just two registers: `rcx` (color 0) and `rbx` (color 1). In the prelude of the `main` function, we push `rbx` onto the stack because it is a callee-saved register and it was assigned to a variable by the register allocator. We subtract 8 from the `rsp` at the end of the prelude to reserve space for the one spilled variable. After that subtraction, the `rsp` is aligned to 16 bytes.

Moving on to the program proper, we see how the registers were allocated. Variables v, x, y, and `tmp_0` were assigned to `rcx`, and variables w and `tmp_1` were assigned to `rbx`. Variable z was spilled to the stack location `-16(%rbp)`. Recall that the prelude saved the callee-save register `rbx` onto the stack. The spilled variables must be placed lower on the stack than the saved callee-save registers, so in this case z is placed at `-16(%rbp)`.

In the conclusion, we undo the work that was done in the prelude. We move the stack pointer up by 8 bytes (the room for spilled variables), then pop the old values of `rbx` and `rbp` (callee-saved registers), and finish with `retq` to return control to the operating system.

Exercise 4.6 Update the `prelude_and_conclusion` pass as described in this section. Run the script to test the complete compiler for $\mathcal{L}_{Var}$ that performs register allocation.

4.7 Challenge: Move Biasing

This section describes an enhancement to the register allocator, called move biasing, for students who are looking for an extra challenge.

To motivate the need for move biasing we return to the running example and recall that in section 4.5 we were able to remove three trivial move instructions from the running example. However, we could remove another trivial move if we were able to allocate y and `tmp_0` to the same register.

We say that two variables p and q are *move related* if they participate together in a `movq` instruction, that is, `movq p, q` or `movq q, p`. Recall that we color variables that are more saturated before coloring variables that are less saturated, and in the case of equally saturated variables, we choose randomly. Now we break such ties by giving preference to variables that have an available color that is the same as the color of a move-related variable. Furthermore, when the register allocator chooses a color for a variable, it should prefer a color that has already been used for a move-related variable if one exists (and assuming that they do not interfere). This preference should not override the preference for registers over stack locations. So,

```
        .globl main
main:
    pushq %rbp
    movq %rsp, %rbp
    pushq %rbx
    subq $8, %rsp
    movq $1, %rcx
    movq $42, %rbx
    addq $7, %rcx
    movq %rcx, -16(%rbp)
    addq %rbx, -16(%rbp)
    negq %rcx
    movq -16(%rbp), %rbx
    addq %rcx, %rbx
    movq %rbx, %rdi
    callq print_int
    addq $8, %rsp
    popq %rbx
    popq %rbp
    retq
```

Figure 4.9
The x86 output from the running example (figure 4.1), limiting allocation to just **rbx** and **rcx**.

this preference should be used as a tie breaker in choosing between two registers or in choosing between two stack locations.

We recommend representing the move relationships in a graph, similarly to how we represented interference. The following is the *move graph* for our example.

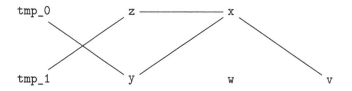

Now we replay the graph coloring, pausing before the coloring of w. Recall the following configuration. The most saturated vertices were tmp_1, w, and y.

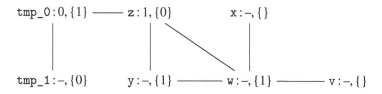

We have arbitrarily chosen to color w instead of tmp_1 or y. Note, however, that w is not move related to any variables, whereas y and tmp_1 are move related to tmp_0 and z, respectively. If we instead choose y and color it 0, we can delete another move instruction.

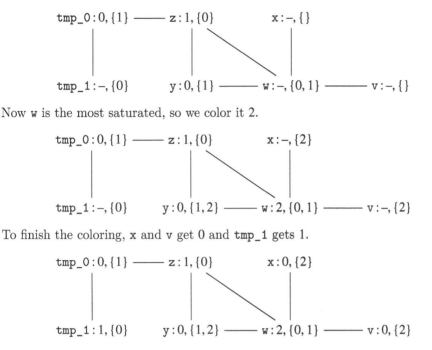

Now w is the most saturated, so we color it 2.

To finish the coloring, x and v get 0 and tmp_1 gets 1.

So, we have the following assignment of variables to registers.

$$\{v \mapsto \texttt{\%rcx}, w \mapsto \texttt{-16(\%rbp)}, x \mapsto \texttt{\%rcx}, y \mapsto \texttt{\%rcx},$$

$$z \mapsto \texttt{-8(\%rbp)}, \texttt{tmp\_0} \mapsto \texttt{\%rcx}, \texttt{tmp\_1} \mapsto \texttt{-8(\%rbp)}\}$$

We apply this register assignment to the running example shown next, on the left, to obtain the code in the middle. The `patch_instructions` then deletes the trivial moves to obtain the code on the right.

```
movq $1, v
movq $42, w
movq v, x
addq $7, x
movq x, y
movq x, z
addq w, z           ⇒
movq y, tmp_0
negq tmp_0
movq z, tmp_1
addq tmp_0, tmp_1
movq tmp_1, %rdi
callq _print_int
```

```
movq $1, %rcx
movq $42, -16(%rbp)
movq %rcx, %rcx
addq $7, %rcx
movq %rcx, %rcx
movq %rcx, -8(%rbp)
addq -16(%rbp), -8(%rbp)    ⇒
movq %rcx, %rcx
negq %rcx
movq -8(%rbp), -8(%rbp)
addq %rcx, -8(%rbp)
movq -8(%rbp), %rdi
callq _print_int
```

```
movq $1, %rcx
movq $42, -16(%rbp)
addq $7, %rcx
movq %rcx, -8(%rbp)
movq -16(%rbp), %rax
addq %rax, -8(%rbp)
negq %rcx
addq %rcx, -8(%rbp)
movq -8(%rbp), %rdi
callq print_int
```

Exercise 4.7 Change your implementation of `allocate_registers` to take move biasing into account. Create two new tests that include at least one opportunity for move biasing, and visually inspect the output x86 programs to make sure that your move biasing is working properly. Make sure that your compiler still passes all the tests.

4.8   Further Reading

Early register allocation algorithms were developed for Fortran compilers in the 1950s (Horwitz et al. 1966; Backus 1978). The use of graph coloring began in the late 1970s and early 1980s with the work of Chaitin et al. (1981) on an optimizing compiler for PL/I. The algorithm is based on the following observation of Kempe (1879). If a graph G has a vertex v with degree lower than k, then G is k colorable if the subgraph of G with v removed is also k colorable. To see why, suppose that the subgraph is k colorable. At worst, the neighbors of v are assigned different colors, but because there are fewer than k neighbors, there will be one or more colors left over to use for coloring v in G.

The algorithm of Chaitin et al. (1981) removes a vertex v of degree less than k from the graph and recursively colors the rest of the graph. Upon returning from the recursion, it colors v with one of the available colors and returns. Chaitin (1982) augments this algorithm to handle spilling as follows. If there are no vertices of degree lower than k then pick a vertex at random, spill it, remove it from the graph, and proceed recursively to color the rest of the graph.

Prior to coloring, Chaitin et al. (1981) merged variables that are move-related and that don't interfere with each other, in a process called *coalescing*. Although coalescing decreases the number of moves, it can make the graph more difficult to color. Briggs, Cooper, and Torczon (1994) proposed *conservative coalescing* in which two variables are merged only if they have fewer than k neighbors of high degree. George and Appel (1996) observes that conservative coalescing is sometimes too conservative and made it more aggressive by iterating the coalescing with the removal of low-degree vertices. Attacking the problem from a different angle, Briggs, Cooper, and Torczon (1994) also proposed *biased coloring*, in which a variable is assigned to the same color as another move-related variable if possible, as discussed in section 4.7. The algorithm of Chaitin et al. (1981) and its successors iteratively performs coalescing, graph coloring, and spill code insertion until all variables have been assigned a location.

Briggs, Cooper, and Torczon (1994) observes that Chaitin (1982) sometimes spilled variables that don't have to be: a high-degree variable can be colorable if many of its neighbors are assigned the same color. Briggs, Cooper, and Torczon (1994) proposed *optimistic coloring*, in which a high-degree vertex is not immediately spilled. Instead the decision is deferred until after the recursive call, when it is apparent whether there is an available color or not. We observe that this algorithm is equivalent to the smallest-last ordering algorithm (Matula, Marble, and Isaacson 1972) if one takes the first k colors to be registers and the rest to be stack locations. Earlier editions of the compiler course at Indiana University (Dybvig and Keep 2010) were based on the algorithm of Briggs, Cooper, and Torczon (1994).

The smallest-last ordering algorithm is one of many *greedy* coloring algorithms. A greedy coloring algorithm visits all the vertices in a particular order and assigns each one the first available color. An *offline* greedy algorithm chooses the ordering up front, prior to assigning colors. The algorithm of Chaitin et al. (1981) should be considered offline because the vertex ordering does not depend on the colors assigned. Other orderings are possible. For example, Chow and Hennessy (1984) ordered variables according to an estimate of runtime cost.

An *online* greedy coloring algorithm uses information about the current assignment of colors to influence the order in which the remaining vertices are colored. The saturation-based algorithm described in this chapter is one such algorithm. We choose to use saturation-based coloring because it is fun to introduce graph coloring via sudoku!

A register allocator may choose to map each variable to just one location, as in Chaitin et al. (1981), or it may choose to map a variable to one or more locations. The latter can be achieved by *live range splitting*, where a variable is replaced by several variables that each handle part of its live range (Chow and Hennessy 1984; Briggs, Cooper, and Torczon 1994; Cooper and Simpson 1998).

Palsberg (2007) observes that many of the interference graphs that arise from Java programs in the JoeQ compiler are *chordal*; that is, every cycle with four or more edges has an edge that is not part of the cycle but that connects two vertices on the cycle. Such graphs can be optimally colored by the greedy algorithm with a vertex ordering determined by maximum cardinality search.

In situations in which compile time is of utmost importance, such as in just-in-time compilers, graph coloring algorithms can be too expensive, and the linear scan algorithm of Poletto and Sarkar (1999) may be more appropriate.

5 Booleans and Conditionals

The $\mathcal{L}_{\mathsf{Var}}$ language has only a single kind of value, the integers. In this chapter we add a second kind of value, the Booleans, to create the $\mathcal{L}_{\mathsf{If}}$ language. In Python, the Boolean values *true* and *false* are written `True` and `False`, respectively. The $\mathcal{L}_{\mathsf{If}}$ language includes several operations that involve Booleans (`and`, `or`, `not`, `==`, `<`, etc.) and the `if` conditional expression and statement. With the addition of `if`, programs can have nontrivial control flow, which impacts liveness analysis and motivates a new pass named `explicate_control`. Also, because we now have two kinds of values, we need to handle programs that apply an operation to the wrong kind of value, such as `not 1`.

There are two language design options for such situations. One option is to signal an error and the other is to provide a wider interpretation of the operation. Python uses a mixture of these two options, depending on the operation and the kind of value. For example, the result of `not 1` is False because Python treats nonzero integers as if they were `True`. On the other hand, `1[0]` results in a runtime error in Python because an "`int` object is not subscriptable."

The MyPy type checker makes similar design choices as Python, except that much of the error detection happens at compile time instead of runtime (Lehtosalo 2021). MyPy accepts `not 1`. But in the case of `1[0]`, MyPy reports a compile-time error stating that a "value of type `int` is not indexable."

The $\mathcal{L}_{\mathsf{If}}$ language performs type checking during compilation just as MyPy. In chapter 10 we study the alternative choice, that is, a dynamically typed language like Python. The $\mathcal{L}_{\mathsf{If}}$ language is a subset of MyPy; for some operations we are more restrictive, for example, rejecting `not 1`. We keep the type checker for $\mathcal{L}_{\mathsf{If}}$ fairly simple because the focus of this book is on compilation and not type systems, about which there are already several excellent books (Pierce 2002, 2004; Harper 2016; Pierce et al. 2018).

This chapter is organized as follows. We begin by defining the syntax and interpreter for the $\mathcal{L}_{\mathsf{If}}$ language (section 5.1). We then introduce the idea of type checking (aka semantic analysis) and define a type checker for $\mathcal{L}_{\mathsf{If}}$ (section 5.2). The remaining sections of this chapter discuss how Booleans and conditional control flow require changes to the existing compiler passes and the addition of new ones. We introduce the `shrink` pass to translate some operators into others, thereby reducing the number of operators that need to be handled in later passes. The main event of this chapter is the `explicate_control` pass that is responsible for translating

$$
\begin{array}{rcl}
\mathit{exp} & ::= & \mathit{int} \mid \texttt{input\_int()} \mid - \mathit{exp} \mid \mathit{exp} + \mathit{exp} \mid \mathit{exp} - \mathit{exp} \mid (\mathit{exp}) \\
\mathit{stmt} & ::= & \texttt{print}(\mathit{exp}) \mid \mathit{exp} \\
\mathit{exp} & ::= & \mathit{var} \\
\mathit{stmt} & ::= & \mathit{var} = \mathit{exp} \\
\end{array}
$$

$$
\begin{array}{rcl}
\mathit{cmp} & ::= & \texttt{==} \mid \texttt{!=} \mid \texttt{<} \mid \texttt{<=} \mid \texttt{>} \mid \texttt{>=} \\
\mathit{exp} & ::= & \texttt{True} \mid \texttt{False} \mid \mathit{exp} \textbf{ and } \mathit{exp} \mid \mathit{exp} \textbf{ or } \mathit{exp} \mid \textbf{not } \mathit{exp} \\
& \mid & \mathit{exp}\ \mathit{cmp}\ \mathit{exp} \mid \mathit{exp} \textbf{ if } \mathit{exp} \textbf{ else } \mathit{exp} \\
\mathit{stmt} & ::= & \texttt{if } \mathit{exp}\texttt{: } \mathit{stmt}^+ \texttt{ else: } \mathit{stmt}^+ \\
\mathcal{L}_{\mathsf{If}} & ::= & \mathit{stmt}^* \\
\end{array}
$$

Figure 5.1
The concrete syntax of $\mathcal{L}_{\mathsf{If}}$, extending $\mathcal{L}_{\mathsf{Var}}$ (figure 2.1) with Booleans and conditionals.

`ifs` into conditional `gotos` (section 5.7). Regarding register allocation, there is the interesting question of how to handle conditional `gotos` during liveness analysis.

5.1 The $\mathcal{L}_{\mathsf{If}}$ Language

Definitions of the concrete syntax and abstract syntax of the $\mathcal{L}_{\mathsf{If}}$ language are shown in figures 5.1 and 5.2, respectively. The $\mathcal{L}_{\mathsf{If}}$ language includes all of $\mathcal{L}_{\mathsf{Var}}$ (shown in gray), the Boolean literals `True` and `False`, the if expression, and the if statement. We expand the set of operators to include

1. the logical operators **and**, **or**, and **not**,
2. the == and != operations for comparing integers or Booleans for equality, and
3. the <, <=, >, and >= operations for comparing integers.

Figure 5.3 shows the definition of the interpreter for $\mathcal{L}_{\mathsf{If}}$, which inherits from the interpreter for $\mathcal{L}_{\mathsf{Var}}$ (figure 2.4). The constants `True` and `False` evaluate to the corresponding Boolean values, behavior that is inherited from the interpreter for $\mathcal{L}_{\mathsf{Int}}$ (figure 2.3). The conditional expression e_2 **if** e_1 **else** e_3 evaluates expression e_1 and then either evaluates e_2 or e_3, depending on whether e_1 produced `True` or `False`. The logical operations **and**, **or**, and **not** behave according to propositional logic. In addition, the **and** and **or** operations perform *short-circuit evaluation*. That is, given the expression e_1 **and** e_2, the expression e_2 is not evaluated if e_1 evaluates to `False`. Similarly, given e_1 **or** e_2, the expression e_2 is not evaluated if e_1 evaluates to `True`.

5.2 Type Checking $\mathcal{L}_{\mathsf{If}}$ Programs

It is helpful to think about type checking in two complementary ways. A type checker predicts the type of value that will be produced by each expression in the

```
exp    ::=   Constant(int) | Call(Name('input_int'),[])
       |     UnaryOp(USub(),exp) | BinOp(exp,Add(),exp)
       |     BinOp(exp,Sub(),exp)
stmt   ::=   Expr(Call(Name('print'),[exp])) | Expr(exp)
```
```
exp    ::=   Name(var)
stmt   ::=   Assign([Name(var)], exp)
```
```
boolop ::=   And() | Or()
cmp    ::=   Eq() | NotEq() | Lt() | LtE() | Gt() | GtE()
bool   ::=   True | False
exp    ::=   Constant(bool) | BoolOp(boolop,[exp,exp])
       |     UnaryOp(Not(),exp) | Compare(exp,[cmp],[exp])
       |     IfExp(exp,exp,exp)
stmt   ::=   If(exp, stmt⁺, stmt⁺)
𝓛ɪf    ::=   Module(stmt*)
```

Figure 5.2
The abstract syntax of $\mathcal{L}_{\text{If}}$.

program. For $\mathcal{L}_{\text{If}}$, we have just two types, int and bool. So, a type checker should predict that

    10 + -(12 + 20)

produces a value of type int, whereas

    (not False) and True

produces a value of type bool.

A second way to think about type checking is that it enforces a set of rules about which operators can be applied to which kinds of values. For example, our type checker for $\mathcal{L}_{\text{If}}$ signals an error for the following expression:

    not (10 + -(12 + 20))

The subexpression (10 + -(12 + 20)) has type int, but the type checker enforces the rule that the argument of not must be an expression of type bool.

We implement type checking using classes and methods because they provide the open recursion needed to reuse code as we extend the type checker in subsequent chapters, analogous to the use of classes and methods for the interpreters (section 2.1.1).

We separate the type checker for the $\mathcal{L}_{\text{Var}}$ subset into its own class, shown in figure 5.5. The type checker for $\mathcal{L}_{\text{If}}$ is shown in figure 5.6, and it inherits from the type checker for $\mathcal{L}_{\text{Var}}$. These type checkers are in the files type_check_Lvar.py and type_check_Lif.py of the support code. Each type checker is a structurally recursive function over the AST. Given an input expression e, the type checker either signals an error or returns its type.

```
class InterpLif(InterpLvar):
  def interp_exp(self, e, env):
    match e:
      case IfExp(test, body, orelse):
        if self.interp_exp(test, env):
          return self.interp_exp(body, env)
        else:
          return self.interp_exp(orelse, env)
      case UnaryOp(Not(), v):
        return not self.interp_exp(v, env)
      case BoolOp(And(), values):
        if self.interp_exp(values[0], env):
          return self.interp_exp(values[1], env)
        else:
          return False
      case BoolOp(Or(), values):
        if self.interp_exp(values[0], env):
          return True
        else:
          return self.interp_exp(values[1], env)
      case Compare(left, [cmp], [right]):
        l = self.interp_exp(left, env)
        r = self.interp_exp(right, env)
        return self.interp_cmp(cmp)(l, r)
      case _:
        return super().interp_exp(e, env)

  def interp_stmt(self, s, env, cont):
    match s:
      case If(test, body, orelse):
        match self.interp_exp(test, env):
          case True:
            return self.interp_stmts(body + cont, env)
          case False:
            return self.interp_stmts(orelse + cont, env)
      case _:
        return super().interp_stmt(s, env, cont)
    ...
```

Figure 5.3
Interpreter for the $\mathcal{L}_{\text{If}}$ language. (See figure 5.4 for interp_cmp.)

Next we discuss the type_check_exp function of $\mathcal{L}_{\text{Var}}$ shown in figure 5.5. The type of an integer constant is int. To handle variables, the type checker uses the environment env to map variables to types. Consider the case for assignment. We type check the initializing expression to obtain its type t. If the variable id is already in the environment because there was a prior assignment, we check that this initializer has the same type as the prior one. If this is the first assignment to

```
class InterpLif(InterpLvar):
  ...
  def interp_cmp(self, cmp):
    match cmp:
      case Lt():
        return lambda x, y: x < y
      case LtE():
        return lambda x, y: x <= y
      case Gt():
        return lambda x, y: x > y
      case GtE():
        return lambda x, y: x >= y
      case Eq():
        return lambda x, y: x == y
      case NotEq():
        return lambda x, y: x != y
```

Figure 5.4
Interpreter for the comparison operators in the $\mathcal{L}_{\text{If}}$ language.

the variable, we associate type t with the variable id in the environment. Thus, when the type checker encounters a use of variable x, it can find its type in the environment. Regarding addition, subtraction, and negation, we recursively analyze the arguments, check that they have type int, and return int.

The auxiliary method **check_type_equal** triggers an error if the two types are not equal.

The definition of the type checker for $\mathcal{L}_{\text{If}}$ is shown in figure 5.6. The type of a Boolean constant is bool. The logical **not** operator requires its argument to be a bool and produces a bool. Similarly for the logical **and** and logical **or** operators. The equality operator requires the two arguments to have the same type, and therefore we handle it separately from the other operators. The other comparisons (less-than, etc.) require their arguments to be of type int, and they produce a bool. The condition of an if must be of bool type, and the two branches must have the same type.

Exercise 5.1 Create ten new test programs in $\mathcal{L}_{\text{If}}$. Half the programs should have a type error. The other half of the test programs should not have type errors. Run the test script to check that these test programs type check as expected.

```
class TypeCheckLvar:
  def check_type_equal(self, t1, t2, e):
    if t1 != t2:
      msg = 'error: ' + repr(t1) + ' != ' + repr(t2) + ' in ' + repr(e)
      raise Exception(msg)

  def type_check_exp(self, e, env):
    match e:
      case BinOp(left, (Add() | Sub()), right):
        l = self.type_check_exp(left, env)
        check_type_equal(l, int, left)
        r = self.type_check_exp(right, env)
        check_type_equal(r, int, right)
        return int
      case UnaryOp(USub(), v):
        t = self.type_check_exp(v, env)
        check_type_equal(t, int, v)
        return int
      case Name(id):
        return env[id]
      case Constant(value) if isinstance(value, int):
        return int
      case Call(Name('input_int'), []):
        return int

  def type_check_stmts(self, ss, env):
    if len(ss) == 0:
      return
    match ss[0]:
      case Assign([Name(id)], value):
        t = self.type_check_exp(value, env)
        if id in env:
          check_type_equal(env[id], t, value)
        else:
          env[id] = t
        return self.type_check_stmts(ss[1:], env)
      case Expr(Call(Name('print'), [arg])):
        t = self.type_check_exp(arg, env)
        check_type_equal(t, int, arg)
        return self.type_check_stmts(ss[1:], env)
      case Expr(value):
        self.type_check_exp(value, env)
        return self.type_check_stmts(ss[1:], env)

  def type_check_P(self, p):
    match p:
      case Module(body):
        self.type_check_stmts(body, {})
```

Figure 5.5

Type checker for the $\mathcal{L}_{Var}$ language.

```
class TypeCheckLif(TypeCheckLvar):
  def type_check_exp(self, e, env):
    match e:
      case Constant(value) if isinstance(value, bool):
        return bool
      case BinOp(left, Sub(), right):
        l = self.type_check_exp(left, env); check_type_equal(l, int, left)
        r = self.type_check_exp(right, env); check_type_equal(r, int, right)
        return int
      case UnaryOp(Not(), v):
        t = self.type_check_exp(v, env); check_type_equal(t, bool, v)
        return bool
      case BoolOp(op, values):
        left = values[0] ; right = values[1]
        l = self.type_check_exp(left, env); check_type_equal(l, bool, left)
        r = self.type_check_exp(right, env); check_type_equal(r, bool, right)
        return bool
      case Compare(left, [cmp], [right]) if isinstance(cmp, Eq) \
                                    or isinstance(cmp, NotEq):
        l = self.type_check_exp(left, env)
        r = self.type_check_exp(right, env)
        check_type_equal(l, r, e)
        return bool
      case Compare(left, [cmp], [right]):
        l = self.type_check_exp(left, env); check_type_equal(l, int, left)
        r = self.type_check_exp(right, env); check_type_equal(r, int, right)
        return bool
      case IfExp(test, body, orelse):
        t = self.type_check_exp(test, env); check_type_equal(bool, t, test)
        b = self.type_check_exp(body, env)
        o = self.type_check_exp(orelse, env)
        check_type_equal(b, o, e)
        return b
      case _:
        return super().type_check_exp(e, env)

  def type_check_stmts(self, ss, env):
    if len(ss) == 0:
      return
    match ss[0]:
      case If(test, body, orelse):
        t = self.type_check_exp(test, env); check_type_equal(bool, t, test)
        b = self.type_check_stmts(body, env)
        o = self.type_check_stmts(orelse, env)
        check_type_equal(b, o, ss[0])
        return self.type_check_stmts(ss[1:], env)
      case _:
        return super().type_check_stmts(ss, env)
```

Figure 5.6
Type checker for the $\mathcal{L}_{\text{If}}$ language.

$$
\begin{array}{rcl}
atm & ::= & int \mid var \mid bool \\
exp & ::= & atm \mid \texttt{input\_int()} \mid - atm \mid atm + atm \mid atm - atm \mid atm\ cmp\ atm \\
stmt & ::= & \texttt{print}(atm) \mid exp \mid var = exp \\
tail & ::= & \texttt{return}\ exp \mid \texttt{goto}\ label \\
& \mid & \texttt{if}\ atm\ cmp\ atm\texttt{: goto}\ label\ \texttt{else: goto}\ label \\
\mathcal{C}_{\mathsf{If}} & ::= & (label\texttt{:}\ stmt^*\ tail) \dots
\end{array}
$$

Figure 5.7
The concrete syntax of the $\mathcal{C}_{\mathsf{If}}$ intermediate language.

$$
\begin{array}{rcl}
atm & ::= & \texttt{Constant}(int) \mid \texttt{Name}(var) \mid \texttt{Constant}(bool) \\
exp & ::= & atm \mid \texttt{Call(Name('input\_int'),[])} \mid \texttt{UnaryOp(USub(),}atm\texttt{)} \\
& \mid & \texttt{BinOp(}atm\texttt{,Sub(),}atm\texttt{)} \mid \texttt{BinOp(}atm\texttt{,Add(),}atm\texttt{)} \\
& \mid & \texttt{Compare(}atm\texttt{,[}cmp\texttt{],[}atm\texttt{])} \\
stmt & ::= & \texttt{Expr(Call(Name('print'),[}atm\texttt{]))} \mid \texttt{Expr(}exp\texttt{)} \\
& \mid & \texttt{Assign([Name(}var\texttt{)],}\ exp\texttt{)} \\
tail & ::= & \texttt{Return(}exp\texttt{)} \mid \texttt{Goto(}label\texttt{)} \\
& \mid & \texttt{If(Compare(}atm\texttt{,[}cmp\texttt{],[}atm\texttt{]), [Goto(}label\texttt{)], [Goto(}label\texttt{)])} \\
\mathcal{C}_{\mathsf{If}} & ::= & \texttt{CProgram(\{}label\texttt{: [}stmt, \dots, tail\texttt{], } \dots \texttt{\})}
\end{array}
$$

Figure 5.8
The abstract syntax of $\mathcal{C}_{\mathsf{If}}$.

5.3 The $\mathcal{C}_{\mathsf{If}}$ Intermediate Language

The output of `explicate_control` is a language similar to the C language (Kernighan and Ritchie 1988) in that it has labels and `goto` statements, so we name it $\mathcal{C}_{\mathsf{If}}$. The $\mathcal{C}_{\mathsf{If}}$ language supports most of the operators in $\mathcal{L}_{\mathsf{If}}$, but the arguments of operators are restricted to atomic expressions. The $\mathcal{C}_{\mathsf{If}}$ language does not include `if` expressions, but it does include a restricted form of `if` statement. The condition must be a comparison, and the two branches may contain only `goto` statements. These restrictions make it easier to translate `if` statements to x86. The $\mathcal{C}_{\mathsf{If}}$ language also adds a **return** statement to finish the program with a specified value. The `CProgram` construct contains a dictionary mapping labels to lists of statements that end with a *tail* statement, which is either a **return** statement, a `goto`, or an `if` statement. A `goto` transfers control to the sequence of statements associated with its label. Figure 5.7 shows the concrete syntax for $\mathcal{C}_{\mathsf{If}}$, and figure 5.8 shows its abstract syntax.

5.4 The x86$_{\mathsf{If}}$ Language

To implement Booleans, the new logical operations, the comparison operations, and the `if` expression and statement, we delve further into the x86 language. Figures 5.9

```
 reg    ::=   rsp | rbp | rax | rbx | rcx | rdx | rsi | rdi |
              r8 | r9 | r10 | r11 | r12 | r13 | r14 | r15
 arg    ::=   $int | %reg | int(%reg)
 instr  ::=   addq arg,arg | subq arg,arg | negq arg | movq arg,arg |
              pushq arg | popq arg | callq label | retq | jmp label |
              label: instr
 bytereg ::=  ah | al | bh | bl | ch | cl | dh | dl
 arg     ::=  %bytereg
 cc      ::=  e | ne | l | le | g | ge
 instr   ::=  xorq arg, arg | cmpq arg, arg | setcc arg | movzbq arg, arg
           |  jcc label
 x86_If  ::=  .globl main
              main: instr ...
```

Figure 5.9
The concrete syntax of x86$_{If}$ (extends x86$_{Int}$ of figure 2.5).

and 5.10 present the definitions of the concrete and abstract syntax for the x86$_{If}$ subset of x86, which includes instructions for logical operations, comparisons, and jumps. The abstract syntax for an x86$_{If}$ program contains a dictionary mapping labels to sequences of instructions, each of which we refer to as a *basic block*.

As x86 does not provide direct support for Booleans, we take the usual approach of encoding Booleans as integers, with **True** as 1 and **False** as 0.

Furthermore, x86 does not provide an instruction that directly implements logical negation (**not** in $\mathcal{L}_{If}$ and $\mathcal{C}_{If}$). However, the **xorq** instruction can be used to encode **not**. The **xorq** instruction takes two arguments, performs a pairwise exclusive-or (XOR) operation on each bit of its arguments, and writes the results into its second argument. Recall the following truth table for exclusive-or:

	0	1
0	0	1
1	1	0

For example, applying XOR to each bit of the binary numbers 0011 and 0101 yields 0110. Notice that in the row of the table for the bit 1, the result is the opposite of the second bit. Thus, the **not** operation can be implemented by **xorq** with 1 as the first argument, as follows, where *arg* is the translation of *atm* to x86:

$$var = \text{not } atm \quad \Rightarrow \quad \begin{array}{l} \text{movq } arg,var \\ \text{xorq } \$1,var \end{array}$$

Next we consider the x86 instructions that are relevant for compiling the comparison operations. The **cmpq** instruction compares its two arguments to determine whether one argument is less than, equal to, or greater than the other argument. The **cmpq** instruction is unusual regarding the order of its arguments and where

$$
\begin{array}{lll}
\textit{reg} & ::= & \texttt{rsp} \mid \texttt{rbp} \mid \texttt{rax} \mid \texttt{rbx} \mid \texttt{rcx} \mid \texttt{rdx} \mid \texttt{rsi} \mid \texttt{rdi} \mid \\
& & \texttt{r8} \mid \texttt{r9} \mid \texttt{r10} \mid \texttt{r11} \mid \texttt{r12} \mid \texttt{r13} \mid \texttt{r14} \mid \texttt{r15} \\
\textit{arg} & ::= & \texttt{Immediate}(\textit{int}) \mid \texttt{Reg}(\textit{reg}) \mid \texttt{Deref}(\textit{reg},\textit{int}) \\
\textit{instr} & ::= & \texttt{Instr('addq',}[\textit{arg},\textit{arg}]) \mid \texttt{Instr('subq',}[\textit{arg},\textit{arg}]) \\
& \mid & \texttt{Instr('negq',}[\textit{arg}]) \mid \texttt{Instr('movq',}[\textit{arg},\textit{arg}]) \\
& \mid & \texttt{Instr('pushq',}[\textit{arg}]) \mid \texttt{Instr('popq',}[\textit{arg}]) \\
& \mid & \texttt{Callq}(\textit{label},\textit{int}) \mid \texttt{Retq}() \mid \texttt{Jump}(\textit{label}) \\
\textit{block} & ::= & \textit{instr}^{+}
\end{array}
$$

$$
\begin{array}{lll}
\textit{bytereg} & ::= & \texttt{'ah'} \mid \texttt{'al'} \mid \texttt{'bh'} \mid \texttt{'bl'} \mid \texttt{'ch'} \mid \texttt{'cl'} \mid \texttt{'dh'} \mid \texttt{'dl'} \\
\textit{arg} & ::= & \texttt{Immediate}(\textit{int}) \mid \texttt{Reg}(\textit{reg}) \mid \texttt{Deref}(\textit{reg},\textit{int}) \mid \texttt{ByteReg}(\textit{bytereg}) \\
\textit{cc} & ::= & \texttt{'e'} \mid \texttt{'ne'} \mid \texttt{'l'} \mid \texttt{'le'} \mid \texttt{'g'} \mid \texttt{'ge'} \\
\textit{instr} & ::= & \texttt{Jump}(\textit{label}) \\
& \mid & \texttt{Instr('xorq',}[\textit{arg},\textit{arg}]) \mid \texttt{Instr('cmpq',}[\textit{arg},\textit{arg}]) \\
& \mid & \texttt{Instr('set'}+\textit{cc},[\textit{arg}]) \mid \texttt{Instr('movzbq',}[\textit{arg},\textit{arg}]) \\
& \mid & \texttt{JumpIf}(\textit{cc},\textit{label}) \\
\text{x86}_{\text{If}} & ::= & \texttt{X86Program}(\{\textit{label} : \textit{block}, \ldots \})
\end{array}
$$

Figure 5.10
The abstract syntax of x86$_{\text{If}}$ (extends x86$_{\text{Int}}$ shown in figure 2.9).

the result is placed. The argument order is backward: if you want to test whether $x<y$, then write cmpq y, x. The result of cmpq is placed in the special EFLAGS register. This register cannot be accessed directly, but it can be queried by a number of instructions, including the **set** instruction. The instruction set*cc* d puts a 1 or 0 into the destination d, depending on whether the contents of the EFLAGS register matches the condition code *cc*: e for equal, l for less, le for less-or-equal, g for greater, ge for greater-or-equal. The **set** instruction has a quirk in that its destination argument must be a single-byte register, such as al (l for lower bits) or ah (h for higher bits), which are part of the rax register. Thankfully, the movzbq instruction can be used to move from a single-byte register to a normal 64-bit register. The abstract syntax for the **set** instruction differs from the concrete syntax in that it separates the instruction name from the condition code.

The x86 instructions for jumping are relevant to the compilation of **if** expressions. The instruction jmp *label* updates the program counter to the address of the instruction after the specified label. The instruction j*cc label* updates the program counter to point to the instruction after *label*, depending on whether the result in the EFLAGS register matches the condition code *cc*; otherwise, the jump instruction falls through to the next instruction. Like the abstract syntax for **set**, the abstract syntax for conditional jump separates the instruction name from the condition code. For example, JumpIf('le' , 'foo') corresponds to jle foo. Because the conditional jump instruction relies on the EFLAGS register, it is common for it to be immediately preceded by a cmpq instruction to set the EFLAGS register.

5.5   Shrink the $\mathcal{L}_{\text{If}}$ Language

The shrink pass translates some of the language features into other features, thereby reducing the kinds of expressions in the language. For example, the short-circuiting nature of the and and or logical operators can be expressed using if as follows.

$$e_1 \text{ and } e_2 \quad \Rightarrow \quad e_2 \text{ if } e_1 \text{ else False}$$

$$e_1 \text{ or } e_2 \quad \Rightarrow \quad \text{True if } e_1 \text{ else } e_2$$

By performing these translations in the front end of the compiler, subsequent passes of the compiler can be shorter.

On the other hand, translations sometimes reduce the efficiency of the generated code by increasing the number of instructions. For example, expressing subtraction in terms of addition and negation

$$e_1 - e_2 \quad \Rightarrow \quad e_1 + - e_2$$

produces code with two x86 instructions (**negq** and **addq**) instead of just one (**subq**). Thus, we do not recommend translating subtraction into addition and negation.

Exercise 5.2   Implement the pass **shrink** to remove and and or from the language by translating them to if expressions in $\mathcal{L}_{\text{If}}$. Create four test programs that involve these operators. Run the script to test your compiler on all the test programs.

5.6   Remove Complex Operands

The output language of **remove_complex_operands** is $\mathcal{L}_{\text{if}}^{mon}$ (figure 5.11), the monadic normal form of $\mathcal{L}_{\text{If}}$. A Boolean constant is an atomic expression, but the if expression is not. All three subexpressions of an if are allowed to be complex expressions, but the operands of the not operator and comparison operators must be atomic. We add a new language form, the **Begin** expression, to aid in the translation of if expressions. When we recursively process the two branches of the if, we generate temporary variables and their initializing expressions. However, these expressions may contain side effects and should be executed only when the condition of the if is true (for the "then" branch) or false (for the "else" branch). The **Begin** expression provides a way to initialize the temporary variables within the two branches of the if expression. In general, the **Begin**(ss, e) form executes the statements ss and then returns the result of expression e.

Add cases to the **rco_exp** and **rco_atom** functions for the new features in $\mathcal{L}_{\text{If}}$. In recursively processing subexpressions, recall that you should invoke **rco_atom** when the output needs to be an *atm* (as specified in the grammar for $\mathcal{L}_{\text{if}}^{mon}$) and invoke **rco_exp** when the output should be *exp*. Regarding if, it is particularly important *not* to replace its condition with a temporary variable, because that would interfere with the generation of high-quality output in the upcoming **explicate_control** pass.

```
atm   ::=  Constant(int) | Name(var)
exp   ::=  atm | Call(Name('input_int'),[])
       |   UnaryOp(USub(),atm) | BinOp(atm,Add(),atm)
       |   BinOp(atm,Sub(),atm)
stmt  ::=  Expr(Call(Name('print'),[atm])) | Expr(exp)
       |   Assign([Name(var)], exp)
atm   ::=  Constant(bool)
exp   ::=  UnaryOp(Not(),exp) | Compare(atm,[cmp],[atm])
       |   IfExp(exp,exp,exp) | Begin(stmt*, exp)
stmt  ::=  If(exp, stmt*, stmt*)
L_If^mon ::= Module(stmt*)
```

Figure 5.11
$\mathcal{L}_{\sf If}^{mon}$ is $\mathcal{L}_{\sf If}$ in monadic normal form (extends $\mathcal{L}_{\sf Var}^{mon}$ in figure 2.11).

Exercise 5.3 Add cases for Boolean constants and `if` to the `rco_atom` and `rco_exp` functions. Create three new $\mathcal{L}_{\sf If}$ programs that exercise the interesting code in this pass.

5.7 Explicate Control

The `explicate_control` pass translates from $\mathcal{L}_{\sf If}$ to $\mathcal{C}_{\sf If}$. The main challenge to overcome is that the condition of an `if` can be an arbitrary expression in $\mathcal{L}_{\sf If}$, whereas in $\mathcal{C}_{\sf If}$ the condition must be a comparison.

As a motivating example, consider the following program that has an `if` expression nested in the condition of another `if`:[1]

```
x = input_int()
y = input_int()
print(y + 2 if (x == 0 if x < 1 else x == 2) else y + 10)
```

The naive way to compile `if` and the comparison operations would be to handle each of them in isolation, regardless of their context. Each comparison would be translated into a `cmpq` instruction followed by several instructions to move the result from the EFLAGS register into a general purpose register or stack location. Each `if` would be translated into a `cmpq` instruction followed by a conditional jump. The generated code for the inner `if` in this example would be as follows:

---

1. Programmers rarely write nested `if` expressions, but they do write nested expressions involving logical **and**, which, as we have seen, translates to `if`.

```
cmpq $1, x
setl %al
movzbq %al, tmp
cmpq $1, tmp
je then_branch_1
jmp else_branch_1
```

Notice that the three instructions starting with `setl` are redundant; the conditional jump could come immediately after the first `cmpq`.

Our goal is to compile `if` expressions so that the relevant comparison instruction appears directly before the conditional jump. For example, we want to generate the following code for the inner `if`:

```
cmpq $1, x
jl then_branch_1
jmp else_branch_1
```

One way to achieve this goal is to reorganize the code at the level of $\mathcal{L}_{\text{If}}$, pushing the outer `if` inside the inner one, yielding the following code:

```
x = input_int()
y = input_int()
print(((y + 2) if x == 0 else (y + 10)) \
      if (x < 1) \
      else ((y + 2) if (x == 2) else (y + 10)))
```

Unfortunately, this approach duplicates the two branches from the outer `if`, and a compiler must never duplicate code! After all, the two branches could be very large expressions.

How can we apply this transformation without duplicating code? In other words, how can two different parts of a program refer to one piece of code? The answer is that we must move away from abstract syntax *trees* and instead use *graphs*. At the level of x86 assembly, this is straightforward because we can label the code for each branch and insert jumps in all the places that need to execute the branch. In this way, jump instructions are edges in the graph and the basic blocks are the nodes. Likewise, our language $\mathcal{C}_{\text{If}}$ provides the ability to label a sequence of statements and to jump to a label via `goto`.

As a preview of what `explicate_control` will do, figure 5.12 shows the output of `explicate_control` on this example. Note how the condition of every `if` is a comparison operation and that we have not duplicated any code but instead have used labels and `goto` to enable sharing of code.

We recommend implementing `explicate_control` using the following four auxiliary functions.

explicate_effect generates code for expressions as statements, so their result is ignored and only their side effects matter.

```
                                         start:
                                             x = input_int()
                                             y = input_int()
                                             if x < 1:
                                                 goto block_6
                                             else:
                                                 goto block_7
                                         block_6:
                                             if x == 0:
                                                 goto block_4
     x = input_int()                         else:
     y = input_int()                             goto block_5
     print(y + 2          \              block_7:
           if (x == 0     \        ⇒        if x == 2:
              if x < 1     \                    goto block_4
              else x == 2) \               else:
           else y + 10)                        goto block_5
                                         block_4:
                                             tmp.82 = (y + 2)
                                             goto block_3
                                         block_5:
                                             tmp.82 = (y + 10)
                                             goto block_3
                                         block_3:
                                             print(tmp.82)
                                             return 0
```

Figure 5.12
Translation from $\mathcal{L}_{\text{If}}$ to $\mathcal{C}_{\text{If}}$ via the `explicate_control`.

explicate_assign generates code for expressions on the right-hand side of an assignment.

explicate_pred generates code for an `if` expression or statement by analyzing the condition expression.

explicate_stmt generates code for statements.

These four functions should build the dictionary of basic blocks. The following auxiliary function **create_block** is used to create a new basic block from a list of statements. If the list just contains a `goto`, then **create_block** returns the list. Otherwise **create_block** creates a new basic block and returns a `goto` to its label.

```
def create_block(stmts, basic_blocks):
  match stmts:
    case [Goto(l)]:
      return stmts
    case _:
      label = label_name(generate_name('block'))
      basic_blocks[label] = stmts
      return [Goto(label)]
```

Figure 5.13 provides a skeleton for the `explicate_control` pass.

The `explicate_effect` function has three parameters: (1) the expression to be compiled; (2) the already-compiled code for this expression's *continuation*, that is, the list of statements that should execute after this expression; and (3) the dictionary of generated basic blocks. The `explicate_effect` function returns a list of C_{If} statements and it may add to the dictionary of basic blocks. Let's consider a few of the cases for the expression to be compiled. If the expression to be compiled is a constant, then it can be discarded because it has no side effects. If it's a `input_int()`, then it has a side effect and should be preserved. So the expression should be translated into a statement using the `Expr` AST class. If the expression to be compiled is an `if` expression, we translate the two branches using `explicate_effect` and then translate the condition expression using `explicate_pred`, which generates code for the entire `if`.

The `explicate_assign` function has four parameters: (1) the right-hand side of the assignment, (2) the left-hand side of the assignment (the variable), (3) the continuation, and (4) the dictionary of basic blocks. The `explicate_assign` function returns a list of C_{If} statements, and it may add to the dictionary of basic blocks.

When the right-hand side is an `if` expression, there is some work to do. In particular, the two branches should be translated using `explicate_assign`, and the condition expression should be translated using `explicate_pred`. Otherwise we can simply generate an assignment statement, with the given left- and right-hand sides, concatenated with its continuation.

The `explicate_pred` function has four parameters: (1) the condition expression, (2) the generated statements for the *then* branch, (3) the generated statements for the *else* branch, and (4) the dictionary of basic blocks. The `explicate_pred` function returns a list of statements, and it adds to the dictionary of basic blocks.

Consider the case for comparison operators. We translate the comparison to an `if` statement whose branches are `goto` statements created by applying `create_block` to the `thn` and `els` parameters. Let us illustrate this translation by returning to the program with an `if` expression in tail position, shown next. We invoke `explicate_pred` on its condition `x == 0`.

```
x = input_int()
42 if x == 0 else 777
```

The two branches `42` and `777` were already compiled to `return` statements, from which we now create the following blocks:

```
def explicate_effect(e, cont, basic_blocks):
  match e:
    case IfExp(test, body, orelse):
      ...
    case Call(func, args):
      ...
    case Begin(body, result):
      ...
    case _:
      ...
def explicate_assign(rhs, lhs, cont, basic_blocks):
  match rhs:
    case IfExp(test, body, orelse):
      ...
    case Begin(body, result):
      ...
    case _:
      return [Assign([lhs], rhs)] + cont
def explicate_pred(cnd, thn, els, basic_blocks):
  match cnd:
    case Compare(left, [op], [right]):
      goto_thn = create_block(thn, basic_blocks)
      goto_els = create_block(els, basic_blocks)
      return [If(cnd, goto_thn, goto_els)]
    case Constant(True):
      return thn;
    case Constant(False):
      return els;
    case UnaryOp(Not(), operand):
      ...
    case IfExp(test, body, orelse):
      ...
    case Begin(body, result):
      ...
    case _:
      return [If(Compare(cnd, [Eq()], [Constant(False)]),
                 create_block(els, basic_blocks),
                 create_block(thn, basic_blocks))]
def explicate_stmt(s, cont, basic_blocks):
  match s:
    case Assign([lhs], rhs):
      return explicate_assign(rhs, lhs, cont, basic_blocks)
    case Expr(value):
      return explicate_effect(value, cont, basic_blocks)
    case If(test, body, orelse):
      ...
def explicate_control(p):
  match p:
    case Module(body):
      new_body = [Return(Constant(0))]
      basic_blocks = {}
      for s in reversed(body):
        new_body = explicate_stmt(s, new_body, basic_blocks)
      basic_blocks[label_name('start')] = new_body
      return CProgram(basic_blocks)
```

Figure 5.13
Skeleton for the explicate_control pass.

```
block_1:
  return 42;
block_2:
  return 777;
```

After that, `explicate_pred` compiles the comparison `x == 0` to the following `if` statement:

```
if x == 0:
  goto block_1;
else
  goto block_2;
```

Next consider the case for Boolean constants. We perform a kind of partial evaluation and output either the **thn** or **els** parameter, depending on whether the constant is **True** or **False**. Let us illustrate this with the following program:

```
42 if True else 777
```

Again, the two branches `42` and `777` were compiled to `return` statements, so `explicate_pred` compiles the constant `True` to the code for the *then* branch.

```
return 42;
```

This case demonstrates that we sometimes discard the **thn** or **els** blocks that are input to `explicate_pred`.

The case for `if` expressions in `explicate_pred` is particularly illuminating because it deals with the challenges discussed previously regarding nested `if` expressions (figure 5.12). The **body** and **orelse** branches of the `if` inherit their context from the current one, that is, predicate context. So, you should recursively apply `explicate_pred` to the **body** and **orelse** branches. For both of those recursive calls, pass **thn** and **els** as the extra parameters. Thus, **thn** and **els** may be used twice, once inside each recursive call. As discussed previously, to avoid duplicating code, we need to add them to the dictionary of basic blocks so that we can instead refer to them by name and execute them with a **goto**.

The last of the auxiliary functions is `explicate_stmt`. It has three parameters: (1) the statement to be compiled, (2) the code for its continuation, and (3) the dictionary of basic blocks. The `explicate_stmt` returns a list of statements, and it may add to the dictionary of basic blocks. The cases for assignment and an expression-statement are given in full in the skeleton code: they simply dispatch to `explicate_assign` and `explicate_effect`, respectively. The case for `if` statements is not given; it is similar to the case for `if` expressions.

The `explicate_control` function itself is given in figure 5.13. It applies `explicate_stmt` to each statement in the program, from back to front. Thus, the result so far, stored in **new_body**, can be used as the continuation parameter in the next call to `explicate_stmt`. The **new_body** is initialized to a **Return** statement. Once complete, we add the **new_body** to the dictionary of basic blocks, labeling it the "start" block.

Figure 5.12 shows the output of the `remove_complex_operands` pass and then the `explicate_control` pass on the example program. We walk through the output program. Following the order of evaluation in the output of `remove_complex_operands`, we first have two calls to `input_int()` and then the comparison x < 1 in the predicate of the inner `if`. In the output of `explicate_control`, in the block labeled `start`, two assignment statements are followed by an `if` statement that branches to `block_6` or `block_7`. The blocks associated with those labels contain the translations of the code x == 0 and x == 2, respectively. In particular, we start `block_6` with the comparison x == 0 and then branch to `block_4` or `block_5`, which correspond to the two branches of the outer `if`, that is, y + 2 and y + 10. The story for `block_7` is similar to that of `block_6`. The `block_3` is the translation of the `print` statement.

Exercise 5.4 Implement `explicate_control` pass with its four auxiliary functions. Create test cases that exercise all the new cases in the code for this pass.

5.8 Select Instructions

The `select_instructions` pass translates C_{If} to $\text{x86}_{\text{If}}^{\text{Var}}$. We begin with the Boolean constants. As previously discussed, we encode them as integers.

$$\texttt{True} \quad \Rightarrow \quad 1 \qquad \texttt{False} \quad \Rightarrow \quad 0$$

For translating statements, we discuss some of the cases. The `not` operation can be implemented in terms of `xorq`, as we discussed at the beginning of this section. Given an assignment, if the left-hand-side variable is the same as the argument of `not`, then just the `xorq` instruction suffices.

$$var = \texttt{not } var \quad \Rightarrow \quad \texttt{xorq \$1, } var$$

Otherwise, a `movq` is needed to adapt to the update-in-place semantics of x86. In the following translation, let *arg* be the result of translating *atm* to x86.

$$var = \texttt{not } atm \quad \Rightarrow \quad \begin{array}{l}\texttt{movq } arg\texttt{, } var \\ \texttt{xorq \$1, } var\end{array}$$

Next consider the cases for equality comparisons. Translating this operation to x86 is slightly involved due to the unusual nature of the `cmpq` instruction that we discussed in section 5.4. We recommend translating an assignment with an equality on the right-hand side into a sequence of three instructions. Let arg_1 be the translation of atm_1 to x86 and likewise for arg_2.

$$var = (atm_1 \texttt{ == } atm_2) \quad \Rightarrow \quad \begin{array}{l}\texttt{cmpq } arg_2\texttt{, } arg_1 \\ \texttt{sete \%al} \\ \texttt{movzbq \%al, } var\end{array}$$

The translations for the other comparison operators are similar to this but use different condition codes for the `set` instruction.

A `goto` statement becomes a jump instruction.

$$\text{goto}\,\ell \quad \Rightarrow \quad \text{jmp}\,\ell$$

An `if` statement becomes a compare instruction followed by a conditional jump (for the *then* branch), and the fall-through is to a regular jump (for the *else* branch). Again, arg_1 and arg_2 are the translations of atm_1 and atm_2, respectively.

```
if atm₁ == atm₂:
    goto ℓ₁
else:
    goto ℓ₂
```

$$\Rightarrow \quad \begin{array}{l} \text{cmpq } arg_2,\ arg_1 \\ \text{je } \ell_1 \\ \text{jmp } \ell_2 \end{array}$$

Again, the translations for the other comparison operators are similar to this but use different condition codes for the conditional jump instruction.

Regarding the **return** statement, we recommend treating it as an assignment to the **rax** register followed by a jump to the conclusion of the **main** function. (See section 5.11 for more about the conclusion of **main**.)

Exercise 5.5 Expand your `select_instructions` pass to handle the new features of the C_{If} language. Run the script to test your compiler on all the test programs.

5.9 Register Allocation

The changes required for compiling $\mathcal{L}_{If}$ affect liveness analysis, building the interference graph, and assigning homes, but the graph coloring algorithm itself does not change.

5.9.1 Liveness Analysis

Recall that for $\mathcal{L}_{Var}$ we implemented liveness analysis for a single basic block (section 4.2). With the addition of `if` expressions to $\mathcal{L}_{If}$, `explicate_control` produces many basic blocks.

The first question is, in what order should we process the basic blocks? Recall that to perform liveness analysis on a basic block we need to know the live-after set for the last instruction in the block. If a basic block has no successors (i.e., contains no jumps to other blocks), then it has an empty live-after set and we can immediately apply liveness analysis to it. If a basic block has some successors, then we need to complete liveness analysis on those blocks first. These ordering constraints are the reverse of a *topological order* on a graph representation of the program. In particular, the *control flow graph* (CFG) (Allen 1970) of a program has a node for each basic block and an edge for each jump from one block to another. It is straightforward to generate a CFG from the dictionary of basic blocks. One then transposes the CFG and applies the topological sort algorithm. We provide implementations of `topological_sort` and `transpose` in the file `graph.py` of the support code. As an aside, a topological ordering is only guaranteed to exist if the graph does not contain any cycles. This is the case for the control-flow graphs that we generate from $\mathcal{L}_{If}$ programs. However, in chapter 6 we add loops to create $\mathcal{L}_{While}$ and learn how to handle cycles in the control-flow graph.

The next question is how to analyze jump instructions. The locations that are live before a `jmp` should be the locations in L_{before} at the target of the jump. So we recommend maintaining a dictionary named `live_before_block` that maps each label to the L_{before} for the first instruction in its block. After performing liveness analysis on each block, we take the live-before set of its first instruction and associate that with the block's label in the `live_before_block` dictionary.

In $x86_{\text{If}}^{\text{Var}}$ we also have the conditional jump `JumpIf(`cc`,`$label$`)` to deal with. Liveness analysis for this instruction is particularly interesting because during compilation, we do not know which way a conditional jump will go. Thus we do not know whether to use the live-before set for the block associated with the *label* or the live-before set for the following instruction. So we use both, by taking the union of the live-before sets from the following instruction and from the mapping for *label* in `live_before_block`.

The auxiliary functions for computing the variables in an instruction's argument and for computing the variables read-from (R) or written-to (W) by an instruction need to be updated to handle the new kinds of arguments and instructions in $x86_{\text{If}}^{\text{Var}}$.

Exercise 5.6 Update the `uncover_live` function to perform liveness analysis, in reverse topological order, on all the basic blocks in the program.

5.9.2 Build the Interference Graph
Many of the new instructions in $x86_{\text{If}}^{\text{Var}}$ can be handled in the same way as the instructions in $x86_{\text{Var}}$. Some instructions, such as the `movzbq` instruction, require special care, similar to the `movq` instruction. Refer to rule number 1 in section 4.3.

Exercise 5.7 Update the `build_interference` pass for $x86_{\text{If}}^{\text{Var}}$.

5.10 Patch Instructions

The new instructions `cmpq` and `movzbq` have some special restrictions that need to be handled in the `patch_instructions` pass. The second argument of the `cmpq` instruction must not be an immediate value (such as an integer). So, if you are comparing two immediates, we recommend inserting a `movq` instruction to put the second argument in `rax`. On the other hand, if you implemented the partial evaluator (section 2.9), you could update it for $\mathcal{L}_{\text{If}}$ and then this situation would not arise. As usual, `cmpq` may have at most one memory reference. The second argument of the `movzbq` must be a register.

Exercise 5.8 Update `patch_instructions` pass for $x86_{\text{If}}^{\text{Var}}$.

5.11 Generate Prelude and Conclusion

The generation of the `main` function with its prelude and conclusion must change to accommodate how the program now consists of one or more basic blocks. After the prelude in `main`, jump to the `start` block. Place the conclusion in a basic block labeled with `conclusion`.

Figure 5.14 shows a simple example program in $\mathcal{L}_{\text{If}}$ translated to x86, showing the results of `explicate_control`, `select_instructions`, and the final x86 assembly.

Figure 5.15 lists all the passes needed for the compilation of $\mathcal{L}_{\text{If}}$.

5.12 Challenge: Optimize Blocks and Remove Jumps

We discuss two challenges that involve optimizing the control-flow of the program.

5.12.1 Optimize Blocks

The algorithm for `explicate_control` that we discussed in section 5.7 sometimes generates too many blocks. It creates a block whenever a continuation *might* get used more than once (for example, whenever the `cont` parameter is passed into two or more recursive calls). However, some continuation arguments may not be used at all. Consider the case for the constant `True` in `explicate_pred`, in which we discard the `els` continuation. The following example program falls into this case, and it creates the unused `block_9`.

```
if True:
  print(0)
else:
  x = 1 if False else 2
  print(x)
```

$\Rightarrow$

```
start:
  print(0)
  goto block_8
block_9:
  print(x)
  goto block_8
block_8:
  return 0
```

The question is, how can we decide whether to create a basic block? *Lazy evaluation* (Friedman and Wise 1976) can solve this conundrum by delaying the creation of a basic block until the point in time at which we know that it will be used. Although Python does not provide direct support for lazy evaluation, it is easy to mimic. We *delay* the evaluation of a computation by wrapping it inside a function with no parameters. We *force* its evaluation by calling the function. However, we might need to force multiple times, so we store the result of calling the function instead of recomputing it each time. The following `Promise` class handles this memoization process.

```
@dataclass
class Promise:
  fun : typing.Any
  cache : list[stmt] = None
  def force(self):
    if self.cache is None:
      self.cache = self.fun(); return self.cache
    else:
      return self.cache
```

However, in some cases of `explicate_pred`, we return a list of statements, and in other cases we return a function that computes a list of statements. To uniformly deal with both regular data and promises, we define the following `force` function

```
print(42 if input_int() == 1 else 0)

⇓

start:
      tmp_0 = input_int()
      if tmp_0 == 1:
        goto block_3
      else:
        goto block_4
block_3:
      tmp_1 = 42
      goto block_2
block_4:
      tmp_1 = 0
      goto block_2
block_2:
      print(tmp_1)
      return 0

⇓                              ⇒

start:
      callq read_int
      movq %rax, tmp_0
      cmpq 1, tmp_0
      je block_3
      jmp block_4
block_3:
      movq 42, tmp_1
      jmp block_2
block_4:
      movq 0, tmp_1
      jmp block_2
block_2:
      movq tmp_1, %rdi
      callq print_int
      movq 0, %rax
      jmp conclusion
```

```
          .globl main
main:
      pushq %rbp
      movq %rsp, %rbp
      subq $0, %rsp
      jmp start
start:
      callq read_int
      movq %rax, %rcx
      cmpq $1, %rcx
      je block_3
      jmp block_4
block_3:
      movq $42, %rcx
      jmp block_2
block_4:
      movq $0, %rcx
      jmp block_2
block_2:
      movq %rcx, %rdi
      callq print_int
      movq $0, %rax
      jmp conclusion
conclusion:
      addq $0, %rsp
      popq %rbp
      retq
```

Figure 5.14

Example compilation of an if expression to x86, showing the results of explicate_control, select_instructions, and the final x86 assembly code.

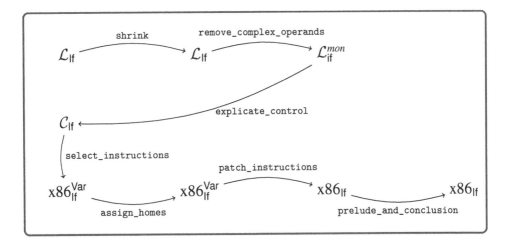

Figure 5.15
Diagram of the passes for $\mathcal{L}_{\text{If}}$, a language with conditionals.

that checks whether its input is delayed (i.e., whether it is a **Promise**) and then either (1) forces the promise or (2) returns the input.

```
def force(promise):
  if isinstance(promise, Promise):
    return promise.force()
  else:
    return promise
```

We use promises for the input and output of the functions `explicate_pred`, `explicate_assign`, `explicate_effect`, and `explicate_stmt`. So, instead of taking and returning lists of statements, they take and return promises. Furthermore, when we come to a situation in which a continuation might be used more than once, as in the case for `if` in `explicate_pred`, we create a delayed computation that creates a basic block for each continuation (if there is not already one) and then returns a `goto` statement to that basic block. When we come to a situation in which we have a promise but need an actual piece of code, for example, to create a larger piece of code with a constructor such as `Seq`, then insert a call to `force`.

Here is the new version of the `create_block` auxiliary function that delays the creation of the new basic block.

```
def create_block(promise, basic_blocks):
  def delay():
    stmts = force(promise)
    match stmts:
      case [Goto(l)]:
        return [Goto(l)]
      case _:
        label = label_name(generate_name('block'))
        basic_blocks[label] = stmts
        return [Goto(label)]
  return Promise(delay)
```

```
      if True:                          start:
        print(0)                          print(0)
      else:                               goto block_4
        x = 1 if False else 2    ⇒
        print(x)                      block_4:
                                          return 0
```

Figure 5.16
Translation from $\mathcal{L}_{If}$ to $\mathcal{C}_{If}$ via the improved `explicate_control`.

Figure 5.16 shows the output of improved `explicate_control` on this example. As you can see, the number of basic blocks has been reduced from three blocks to two blocks.

Exercise 5.9 Implement the improvements to the `explicate_control` pass. Check that it removes trivial blocks in a few example programs. Then check that your compiler still passes all your tests.

5.12.2 Remove Jumps

There is an opportunity for removing jumps that is apparent in the example of figure 5.14. The `start` block ends with a jump to `block_4`, and there are no other jumps to `block_4` in the rest of the program. In this situation we can avoid the run-time overhead of this jump by merging `block_4` into the preceding block, which in this case is the `start` block. Figure 5.17 shows the output of `allocate_registers` on the left and the result of this optimization on the right.

Exercise 5.10 Implement a pass named `remove_jumps` that merges basic blocks into their preceding basic block, when there is only one preceding block. The pass should translate from x86$_{If}^{Var}$ to x86$_{If}^{Var}$. Run the script to test your compiler. Check that `remove_jumps` accomplishes the goal of merging basic blocks on several test programs.

5.13 Further Reading

The algorithm for `explicate_control` is based on the `expose-basic-blocks` pass in the course notes of Dybvig and Keep (2010). It has similarities to the algorithms of Danvy (2003) and Appel and Palsberg (2003), and is related to translations into continuation passing style (van Wijngaarden 1966; Fischer 1972; Reynolds 1972; Plotkin 1975; Friedman, Wand, and Haynes 2001). The treatment of conditionals in the `explicate_control` pass is similar to short-cut Boolean evaluation (Logothetis and Mishra 1981; Aho et al. 2006; Clarke 1989; Danvy 2003) and the case-of-case transformation (Peyton Jones and Santos 1998).

```
start:                                      start:
        callq read_int                              callq read_int
        movq %rax, tmp_0                            movq %rax, tmp_0
        cmpq 1, tmp_0                               cmpq 1, tmp_0
        je block_3                                  je block_3
        jmp block_4                                 movq 0, tmp_1
block_3:                                            jmp block_2
        movq 42, tmp_1                      block_3:
        jmp block_2                ⇒               movq 42, tmp_1
block_4:                                            jmp block_2
        movq 0, tmp_1                       block_2:
        jmp block_2                                 movq tmp_1, %rdi
block_2:                                            callq print_int
        movq tmp_1, %rdi                            movq 0, %rax
        callq print_int                            jmp conclusion
        movq 0, %rax
        jmp conclusion
```

Figure 5.17
Merging basic blocks by removing unnecessary jumps.

6   Loops and Dataflow Analysis

In this chapter we study loops, one of the hallmarks of imperative programming languages. The following example demonstrates the `while` loop by computing the sum of the first five positive integers.

```
sum = 0
i = 5
while i > 0:
  sum = sum + i
  i = i - 1
print(sum)
```

The `while` loop consists of a condition and a body (a sequence of statements). The body is evaluated repeatedly so long as the condition remains true.

6.1   The $\mathcal{L}_{\mathsf{While}}$ Language

Figure 6.1 shows the definition of the concrete syntax of $\mathcal{L}_{\mathsf{While}}$, and figure 6.2 shows the definition of its abstract syntax. The definitional interpreter for $\mathcal{L}_{\mathsf{While}}$ is shown in figure 6.3. We add a new case for `While` in the `interp_stmts` function, in which we repeatedly interpret the `body` so long as the `test` expression remains true.

The definition of the type checker for $\mathcal{L}_{\mathsf{While}}$ is shown in figure 6.4. A `while` loop is well typed if the type of the `test` expression is `bool` and the statements in the `body` are well typed.

At first glance, the translation of `while` loops to x86 seems straightforward because the $\mathcal{C}_{\mathsf{If}}$ intermediate language already supports `goto` and conditional branching. However, there are complications that arise, which we discuss in the next section. After that we introduce the changes necessary to the existing passes.

6.2   Cyclic Control Flow and Dataflow Analysis

Up until this point, the programs generated in `explicate_control` were guaranteed to be acyclic. However, each `while` loop introduces a cycle. Does that matter? Indeed, it does. Recall that for register allocation, the compiler performs liveness analysis to determine which variables can share the same register. To accomplish this, we analyzed the control-flow graph in reverse topological order (section 5.9.1), but topological order is well defined only for acyclic graphs.

$$
\begin{array}{rcl}
exp & ::= & int \mid \texttt{input\_int()} \mid - exp \mid exp + exp \mid exp - exp \mid (exp) \\
stmt & ::= & \texttt{print}(exp) \mid exp \\
\hline
exp & ::= & var \\
stmt & ::= & var = exp \\
\hline
cmp & ::= & \texttt{==} \mid \texttt{!=} \mid \texttt{<} \mid \texttt{<=} \mid \texttt{>} \mid \texttt{>=} \\
exp & ::= & \texttt{True} \mid \texttt{False} \mid exp \text{ and } exp \mid exp \text{ or } exp \mid \texttt{not } exp \\
 & \mid & exp \ cmp \ exp \mid exp \text{ if } exp \text{ else } exp \\
stmt & ::= & \texttt{if } exp: stmt^+ \texttt{ else: } stmt^+ \\
\hline
stmt & ::= & \texttt{while } exp: stmt^+ \\
\mathcal{L}_{\text{While}} & ::= & stmt^*
\end{array}
$$

Figure 6.1
The concrete syntax of $\mathcal{L}_{\text{While}}$, extending $\mathcal{L}_{\text{If}}$ (figure 5.1).

$$
\begin{array}{rcl}
exp & ::= & \texttt{Constant}(int) \mid \texttt{Call(Name('input\_int'),[])} \\
 & \mid & \texttt{UnaryOp(USub(),}exp\texttt{)} \mid \texttt{BinOp(}exp\texttt{,Add(),}exp\texttt{)} \\
 & \mid & \texttt{BinOp(}exp\texttt{,Sub(),}exp\texttt{)} \\
stmt & ::= & \texttt{Expr(Call(Name('print'),[}exp\texttt{]))} \mid \texttt{Expr(}exp\texttt{)} \\
\hline
exp & ::= & \texttt{Name(}var\texttt{)} \\
stmt & ::= & \texttt{Assign([Name(}var\texttt{)], }exp\texttt{)} \\
\hline
boolop & ::= & \texttt{And()} \mid \texttt{Or()} \\
cmp & ::= & \texttt{Eq()} \mid \texttt{NotEq()} \mid \texttt{Lt()} \mid \texttt{LtE()} \mid \texttt{Gt()} \mid \texttt{GtE()} \\
bool & ::= & \texttt{True} \mid \texttt{False} \\
exp & ::= & \texttt{Constant(}bool\texttt{)} \mid \texttt{BoolOp(}boolop\texttt{,[}exp\texttt{,}exp\texttt{])} \\
 & \mid & \texttt{UnaryOp(Not(),}exp\texttt{)} \mid \texttt{Compare(}exp\texttt{,[}cmp\texttt{],[}exp\texttt{])} \\
 & \mid & \texttt{IfExp(}exp\texttt{,}exp\texttt{,}exp\texttt{)} \\
stmt & ::= & \texttt{If(}exp\texttt{, }stmt^+\texttt{, }stmt^+\texttt{)} \\
\hline
stmt & ::= & \texttt{While(}exp\texttt{, }stmt^+\texttt{, [])} \\
\mathcal{L}_{\text{While}} & ::= & \texttt{Module(}stmt^*\texttt{)}
\end{array}
$$

Figure 6.2
The abstract syntax of $\mathcal{L}_{\text{While}}$, extending $\mathcal{L}_{\text{If}}$ (figure 5.2).

```python
class InterpLwhile(InterpLif):
  def interp_stmt(self, s, env, cont):
    match s:
      case While(test, body, []):
        if self.interp_exp(test, env):
           self.interp_stmts(body + [s] + cont, env)
        else:
          return self.interp_stmts(cont, env)
      case _:
        return super().interp_stmt(s, env, cont)
```

Figure 6.3
Interpreter for $\mathcal{L}_{\text{While}}$.

```
class TypeCheckLwhile(TypeCheckLif):
  def type_check_stmts(self, ss, env):
    if len(ss) == 0:
      return
    match ss[0]:
      case While(test, body, []):
        test_t = self.type_check_exp(test, env)
        check_type_equal(bool, test_t, test)
        body_t = self.type_check_stmts(body, env)
        return self.type_check_stmts(ss[1:], env)
      case _:
        return super().type_check_stmts(ss, env)
```

Figure 6.4
Type checker for the $\mathcal{L}_{\text{While}}$ language.

Let us return to the example of computing the sum of the first five positive integers. Here is the program after instruction selection but before register allocation.

```
mainstart:
    movq $0, sum
    movq $5, i
    jmp block5
block5:
    cmpq $0, i
    jg block7
    jmp block8
```

```
block7:
    addq i, sum
    subq $1, i
    jmp block5
block8:
    movq sum, %rdi
    callq print_int
    movq $0, %rax
    jmp mainconclusion
```

Recall that liveness analysis works backward, starting at the end of each function. For this example we could start with `block8` because we know what is live at the beginning of the conclusion: only `rax` and `rsp`. So the live-before set for `block8` is `{rsp,sum}`. Next we might try to analyze `block5` or `block7`, but `block5` jumps to `block7` and vice versa, so it seems that we are stuck.

The way out of this impasse is to realize that we can compute an underapproximation of each live-before set by starting with empty live-after sets. By *underapproximation*, we mean that the set contains only variables that are live for some execution of the program, but the set may be missing some variables that are live. Next, the underapproximations for each block can be improved by (1) updating the live-after set for each block using the approximate live-before sets from the other blocks, and (2) performing liveness analysis again on each block. In fact, by iterating this process, the underapproximations eventually become the correct solutions! This approach of iteratively analyzing a control-flow graph is applicable to many static analysis problems and goes by the name *dataflow analysis*. It was invented by Kildall (1973) in his PhD thesis at the University of Washington.

Let us apply this approach to the previously presented example. We use the empty set for the initial live-before set for each block. Let m_0 be the following mapping from label names to sets of locations (variables and registers):

mainstart: {}, block5: {}, block7: {}, block8: {}

Using the above live-before approximations, we determine the live-after for each block and then apply liveness analysis to each block. This produces our next approximation m_1 of the live-before sets.

mainstart: {}, block5: {i}, block7: {i, sum}, block8: {rsp, sum}

For the second round, the live-after for **mainstart** is the current live-before for **block5**, which is {i}. Therefore the liveness analysis for **mainstart** computes the empty set. The live-after for **block5** is the union of the live-before sets for **block7** and **block8**, which is {i, rsp, sum}. So the liveness analysis for **block5** computes {i, rsp, sum}. The live-after for **block7** is the live-before for **block5** (from the previous iteration), which is {i}. So the liveness analysis for **block7** remains {i, sum}. Together these yield the following approximation m_2 of the live-before sets:

mainstart: {}, block5: {i, rsp, sum}, block7: {i, sum}, block8: {rsp, sum}

In the preceding iteration, only **block5** changed, so we can limit our attention to **mainstart** and **block7**, the two blocks that jump to **block5**. As a result, the live-before sets for **mainstart** and **block7** are updated to include **rsp**, yielding the following approximation m_3:

mainstart: {rsp}, block5: {i,rsp,sum}, block7: {i,rsp,sum}, block8: {rsp,sum}

Because **block7** changed, we analyze **block5** once more, but its live-before set remains {i,rsp,sum}. At this point our approximations have converged, so m_3 is the solution.

This iteration process is guaranteed to converge to a solution by the Kleene fixed-point theorem, a general theorem about functions on lattices (Kleene 1952). Roughly speaking, a *lattice* is any collection that comes with a partial ordering $\sqsubseteq$ on its elements, a least element $\bot$ (pronounced *bottom*), and a join operator $\sqcup$.[1] When two elements are ordered $m_i \sqsubseteq m_j$, it means that m_j contains at least as much information as m_i, so we can think of m_j as a better-than-or-equal-to approximation in relation to m_i. The bottom element $\bot$ represents the complete lack of information, that is, the worst approximation. The join operator takes two lattice elements and combines their information; that is, it produces the least upper bound of the two.

A dataflow analysis typically involves two lattices: one lattice to represent abstract states and another lattice that aggregates the abstract states of all the

---

1. Technically speaking, we will be working with join semilattices.

blocks in the control-flow graph. For liveness analysis, an abstract state is a set of locations. We form the lattice L by taking its elements to be sets of locations, the ordering to be set inclusion ($\subseteq$), the bottom to be the empty set, and the join operator to be set union. We form a second lattice M by taking its elements to be mappings from the block labels to sets of locations (elements of L). We order the mappings point-wise, using the ordering of L. So, given any two mappings m_i and m_j, $m_i \sqsubseteq_M m_j$ when $m_i(\ell) \subseteq m_j(\ell)$ for every block label ℓ in the program. The bottom element of M is the mapping $\perp_M$ that sends every label to the empty set, $\perp_M(\ell) = \emptyset$.

We can think of one iteration of liveness analysis applied to the whole program as being a function f on the lattice M. It takes a mapping as input and computes a new mapping.

$$f(m_i) = m_{i+1}$$

Next let us think for a moment about what a final solution m_s should look like. If we perform liveness analysis using the solution m_s as input, we should get m_s again as the output. That is, the solution should be a *fixed point* of the function f.

$$f(m_s) = m_s$$

Furthermore, the solution should include only locations that are forced to be there by performing liveness analysis on the program, so the solution should be the *least* fixed point.

The Kleene fixed-point theorem states that if a function f is monotone (better inputs produce better outputs), then the least fixed point of f is the least upper bound of the *ascending Kleene chain* that starts at $\perp$ and iterates f as follows:

$$\perp \sqsubseteq f(\perp) \sqsubseteq f(f(\perp)) \sqsubseteq \cdots \sqsubseteq f^n(\perp) \sqsubseteq \cdots$$

When a lattice contains only finitely long ascending chains, then every Kleene chain tops out at some fixed point after some number of iterations of f.

$$\perp \sqsubseteq f(\perp) \sqsubseteq f(f(\perp)) \sqsubseteq \cdots \sqsubseteq f^k(\perp) = f^{k+1}(\perp) = m_s$$

The liveness analysis is indeed a monotone function and the lattice M has finitely long ascending chains because there are only a finite number of variables and blocks in the program. Thus we are guaranteed that iteratively applying liveness analysis to all blocks in the program will eventually produce the least fixed point solution.

Next let us consider dataflow analysis in general and discuss the generic work list algorithm (figure 6.5). The algorithm has four parameters: the control-flow graph G, a function `transfer` that applies the analysis to one block, and the `bottom` and `join` operators for the lattice of abstract states. The `analyze_dataflow` function is formulated as a *forward* dataflow analysis; that is, the inputs to the transfer function come from the predecessor nodes in the control-flow graph. However, liveness analysis is a *backward* dataflow analysis, so in that case one must supply the `analyze_dataflow` function with the transpose of the control-flow graph.

The algorithm begins by creating the bottom mapping, represented by a hash table. It then pushes all the nodes in the control-flow graph onto the work list (a queue). The algorithm repeats the `while` loop as long as there are items in the

```
def analyze_dataflow(G, transfer, bottom, join):
  trans_G = transpose(G)
  mapping = dict((v, bottom) for v in G.vertices())
  worklist = deque(G.vertices)
  while worklist:
    node = worklist.pop()
    inputs = [mapping[v] for v in trans_G.adjacent(node)]
    input = reduce(join, inputs, bottom)
    output = transfer(node, input)
    if output != mapping[node]:
      mapping[node] = output
      worklist.extend(G.adjacent(node))
```

Figure 6.5
Generic work list algorithm for dataflow analysis.

work list. In each iteration, a node is popped from the work list and processed. The `input` for the node is computed by taking the join of the abstract states of all the predecessor nodes. The `transfer` function is then applied to obtain the `output` abstract state. If the output differs from the previous state for this block, the mapping for this block is updated and its successor nodes are pushed onto the work list.

Having discussed the complications that arise from adding support for assignment and loops, we turn to discussing the individual compilation passes.

6.3 Remove Complex Operands

The change needed for this pass is to add a case for the `while` statement. The condition of a loop is allowed to be a complex expression, just like the condition of the `if` statement. Figure 6.6 defines the output language $\mathcal{L}_{\mathsf{While}}^{mon}$ of this pass.

6.4 Explicate Control

The output of this pass is the language $\mathcal{C}_{\mathsf{If}}$. No new language features are needed in the output, because a `while` loop can be expressed in terms of `goto` and `if` statements, which are already in $\mathcal{C}_{\mathsf{If}}$. Add a case for the `while` statement to the `explicate_stmt` method, using `explicate_pred` to process the condition expression.

6.5 Register Allocation

As discussed in section 6.2, the presence of loops in $\mathcal{L}_{\mathsf{While}}$ means that the control-flow graphs may contain cycles, which complicates the liveness analysis needed for register allocation. We recommend using the generic `analyze_dataflow` function

$$
\begin{array}{lll}
atm & ::= & \texttt{Constant}(int) \mid \texttt{Name}(var) \\
exp & ::= & atm \mid \texttt{Call}(\texttt{Name}(\texttt{'input\_int'}),\texttt{[]}) \\
& \mid & \texttt{UnaryOp}(\texttt{USub}(),atm) \mid \texttt{BinOp}(atm,\texttt{Add}(),atm) \\
& \mid & \texttt{BinOp}(atm,\texttt{Sub}(),atm) \\
stmt & ::= & \texttt{Expr}(\texttt{Call}(\texttt{Name}(\texttt{'print'}),[atm])) \mid \texttt{Expr}(exp) \\
& \mid & \texttt{Assign}([\texttt{Name}(var)],\ exp)
\end{array}
$$

$$
\begin{array}{lll}
atm & ::= & \texttt{Constant}(bool) \\
exp & ::= & \texttt{UnaryOp}(\texttt{Not}(),exp) \mid \texttt{Compare}(atm,[cmp],[atm]) \\
& \mid & \texttt{IfExp}(exp,exp,exp) \mid \texttt{Begin}(stmt^*,\ exp) \\
stmt & ::= & \texttt{If}(exp,\ stmt^*,\ stmt^*)
\end{array}
$$

$$
\begin{array}{lll}
\mathbf{stmt} & ::= & \texttt{While}(exp,\ stmt^+,\ \texttt{[]}) \\
\mathcal{L}_{\textsf{While}}^{mon} & ::= & \texttt{Module}(stmt^*)
\end{array}
$$

Figure 6.6
$\mathcal{L}_{\textsf{While}}^{mon}$ is $\mathcal{L}_{\textsf{While}}$ in monadic normal form.

that was presented at the end of section 6.2 to perform liveness analysis, replacing the code in **uncover_live** that processed the basic blocks in topological order (section 5.9.1).

The **analyze_dataflow** function has the following four parameters.

1. The first parameter **G** should be passed the transpose of the control-flow graph.
2. The second parameter **transfer** should be passed a function that applies liveness analysis to a basic block. It takes two parameters: the label for the block to analyze and the live-after set for that block. The transfer function should return the live-before set for the block. Also, as a side effect, it should update the live-before and live-after sets for each instruction. To implement the **transfer** function, you should be able to reuse the code you already have for analyzing basic blocks.
3. The third and fourth parameters of **analyze_dataflow** are **bottom** and **join** for the lattice of abstract states, that is, sets of locations. For liveness analysis, the bottom of the lattice is the empty set, and the join operator is set union.

Figure 6.7 provides an overview of all the passes needed for the compilation of $\mathcal{L}_{\textsf{While}}$.

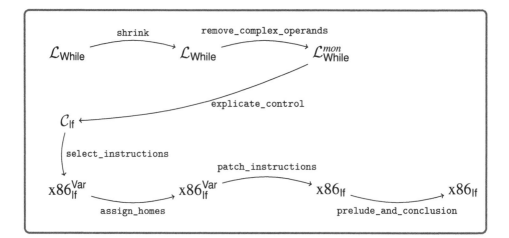

Figure 6.7
Diagram of the passes for $\mathcal{L}_{\mathsf{While}}$.

7 Tuples and Garbage Collection

In this chapter we study the implementation of tuples. A tuple is a fixed-length sequence of elements in which each element may have a different type. This language feature is the first to use the computer's *heap*, because the lifetime of a tuple is indefinite; that is, a tuple lives forever from the programmer's viewpoint. Of course, from an implementer's viewpoint, it is important to reclaim the space associated with a tuple when it is no longer needed, which is why we also study *garbage collection* techniques in this chapter.

Section 7.1 introduces the $\mathcal{L}_{\mathsf{Tup}}$ language, including its interpreter and type checker. The $\mathcal{L}_{\mathsf{Tup}}$ language extends the $\mathcal{L}_{\mathsf{While}}$ language (chapter 6) with tuples. Section 7.2 describes a garbage collection algorithm based on copying live tuples back and forth between two halves of the heap. The garbage collector requires coordination with the compiler so that it can find all the live tuples. Sections 7.3 through 7.8 discuss the necessary changes and additions to the compiler passes, including a new compiler pass named `expose_allocation`.

7.1 The $\mathcal{L}_{\mathsf{Tup}}$ Language

Figure 7.1 shows the definition of the concrete syntax for $\mathcal{L}_{\mathsf{Tup}}$, and figure 7.2 shows the definition of the abstract syntax. The $\mathcal{L}_{\mathsf{Tup}}$ language adds (1) tuple creation via a comma-separated list of expressions; (2) accessing an element of a tuple with the square bracket notation (i.e., `t[n]` returns the element at index `n` of tuple `t`); (3) the `is` comparison operator; and (4) obtaining the number of elements (the length) of a tuple. In this chapter, we restrict access indices to constant integers. The following program shows an example of the use of tuples. It creates a tuple `t` containing the elements 40, `True`, and another tuple that contains just 2. The element at index 1 of `t` is `True`, so the *then* branch of the `if` is taken. The element at index 0 of `t` is 40, to which we add 2, the element at index 0 of the tuple. The result of the program is 42.

```
t = 40, True, (2,)
print(t[0] + t[2][0] if t[1] else 44)
```

Tuples raise several interesting new issues. First, variable binding performs a shallow copy in dealing with tuples, which means that different variables can refer to the same tuple; that is, two variables can be *aliases* for the same entity. Consider

$$
\begin{array}{rcl}
exp & ::= & int \mid \texttt{input\_int()} \mid -exp \mid exp + exp \mid exp - exp \mid (exp) \\
stmt & ::= & \texttt{print}(exp) \mid exp \\
\hline
exp & ::= & var \\
stmt & ::= & var = exp \\
\hline
cmp & ::= & \texttt{==} \mid \texttt{!=} \mid \texttt{<} \mid \texttt{<=} \mid \texttt{>} \mid \texttt{>=} \\
exp & ::= & \texttt{True} \mid \texttt{False} \mid exp \texttt{ and } exp \mid exp \texttt{ or } exp \mid \texttt{not } exp \\
 & \mid & exp \; cmp \; exp \mid exp \texttt{ if } exp \texttt{ else } exp \\
stmt & ::= & \texttt{if } exp\texttt{: } stmt^+ \texttt{ else: } stmt^+ \\
\hline
stmt & ::= & \texttt{while } exp\texttt{: } stmt^+ \\
\hline
cmp & ::= & \texttt{is} \\
exp & ::= & exp, \dots ,exp \mid exp\texttt{[}int\texttt{]} \mid \texttt{len}(exp) \\
\mathcal{L}_{\mathsf{Tup}} & ::= & stmt^*
\end{array}
$$

Figure 7.1
The concrete syntax of $\mathcal{L}_{\mathsf{Tup}}$, extending $\mathcal{L}_{\mathsf{While}}$ (figure 6.1).

$$
\begin{array}{rcl}
exp & ::= & \texttt{Constant}(int) \mid \texttt{Call(Name('input\_int'),[])} \\
 & \mid & \texttt{UnaryOp(USub(),}exp\texttt{)} \mid \texttt{BinOp(}exp\texttt{,Add(),}exp\texttt{)} \\
 & \mid & \texttt{BinOp(}exp\texttt{,Sub(),}exp\texttt{)} \\
stmt & ::= & \texttt{Expr(Call(Name('print'),[}exp\texttt{]))} \mid \texttt{Expr(}exp\texttt{)} \\
\hline
exp & ::= & \texttt{Name(}var\texttt{)} \\
stmt & ::= & \texttt{Assign([Name(}var\texttt{)], }exp\texttt{)} \\
\hline
boolop & ::= & \texttt{And() } \mid \texttt{ Or()} \\
cmp & ::= & \texttt{Eq() } \mid \texttt{ NotEq() } \mid \texttt{ Lt() } \mid \texttt{ LtE() } \mid \texttt{ Gt() } \mid \texttt{ GtE()} \\
bool & ::= & \texttt{True } \mid \texttt{ False} \\
exp & ::= & \texttt{Constant(}bool\texttt{)} \mid \texttt{BoolOp(}boolop\texttt{,[}exp\texttt{,}exp\texttt{])} \\
 & \mid & \texttt{UnaryOp(Not(),}exp\texttt{)} \mid \texttt{Compare(}exp\texttt{,[}cmp\texttt{],[}exp\texttt{])} \\
 & \mid & \texttt{IfExp(}exp\texttt{,}exp\texttt{,}exp\texttt{)} \\
stmt & ::= & \texttt{If(}exp\texttt{, }stmt^+\texttt{, }stmt^+\texttt{)} \\
\hline
stmt & ::= & \texttt{While(}exp\texttt{, }stmt^+\texttt{, [])} \\
\hline
cmp & ::= & \texttt{Is()} \\
exp & ::= & \texttt{Tuple(}exp^+\texttt{,Load())} \mid \texttt{Subscript(}exp\texttt{,Constant(}int\texttt{),Load())} \\
 & \mid & \texttt{Call(Name('len'),[}exp\texttt{])} \\
\mathcal{L}_{\mathsf{Tup}} & ::= & \texttt{Module(}stmt^*\texttt{)}
\end{array}
$$

Figure 7.2
The abstract syntax of $\mathcal{L}_{\mathsf{Tup}}$.

the following example, in which t1 and t2 refer to the same tuple value and t3 refers to a different tuple value with equal elements. The result of the program is 42.

```
t1 = 3, 7
t2 = t1
t3 = 3, 7
print(42 if (t1 is t2) and not (t1 is t3) else 0)
```

```
class InterpLtup(InterpLwhile):
  def interp_cmp(self, cmp):
    match cmp:
      case Is():
        return lambda x, y: x is y
      case _:
        return super().interp_cmp(cmp)
  def interp_exp(self, e, env):
    match e:
      case Tuple(es, Load()):
        return tuple([self.interp_exp(e, env) for e in es])
      case Subscript(tup, index, Load()):
        t = self.interp_exp(tup, env)
        n = self.interp_exp(index, env)
        return t[n]
      case _:
        return super().interp_exp(e, env)
```

Figure 7.3
Interpreter for the $\mathcal{L}_{\mathsf{Tup}}$ language.

The next issue concerns the lifetime of tuples. When does a tuple's lifetime end? Notice that $\mathcal{L}_{\mathsf{Tup}}$ does not include an operation for deleting tuples. Furthermore, the lifetime of a tuple is not tied to any notion of static scoping. For example, the following program returns 42 even though the variable x goes out of scope when the function returns, prior to reading the tuple element at index 0. (We study the compilation of functions in chapter 8.)

```
def f():
    x = 42, 43
    return x
t = f()
print(t[0])
```

From the perspective of programmer-observable behavior, tuples live forever. However, if they really lived forever then many long-running programs would run out of memory. To solve this problem, the language's runtime system performs automatic garbage collection.

Figure 7.3 shows the definitional interpreter for the $\mathcal{L}_{\mathsf{Tup}}$ language. We represent tuples with Python lists in the interpreter because we need to write to them (section 7.3). (Python tuples are immutable.) We define element access, the is operator, and the len operator for $\mathcal{L}_{\mathsf{Tup}}$ in terms of the corresponding operations in Python.

Figure 7.4 shows the type checker for $\mathcal{L}_{\mathsf{Tup}}$. The type of a tuple is a TupleType type that contains a type for each of its elements. The type of accessing the ith element of a tuple is the ith element type of the tuple's type, if there is one. If not,

```
class TypeCheckLtup(TypeCheckLwhile):
  def type_check_exp(self, e, env):
    match e:
      case Compare(left, [cmp], [right]) if isinstance(cmp, Is):
        l = self.type_check_exp(left, env)
        r = self.type_check_exp(right, env)
        check_type_equal(l, r, e)
        return bool
      case Tuple(es, Load()):
        ts = [self.type_check_exp(e, env) for e in es]
        e.has_type = TupleType(ts)
        return e.has_type
      case Subscript(tup, Constant(i), Load()):
        tup_ty = self.type_check_exp(tup, env)
        i_ty = self.type_check_exp(Constant(i), env)
        check_type_equal(i_ty, int, i)
        match tup_ty:
          case TupleType(ts):
            return ts[i]
          case _:
            raise Exception('expected a tuple, not ' + repr(tup_ty))
      case _:
        return super().type_check_exp(e, env)
```

Figure 7.4
Type checker for the $\mathcal{L}_{\mathsf{Tup}}$ language.

an error is signaled. Note that the index i is required to be a constant integer (and not, for example, a call to input_int) so that the type checker can determine the element's type given the tuple type.

7.2 Garbage Collection

Garbage collection is a runtime technique for reclaiming space on the heap that will not be used in the future of the running program. We use the term *object* to refer to any value that is stored in the heap, which for now includes only tuples.[1] Unfortunately, it is impossible to know precisely which objects will be accessed in the future and which will not. Instead, garbage collectors overapproximate the set of objects that will be accessed by identifying which objects can possibly be accessed. The running program can directly access objects that are in registers and on the procedure call stack. It can also transitively access the elements of tuples, starting with a tuple whose address is in a register or on the procedure call stack. We define the *root set* to be all the tuple addresses that are in registers or on the procedure

---

1. The term *object* as it is used in the context of object-oriented programming has a more specific meaning than the way in which we use the term here.

call stack. We define the *live objects* to be the objects that are reachable from the root set. Garbage collectors reclaim the space that is allocated to objects that are no longer live. That means that some objects may not get reclaimed as soon as they could be, but at least garbage collectors do not reclaim the space dedicated to objects that will be accessed in the future! The programmer can influence which objects get reclaimed by causing them to become unreachable.

So the goal of the garbage collector is twofold:

1. to preserve all the live objects, and
2. to reclaim the memory of everything else, that is, the *garbage*.

7.2.1 Two-Space Copying Collector

Here we study a relatively simple algorithm for garbage collection that is the basis of many state-of-the-art garbage collectors (Lieberman and Hewitt 1983; Ungar 1984; Jones and Lins 1996; Detlefs et al. 2004; Dybvig 2006; Tene, Iyengar, and Wolf 2011). In particular, we describe a two-space copying collector (Wilson 1992) that uses Cheney's algorithm to perform the copy (Cheney 1970). Figure 7.5 gives a coarse-grained depiction of what happens in a two-space collector, showing two time steps, prior to garbage collection (on the top) and after garbage collection (on the bottom). In a two-space collector, the heap is divided into two parts named the FromSpace and the ToSpace. Initially, all allocations go to the FromSpace until there is not enough room for the next allocation request. At that point, the garbage collector goes to work to make room for the next allocation.

A copying collector makes more room by copying all the live objects from the FromSpace into the ToSpace and then performs a sleight of hand, treating the ToSpace as the new FromSpace and the old FromSpace as the new ToSpace. In the example shown in figure 7.5, the root set consists of three pointers, one in a register and two on the stack. All the live objects have been copied to the ToSpace (the right-hand side of figure 7.5) in a way that preserves the pointer relationships. For example, the pointer in the register still points to a tuple that in turn points to two other tuples. There are four tuples that are not reachable from the root set and therefore do not get copied into the ToSpace.

The exact situation shown in figure 7.5 cannot be created by a well-typed program in $\mathcal{L}_{\mathsf{Tup}}$ because it contains a cycle. However, creating cycles will be possible once we get to $\mathcal{L}_{\mathsf{Dyn}}$ (chapter 10). We design the garbage collector to deal with cycles to begin with, so we will not need to revisit this issue.

7.2.2 Graph Copying via Cheney's Algorithm

Let us take a closer look at the copying of the live objects. The allocated objects and pointers can be viewed as a graph, and we need to copy the part of the graph that is reachable from the root set. To make sure that we copy all the reachable vertices in the graph, we need an exhaustive graph traversal algorithm, such as depth-first search or breadth-first search (Moore 1959; Cormen et al. 2001). Recall that such algorithms take into account the possibility of cycles by marking which vertices have already been visited, so to ensure termination of the algorithm. These

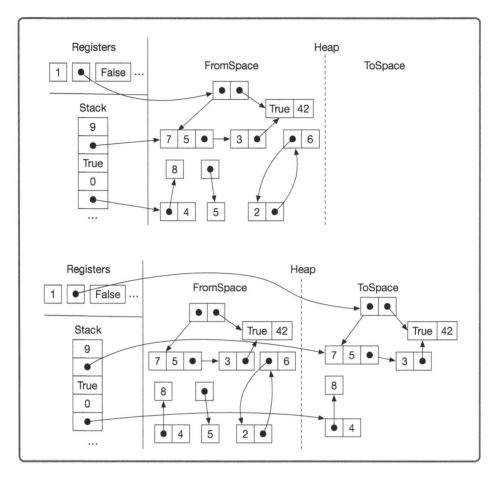

Figure 7.5
A copying collector in action.

search algorithms also use a data structure such as a stack or queue as a to-do list to keep track of the vertices that need to be visited. We use breadth-first search and a trick due to Cheney (1970) for simultaneously representing the queue and copying tuples into the ToSpace.

Figure 7.6 shows several snapshots of the ToSpace as the copy progresses. The queue is represented by a chunk of contiguous memory at the beginning of the ToSpace, using two pointers to track the front and the back of the queue, called the *free pointer* and the *scan pointer*, respectively. The algorithm starts by copying all tuples that are immediately reachable from the root set into the ToSpace to form the initial queue. When we copy a tuple, we mark the old tuple to indicate that it has been visited. We discuss how this marking is accomplished in section 7.2.3. Note that any pointers inside the copied tuples in the queue still point back to the FromSpace. Once the initial queue has been created, the algorithm enters a loop in which it repeatedly processes the tuple at the front of the queue and pops it off the queue. To process a tuple, the algorithm copies all the objects that are

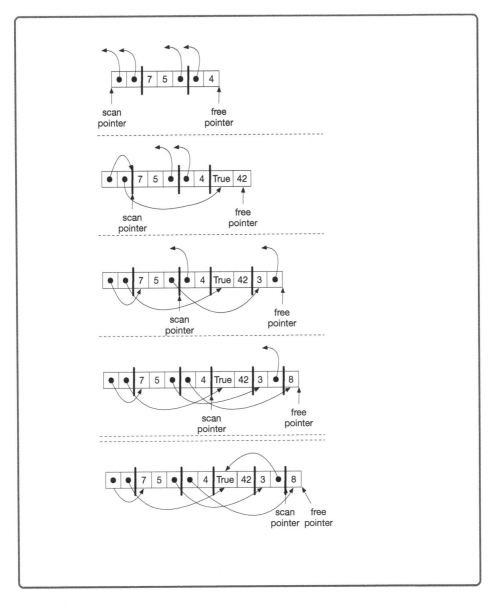

Figure 7.6
Depiction of the Cheney algorithm copying the live tuples.

directly reachable from it to the ToSpace, placing them at the back of the queue. The algorithm then updates the pointers in the popped tuple so that they point to the newly copied objects.

As shown in figure 7.6, in the first step we copy the tuple whose second element is 42 to the back of the queue. The other pointer goes to a tuple that has already been copied, so we do not need to copy it again, but we do need to update the pointer to the new location. This can be accomplished by storing a *forwarding pointer* to the new location in the old tuple, when we initially copied the tuple into the ToSpace.

This completes one step of the algorithm. The algorithm continues in this way until the queue is empty; that is, when the scan pointer catches up with the free pointer.

7.2.3 Data Representation

The garbage collector places some requirements on the data representations used by our compiler. First, the garbage collector needs to distinguish between pointers and other kinds of data such as integers. The following are three ways to accomplish this:

1. Attach a tag to each object that identifies what type of object it is (McCarthy 1960).
2. Store different types of objects in different regions (Steele 1977).
3. Use type information from the program to either (a) generate type-specific code for collecting, or (b) generate tables that guide the collector (Appel 1989; Goldberg 1991; Diwan, Moss, and Hudson 1992).

Dynamically typed languages, such as Python, need to tag objects in any case, so option 1 is a natural choice for those languages. However, $\mathcal{L}_{\mathsf{Tup}}$ is a statically typed language, so it would be unfortunate to require tags on every object, especially small and pervasive objects like integers and Booleans. Option 3 is the best-performing choice for statically typed languages, but it comes with a relatively high implementation complexity. To keep this chapter within a reasonable scope of complexity, we recommend a combination of options 1 and 2, using separate strategies for the stack and the heap.

Regarding the stack, we recommend using a separate stack for pointers, which we call the *root stack* (aka *shadow stack*) (Siebert 2001; Henderson 2002; Baker et al. 2009). That is, when a local variable needs to be spilled and is of type `TupleType`, we put it on the root stack instead of putting it on the procedure call stack. Furthermore, we always spill tuple-typed variables if they are live during a call to the collector, thereby ensuring that no pointers are in registers during a collection. Figure 7.7 reproduces the example shown in figure 7.5 and contrasts it with the data layout using a root stack. The root stack contains the two pointers from the regular stack and also the pointer in the second register.

The problem of distinguishing between pointers and other kinds of data also arises inside each tuple on the heap. We solve this problem by attaching a tag, an extra 64 bits, to each tuple. Figure 7.8 shows a zoomed-in view of the tags for two of the tuples in the example given in figure 7.5. Note that we have drawn the bits in a big-endian way, from right to left, with bit location 0 (the least significant bit) on the far right, which corresponds to the direction of the x86 shifting instructions `salq` (shift left) and `sarq` (shift right). Part of each tag is dedicated to specifying which elements of the tuple are pointers, the part labeled *pointer mask*. Within the pointer mask, a 1 bit indicates that there is a pointer, and a 0 bit indicates some other kind of data. The pointer mask starts at bit location 7. We limit tuples to

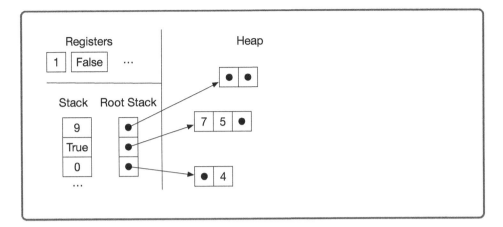

Figure 7.7
Maintaining a root stack to facilitate garbage collection.

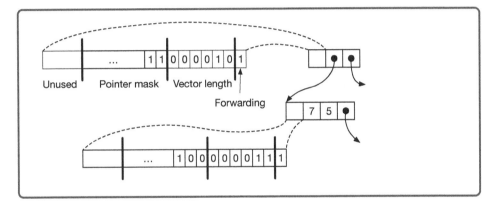

Figure 7.8
Representation of tuples in the heap.

a maximum size of fifty elements, so we need 50 bits for the pointer mask.[2] The tag also contains two other pieces of information. The length of the tuple (number of elements) is stored in bits at locations 1 through 6. Finally, the bit at location 0 indicates whether the tuple has yet to be copied to the ToSpace. If the bit has value 1, then this tuple has not yet been copied. If the bit has value 0, then the entire tag is a forwarding pointer. (The lower 3 bits of a pointer are always zero in any case, because our tuples are 8-byte aligned.)

---

2. A production-quality compiler would handle arbitrarily sized tuples and use a more complex approach.

```
void initialize(uint64_t rootstack_size, uint64_t heap_size);
void collect(int64_t** rootstack_ptr, uint64_t bytes_requested);
int64_t* free_ptr;
int64_t* fromspace_begin;
int64_t* fromspace_end;
int64_t** rootstack_begin;
```

Figure 7.9
The compiler's interface to the garbage collector.

7.2.4 Implementation of the Garbage Collector

An implementation of the copying collector is provided in the `runtime.c` file. Figure 7.9 defines the interface to the garbage collector that is used by the compiler. The `initialize` function creates the FromSpace, ToSpace, and root stack and should be called in the prelude of the `main` function. The arguments of `initialize` are the root stack size and the heap size. Both need to be multiples of sixty-four, and 16, 384 is a good choice for both. The `initialize` function puts the address of the beginning of the FromSpace into the global variable `free_ptr`. The global variable `fromspace_end` points to the address that is one past the last element of the FromSpace. We use half-open intervals to represent chunks of memory (Dijkstra 1982). The `rootstack_begin` variable points to the first element of the root stack.

As long as there is room left in the FromSpace, your generated code can allocate tuples simply by moving the `free_ptr` forward. The amount of room left in the FromSpace is the difference between the `fromspace_end` and the `free_ptr`. The `collect` function should be called when there is not enough room left in the FromSpace for the next allocation. The `collect` function takes a pointer to the current top of the root stack (one past the last item that was pushed) and the number of bytes that need to be allocated. The `collect` function performs the copying collection and leaves the heap in a state such that there is enough room for the next allocation.

The introduction of garbage collection has a nontrivial impact on our compiler passes. We introduce a new compiler pass named `expose_allocation` that elaborates the code for allocating tuples. We also make significant changes to `select_instructions`, `build_interference`, `allocate_registers`, and `prelude_and_conclusion` and make minor changes in several more passes.

The following program serves as our running example. It creates two tuples, one nested inside the other. Both tuples have length one. The program accesses the element in the inner tuple.

```
v1 = (42,)
v2 = (v1,)
print(v2[0][0])
```

7.3 Expose Allocation

The pass `expose_allocation` lowers tuple creation into making a conditional call to the collector followed by allocating the appropriate amount of memory and initializing it. We choose to place the `expose_allocation` pass before `remove_complex_operands` because it generates code that contains complex operands. However, with some care it can also be placed before `remove_complex_operands`, which would simplify tuple creation by removing the need to assign the initializing expressions to temporary variables (see below).

The output of `expose_allocation` is a language $\mathcal{L}_{Alloc}$ that replaces tuple creation with new lower-level forms that we use in the translation of tuple creation.

$$exp \quad ::= \quad \text{collect}(int) \mid \text{allocate}(int, type) \mid \text{global\_value}(name)$$
$$stmt \quad ::= \quad exp[int] = exp$$

The `collect`(n) form runs the garbage collector, requesting that there be n bytes ready to be allocated. During instruction selection, the `collect`(n) form will become a call to the `collect` function in `runtime.c`. The `allocate`$(n,type)$ form obtains memory for n elements (and space at the front for the 64-bit tag), but the elements are not initialized. The *type* parameter is the type of the tuple: `TupleType`$([type_1, \ldots, type_n])$ where $type_i$ is the type of the ith element. The `global_value`$(name)$ form reads the value of a global variable, such as `free_ptr`.

The following shows the transformation of tuple creation into (1) a sequence of temporary variable bindings for the initializing expressions, (2) a conditional call to `collect`, (3) a call to `allocate`, and (4) the initialization of the tuple. The *len* placeholder refers to the length of the tuple, and *bytes* is the total number of bytes that need to be allocated for the tuple, which is 8 for the tag plus *len* times 8. The *type* needed for the second argument of the `allocate` form can be obtained from the `has_type` field of the tuple AST node, which is stored there by running the type checker for $\mathcal{L}_{Tup}$ immediately before this pass.

```
(e_0, ..., e_{n-1})
⟹
begin:
    x_0 = e_0
        ⋮
    x_{n-1} = e_{n-1}
    if global_value(free_ptr) + bytes < global_value(fromspace_end):
        0
    else:
        collect(bytes)
    v = allocate(len, type)
    v[0] = x_0
        ⋮
    v[n-1] = x_{n-1}
    v
```

```
v1 = begin:
      init.514 = 42
      if (free_ptr + 16) < fromspace_end:
      else:
        collect(16)
      alloc.513 = allocate(1,tuple[int])
      alloc.513[0] = init.514
      alloc.513
v2 = begin:
      init.516 = v1
      if (free_ptr + 16) < fromspace_end:
      else:
        collect(16)
      alloc.515 = allocate(1,tuple[tuple[int]])
      alloc.515[0] = init.516
      alloc.515
print(v2[0][0])
```

Figure 7.10
Output of the `expose_allocation` pass.

The sequencing of the initializing expressions $e_0, \ldots, e_{n-1}$ prior to the `allocate` is important because they may trigger garbage collection and we cannot have an allocated but uninitialized tuple on the heap during a collection.

Figure 7.10 shows the output of the `expose_allocation` pass on our running example.

7.4 Remove Complex Operands

The expressions `allocate`, `begin`, and tuple access should be treated as complex operands. The subexpressions of tuple access must be atomic. The `global_value` AST node is atomic. Figure 7.11 shows the grammar for the output language $\mathcal{L}_{\mathsf{Alloc}}^{mon}$ of this pass, which is $\mathcal{L}_{\mathsf{Alloc}}$ in monadic normal form.

7.5 Explicate Control and the $\mathcal{C}_{\mathsf{Tup}}$ Language

The output of `explicate_control` is a program in the intermediate language $\mathcal{C}_{\mathsf{Tup}}$, for which figure 7.12 shows the definition of the abstract syntax. The new expressions of $\mathcal{C}_{\mathsf{Tup}}$ include `allocate`, accessing tuple elements, and `global_value`. $\mathcal{C}_{\mathsf{Tup}}$ also includes the `collect` statement and assignment to a tuple element. The `explicate_control` pass can treat these new forms much like the other forms that we've already encountered. The output of the `explicate_control` pass on the running example is shown on the left side of figure 7.15 in the next section.

```
    atm   ::=  Constant(int) | Name(var)
    exp   ::=  atm | Call(Name('input_int'),[])
          |    UnaryOp(USub(),atm) | BinOp(atm,Add(),atm)
          |    BinOp(atm,Sub(),atm)
    stmt  ::=  Expr(Call(Name('print'),[atm])) | Expr(exp)
          |    Assign([Name(var)], exp)
    ─────────────────────────────────────────────────────────────
    atm   ::=  Constant(bool)
    exp   ::=  UnaryOp(Not(),exp) | Compare(atm,[cmp],[atm])
          |    IfExp(exp,exp,exp) | Begin(stmt*, exp)
    stmt  ::=  If(exp, stmt*, stmt*)
    ─────────────────────────────────────────────────────────────
    stmt  ::=  While(exp, stmt⁺, [])
    ─────────────────────────────────────────────────────────────
    atm   ::=  GlobalValue(var)
    exp   ::=  Subscript(atm,atm,Load()) | Call(Name('len'),[atm])
          |    Allocate(int,type)
    stmt  ::=  Assign([Subscript(atm,atm,Store())], atm)
          |    Collect(int)
    ℒ_Alloc^mon ::= Module(stmt*)
```

Figure 7.11
$\mathcal{L}_{\text{Alloc}}^{mon}$ is $\mathcal{L}_{\text{Alloc}}$ in monadic normal form.

```
    atm   ::=  Constant(int) | Name(var) | Constant(bool)
    exp   ::=  atm | Call(Name('input_int'),[]) | UnaryOp(USub(),atm)
          |    BinOp(atm,Sub(),atm) | BinOp(atm,Add(),atm)
          |    Compare(atm,[cmp],[atm])
    stmt  ::=  Expr(Call(Name('print'),[atm])) | Expr(exp)
          |    Assign([Name(var)], exp)
    tail  ::=  Return(exp) | Goto(label)
          |    If(Compare(atm,[cmp],[atm]), [Goto(label)], [Goto(label)])
    ─────────────────────────────────────────────────────────────
    atm   ::=  GlobalValue(var)
    exp   ::=  Subscript(atm,atm,Load()) | Allocate(int,type)
          |    Call(Name('len'),[atm])
    stmt  ::=  Collect(int) | Assign([Subscript(atm,atm,Store())], atm)
    C_Tup ::=  CProgram({label: stmt* tail, … })
```

Figure 7.12
The abstract syntax of C_{Tup}, extending C_{If} (figure 5.8).

7.6 Select Instructions and the x86$_{\text{Global}}$ Language

In this pass we generate x86 code for most of the new operations that are needed to compile tuples, including `Allocate`, `Collect`, accessing tuple elements, and the `Is` comparison. We compile `GlobalValue` to `Global` because the latter has a different concrete syntax (see figures 7.13 and 7.14).

The tuple read and write forms translate into `movq` instructions. (The +1 in the offset serves to move past the tag at the beginning of the tuple representation.)

lhs = *tup* [*n*]
$\Longrightarrow$
movq *tup*′, %r11
movq 8(*n* + 1)(%r11), *lhs*′

tup [*n*] = *rhs*
$\Longrightarrow$
movq *tup*′, %r11
movq *rhs*′, 8(*n* + 1)(%r11)

The *tup*′ and *rhs*′ are obtained by translating from C_{Tup} to x86. The move of *tup*′ to register r11 ensures that the offset expression 8(*n* + 1)(%r11) contains a register operand. This requires removing r11 from consideration by the register allocator.

Why not use `rax` instead of `r11`? Suppose that we instead used `rax`. Then the generated code for tuple assignment would be

movq *tup*′, %rax
movq *rhs*′, 8(*n* + 1)(%rax)

Next, suppose that *rhs*′ ends up as a stack location, so `patch_instructions` would insert a move through `rax` as follows:

movq *tup*′, %rax
movq *rhs*′, %rax
movq %rax, 8(*n* + 1)(%rax)

However, this sequence of instructions does not work because we're trying to use `rax` for two different values (*tup*′ and *rhs*′) at the same time!

The `len` operation should be translated into a sequence of instructions that read the tag of the tuple and extract the 6 bits that represent the tuple length, which are the bits starting at index 1 and going up to and including bit 6. The x86 instructions `andq` (for bitwise-and) and `sarq` (shift right) can be used to accomplish this.

We compile the `allocate` form to operations on the `free_ptr`, as shown next. This approach is called *inline allocation* because it implements allocation without a function call by simply incrementing the allocation pointer. It is much more efficient than calling a function for each allocation. The address in the `free_ptr` is the next free address in the FromSpace, so we copy it into r11 and then move it forward by enough space for the tuple being allocated, which is 8(*len* + 1) bytes because each element is 8 bytes (64 bits) and we use 8 bytes for the tag. We then initialize the *tag* and finally copy the address in r11 to the left-hand side. Refer to figure 7.8 to see how the tag is organized. We recommend using the bitwise-or operator | and the shift-left operator « to compute the tag during compilation. The type annotation in the `allocate` form is used to determine the pointer mask region of the tag. The addressing mode `free_ptr(%rip)` essentially stands for the address of the `free_ptr` global variable using a special instruction-pointer-relative addressing mode of the x86-64 processor. In particular, the assembler computes the distance *d* between the address of `free_ptr` and where the `rip` would be at that moment and then changes the `free_ptr(%rip)` argument to *d*`(%rip)`, which at runtime will compute the address of `free_ptr`.

```
lhs = allocate(len, TupleType([type, ...]));
⟹
movq free_ptr(%rip), %r11
addq 8(len + 1), free_ptr(%rip)
movq $tag, 0(%r11)
movq %r11, lhs'
```

The `collect` form is compiled to a call to the `collect` function in the runtime. The arguments to `collect` are (1) the top of the root stack, and (2) the number of bytes that need to be allocated. We use another dedicated register, `r15`, to store the pointer to the top of the root stack. Therefore `r15` is not available for use by the register allocator.

```
collect(bytes)
⟹
movq %r15, %rdi
movq $bytes, %rsi
callq collect
```

The `is` comparison is compiled similarly to the other comparison operators, using the `cmpq` instruction. Because the value of a tuple is its address, we can translate `is` into a simple check for equality using the `e` condition code.

$$var = (atm_1 \text{ is } atm_2) \quad \Rightarrow \quad \begin{array}{l} \texttt{cmpq } arg_2, arg_1 \\ \texttt{sete \%al} \\ \texttt{movzbq \%al, } var \end{array}$$

The definitions of the concrete and abstract syntax of the x86$_{\text{Global}}$ language are shown in figures 7.13 and 7.14. It differs from x86$_{\text{If}}$ only in the addition of global variables. Figure 7.15 shows the output of the `select_instructions` pass on the running example.

$$
\begin{array}{rcl}
\textit{reg} & ::= & \texttt{rsp} \mid \texttt{rbp} \mid \texttt{rax} \mid \texttt{rbx} \mid \texttt{rcx} \mid \texttt{rdx} \mid \texttt{rsi} \mid \texttt{rdi} \mid \\
&& \texttt{r8} \mid \texttt{r9} \mid \texttt{r10} \mid \texttt{r11} \mid \texttt{r12} \mid \texttt{r13} \mid \texttt{r14} \mid \texttt{r15} \\
\textit{arg} & ::= & \$ \textit{int} \mid \% \textit{reg} \mid \textit{int}(\% \textit{reg}) \\
\textit{instr} & ::= & \texttt{addq}\,\textit{arg},\textit{arg} \mid \texttt{subq}\,\textit{arg},\textit{arg} \mid \texttt{negq}\,\textit{arg} \mid \texttt{movq}\,\textit{arg},\textit{arg} \mid \\
&& \texttt{pushq}\,\textit{arg} \mid \texttt{popq}\,\textit{arg} \mid \texttt{callq}\,\textit{label} \mid \texttt{retq} \mid \texttt{jmp}\,\textit{label} \mid \\
&& \textit{label} : \textit{instr}
\end{array}
$$

$$
\begin{array}{rcl}
\textit{bytereg} & ::= & \texttt{ah} \mid \texttt{al} \mid \texttt{bh} \mid \texttt{bl} \mid \texttt{ch} \mid \texttt{cl} \mid \texttt{dh} \mid \texttt{dl} \\
\textit{arg} & ::= & \% \textit{bytereg} \\
\textit{cc} & ::= & \texttt{e} \mid \texttt{ne} \mid \texttt{l} \mid \texttt{le} \mid \texttt{g} \mid \texttt{ge} \\
\textit{instr} & ::= & \texttt{xorq}\,\textit{arg},\,\textit{arg} \mid \texttt{cmpq}\,\textit{arg},\,\textit{arg} \mid \texttt{set}cc\,\textit{arg} \mid \texttt{movzbq}\,\textit{arg},\,\textit{arg} \\
& \mid & \texttt{j}cc\,\textit{label}
\end{array}
$$

$$
\begin{array}{rcl}
\textit{arg} & ::= & \textit{label}(\texttt{\%rip}) \\
\text{x86}_{\text{Global}} & ::= & \texttt{.globl main} \\
&& \texttt{main}: \textit{instr}^*
\end{array}
$$

Figure 7.13
The concrete syntax of x86$_{\text{Global}}$ (extends x86$_{\text{If}}$ shown in figure 5.9).

$$
\begin{array}{rcl}
\textit{reg} & ::= & \texttt{rsp} \mid \texttt{rbp} \mid \texttt{rax} \mid \texttt{rbx} \mid \texttt{rcx} \mid \texttt{rdx} \mid \texttt{rsi} \mid \texttt{rdi} \mid \\
&& \texttt{r8} \mid \texttt{r9} \mid \texttt{r10} \mid \texttt{r11} \mid \texttt{r12} \mid \texttt{r13} \mid \texttt{r14} \mid \texttt{r15} \\
\textit{arg} & ::= & \texttt{Immediate}(\textit{int}) \mid \texttt{Reg}(\textit{reg}) \mid \texttt{Deref}(\textit{reg},\textit{int}) \\
\textit{instr} & ::= & \texttt{Instr('addq',}[\textit{arg},\textit{arg}]) \mid \texttt{Instr('subq',}[\textit{arg},\textit{arg}]) \\
& \mid & \texttt{Instr('negq',}[\textit{arg}]) \mid \texttt{Instr('movq',}[\textit{arg},\textit{arg}]) \\
& \mid & \texttt{Instr('pushq',}[\textit{arg}]) \mid \texttt{Instr('popq',}[\textit{arg}]) \\
& \mid & \texttt{Callq}(\textit{label},\textit{int}) \mid \texttt{Retq()} \mid \texttt{Jump}(\textit{label}) \\
\textit{block} & ::= & \textit{instr}^+
\end{array}
$$

$$
\begin{array}{rcl}
\textit{bytereg} & ::= & \texttt{'ah'} \mid \texttt{'al'} \mid \texttt{'bh'} \mid \texttt{'bl'} \mid \texttt{'ch'} \mid \texttt{'cl'} \mid \texttt{'dh'} \mid \texttt{'dl'} \\
\textit{arg} & ::= & \texttt{Immediate}(\textit{int}) \mid \texttt{Reg}(\textit{reg}) \mid \texttt{Deref}(\textit{reg},\textit{int}) \mid \texttt{ByteReg}(\textit{bytereg}) \\
\textit{cc} & ::= & \texttt{'e'} \mid \texttt{'ne'} \mid \texttt{'l'} \mid \texttt{'le'} \mid \texttt{'g'} \mid \texttt{'ge'} \\
\textit{instr} & ::= & \texttt{Jump}(\textit{label}) \\
& \mid & \texttt{Instr('xorq',}[\textit{arg},\textit{arg}]) \mid \texttt{Instr('cmpq',}[\textit{arg},\textit{arg}]) \\
& \mid & \texttt{Instr('set'+}cc,[\textit{arg}]) \mid \texttt{Instr('movzbq',}[\textit{arg},\textit{arg}]) \\
& \mid & \texttt{JumpIf}(cc,\textit{label})
\end{array}
$$

$$
\begin{array}{rcl}
\textit{arg} & ::= & \texttt{Global}(\textit{label}) \\
\text{x86}_{\text{Global}} & ::= & \texttt{X86Program}(\{\textit{label} : \textit{block}, \dots\})
\end{array}
$$

Figure 7.14
The abstract syntax of x86$_{\text{Global}}$ (extends x86$_{\text{If}}$ shown in figure 5.10).

```
                                                        start:
                                                            movq $42, init.514
                                                            movq free_ptr(%rip), tmp.517
                                                            movq tmp.517, tmp.518
                                                            addq $16, tmp.518
                                                            movq fromspace_end(%rip), tmp.519
                                                            cmpq tmp.519, tmp.518
                                                            jl block.529
                                                            jmp block.530

start:                                                  block.529:
    init.514 = 42                                           jmp block.528
    tmp.517 = free_ptr
    tmp.518 = (tmp.517 + 16)                            block.530:
    tmp.519 = fromspace_end                                 movq %r15, %rdi
    if tmp.518 < tmp.519:                                   movq $16, %rsi
      goto block.529                                        callq collect
    else:                                                   jmp block.528
      goto block.530
                                                        block.528:
block.529:                                                  movq free_ptr(%rip), %r11
    goto block.528                                          addq $16, free_ptr(%rip)
                                                            movq $3, 0(%r11)
block.530:                                                  movq %r11, alloc.513
    collect(16)                                             movq alloc.513, %r11
    goto block.528                                          movq init.514, 8(%r11)
                                                            movq alloc.513, v1
block.528:                                                  movq v1, init.516
    alloc.513 = allocate(1,tuple[int])                      movq free_ptr(%rip), tmp.520
    alloc.513:tuple[int][0] = init.514                      movq tmp.520, tmp.521
    v1 = alloc.513                                          addq $16, tmp.521
    init.516 = v1                                 ⟹      movq fromspace_end(%rip), tmp.522
    tmp.520 = free_ptr                                     cmpq tmp.522, tmp.521
    tmp.521 = (tmp.520 + 16)                               jl block.526
    tmp.522 = fromspace_end                                jmp block.527
    if tmp.521 < tmp.522:
      goto block.526                                   block.526:
    else:                                                  jmp block.525
      goto block.527
                                                        block.527:
block.526:                                                  movq %r15, %rdi
    goto block.525                                          movq $16, %rsi
                                                            callq collect
block.527:                                                  jmp block.525
    collect(16)
    goto block.525                                      block.525:
                                                            movq free_ptr(%rip), %r11
block.525:                                                  addq $16, free_ptr(%rip)
    alloc.515 = allocate(1,tuple[tuple[int]])               movq $131, 0(%r11)
    alloc.515:tuple[tuple[int]][0] = init.516               movq %r11, alloc.515
    v2 = alloc.515                                          movq alloc.515, %r11
    tmp.523 = v2[0]                                         movq init.516, 8(%r11)
    tmp.524 = tmp.523[0]                                    movq alloc.515, v2
    print(tmp.524)                                          movq v2, %r11
    return 0                                                movq 8(%r11), %r11
                                                            movq %r11, tmp.523
                                                            movq tmp.523, %r11
                                                            movq 8(%r11), %r11
                                                            movq %r11, tmp.524
                                                            movq tmp.524, %rdi
                                                            callq print_int
                                                            movq $0, %rax
                                                            jmp conclusion
```

Figure 7.15
Output of explicate_control (*left*) and select_instructions (*right*) on the running example.

7.7   Register Allocation

As discussed previously in this chapter, the garbage collector needs to access all the pointers in the root set, that is, all variables that are tuples. It will be the responsibility of the register allocator to make sure that

1. the root stack is used for spilling tuple-typed variables, and
2. if a tuple-typed variable is live during a call to the collector, it must be spilled to ensure that it is visible to the collector.

The latter responsibility can be handled during construction of the interference graph, by adding interference edges between the call-live tuple-typed variables and all the callee-saved registers. (They already interfere with the caller-saved registers.) The type information for variables is generated by the type checker for $\mathcal{C}_{\mathsf{Tup}}$, stored in a field named `var_types` in the `CProgram` AST mode. You'll need to propagate that information so that it is available in this pass.

The spilling of tuple-typed variables to the root stack can be handled after graph coloring, in choosing how to assign the colors (integers) to registers and stack locations. The `CProgram` output of this pass changes to also record the number of spills to the root stack.

7.8   Generate Prelude and Conclusion

Figure 7.16 shows the output of the `prelude_and_conclusion` pass on the running example. In the prelude of the `main` function, we allocate space on the root stack to make room for the spills of tuple-typed variables. We do so by incrementing the root stack pointer (`r15`), taking care that the root stack grows up instead of down. For the running example, there was just one spill, so we increment `r15` by 8 bytes. In the conclusion we subtract 8 bytes from `r15`.

One issue that deserves special care is that there may be a call to `collect` prior to the initializing assignments for all the variables in the root stack. We do not want the garbage collector to mistakenly determine that some uninitialized variable is a pointer that needs to be followed. Thus, we zero out all locations on the root stack in the prelude of `main`. In figure 7.16, the instruction `movq $0, 0(%r15)` is sufficient to accomplish this task because there is only one spill. In general, we have to clear as many words as there are spills of tuple-typed variables. The garbage collector tests each root to see if it is null prior to dereferencing it.

Figure 7.17 gives an overview of all the passes needed for the compilation of $\mathcal{L}_{\mathsf{Tup}}$.

```
        .globl main
main:
    pushq %rbp
    movq %rsp, %rbp
    pushq %rbx
    subq $8, %rsp
    movq $65536, %rdi
    movq $16, %rsi
    callq initialize
    movq rootstack_begin(%rip), %r15
    movq $0, 0(%r15)
    addq $8, %r15
    jmp start

conclusion:
    subq $8, %r15
    addq $8, %rsp
    popq %rbx
    popq %rbp
    retq
```

Figure 7.16
The prelude and conclusion for the running example.

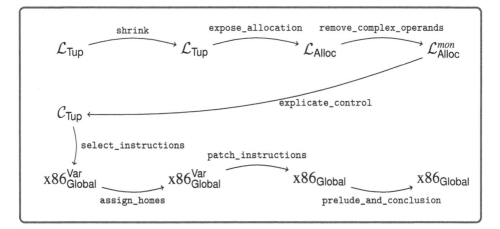

Figure 7.17
Diagram of the passes for $\mathcal{L}_{\text{Tup}}$, a language with tuples.

$$
\begin{array}{rcl}
exp & ::= & int \mid \texttt{input\_int()} \mid -exp \mid exp + exp \mid exp - exp \mid (exp) \\
stmt & ::= & \texttt{print}(exp) \mid exp \\
\hline
exp & ::= & var \\
stmt & ::= & var = exp \\
\hline
cmp & ::= & \texttt{==} \mid \texttt{!=} \mid \texttt{<} \mid \texttt{<=} \mid \texttt{>} \mid \texttt{>=} \\
exp & ::= & \texttt{True} \mid \texttt{False} \mid exp \texttt{ and } exp \mid exp \texttt{ or } exp \mid \texttt{not } exp \\
 & \mid & exp \; cmp \; exp \mid exp \texttt{ if } exp \texttt{ else } exp \\
stmt & ::= & \texttt{if } exp\texttt{: } stmt^{+} \texttt{ else: } stmt^{+} \\
\hline
stmt & ::= & \texttt{while } exp\texttt{: } stmt^{+} \\
\hline
cmp & ::= & \texttt{is} \\
exp & ::= & exp, \dots , exp \mid exp\,[int] \mid \texttt{len}(exp) \\
\hline
type & ::= & \texttt{list}[type] \\
exp & ::= & exp * exp \mid exp\,[exp] \mid [exp, \dots] \\
stmt & ::= & exp\,[exp] = exp \\
\mathcal{L}_{\mathsf{Array}} & ::= & stmt^{*}
\end{array}
$$

Figure 7.18
The concrete syntax of $\mathcal{L}_{\mathsf{Array}}$, extending $\mathcal{L}_{\mathsf{Tup}}$ (figure 7.1).

7.9   Challenge: Arrays

In this chapter we have studied tuples, that is, heterogeneous sequences of elements whose length is determined at compile time. This challenge is also about sequences, but this time the length is determined at runtime and all the elements have the same type (they are homogeneous). We use the traditional term *array* for this latter kind of sequence. Arrays correspond to the **list** type in the Python language.

Figure 7.18 presents the definition of the concrete syntax for $\mathcal{L}_{\mathsf{Array}}$, and figure 7.19 presents the definition of the abstract syntax, extending $\mathcal{L}_{\mathsf{Tup}}$ with the **list** type and the bracket notation for creating an array literal. The subscript operator becomes overloaded for use with arrays and tuples and now may appear on the left-hand side of an assignment. Note that the index of the subscript, when applied to an array, may be an arbitrary expression and not exclusively a constant integer. The **len** function is also applicable to arrays. We include integer multiplication in $\mathcal{L}_{\mathsf{Array}}$ because it is useful in many examples involving arrays such as computing the inner product of two arrays (figure 7.20).

The type checker for $\mathcal{L}_{\mathsf{Array}}$ is defined in figures 7.21 and 7.22. The result type of a list literal is **list[T]**, where T is the type of the initializing expressions. The type checking of the **len** function and the subscript operator are updated to handle lists. The type checker now also handles a subscript on the left-hand side of an assignment. Regarding multiplication, it takes two integers and returns an integer.

The definition of the interpreter for $\mathcal{L}_{\mathsf{Array}}$ is shown in figure 7.23. We implement array creation with a Python list comprehension, and multiplication is implemented with 64-bit multiplication. We add a case for a subscript on the left-hand side of assignment. Other uses of subscript can be handled by the existing code for tuples.

$$
\begin{array}{lll}
\mathit{exp} & ::= & \texttt{Constant}(\mathit{int}) \mid \texttt{Call(Name('input\_int'),[])} \\
 & \mid & \texttt{UnaryOp(USub(),}\mathit{exp}) \mid \texttt{BinOp(}\mathit{exp}\texttt{,Add(),}\mathit{exp}) \\
 & \mid & \texttt{BinOp(}\mathit{exp}\texttt{,Sub(),}\mathit{exp}) \\
\mathit{stmt} & ::= & \texttt{Expr(Call(Name('print'),[}\mathit{exp}\texttt{]))} \mid \texttt{Expr(}\mathit{exp}) \\
\hline
\mathit{exp} & ::= & \texttt{Name(}\mathit{var}) \\
\mathit{stmt} & ::= & \texttt{Assign([Name(}\mathit{var}\texttt{)], }\mathit{exp}) \\
\hline
\mathit{boolop} & ::= & \texttt{And() | Or()} \\
\mathit{cmp} & ::= & \texttt{Eq() | NotEq() | Lt() | LtE() | Gt() | GtE()} \\
\mathit{bool} & ::= & \texttt{True | False} \\
\mathit{exp} & ::= & \texttt{Constant(}\mathit{bool}\texttt{)} \mid \texttt{BoolOp(}\mathit{boolop}\texttt{,[}\mathit{exp}\texttt{,}\mathit{exp}\texttt{])} \\
 & \mid & \texttt{UnaryOp(Not(),}\mathit{exp}\texttt{)} \mid \texttt{Compare(}\mathit{exp}\texttt{,[}\mathit{cmp}\texttt{],[}\mathit{exp}\texttt{])} \\
 & \mid & \texttt{IfExp(}\mathit{exp}\texttt{,}\mathit{exp}\texttt{,}\mathit{exp}\texttt{)} \\
\mathit{stmt} & ::= & \texttt{If(}\mathit{exp}\texttt{, }\mathit{stmt}^{+}\texttt{, }\mathit{stmt}^{+}\texttt{)} \\
\hline
\mathit{stmt} & ::= & \texttt{While(}\mathit{exp}\texttt{, }\mathit{stmt}^{+}\texttt{, [])} \\
\hline
\mathit{cmp} & ::= & \texttt{Is()} \\
\mathit{exp} & ::= & \texttt{Tuple(}\mathit{exp}^{+}\texttt{,Load())} \mid \texttt{Subscript(}\mathit{exp}\texttt{,Constant(}\mathit{int}\texttt{),Load())} \\
 & \mid & \texttt{Call(Name('len'),[}\mathit{exp}\texttt{])} \\
\hline
\mathit{type} & ::= & \texttt{ListType(}\mathit{type}\texttt{)} \\
\mathit{exp} & ::= & \texttt{BinOp(}\mathit{exp}\texttt{,Mult(),}\mathit{exp}\texttt{)} \mid \texttt{Subscript(}\mathit{exp}\texttt{,}\mathit{exp}\texttt{,Load())} \\
 & \mid & \texttt{List(}\mathit{exp}\texttt{, ... , Load())} \\
\mathit{stmt} & ::= & \texttt{Assign([Subscript(}\mathit{exp}\texttt{,}\mathit{exp}\texttt{,Store())], }\mathit{exp}\texttt{)} \\
\mathcal{L}_{\mathsf{Array}} & ::= & \mathit{stmt}^{*} \\
\end{array}
$$

Figure 7.19
The abstract syntax of $\mathcal{L}_{\mathsf{Array}}$, extending $\mathcal{L}_{\mathsf{Tup}}$ (figure 7.2).

```
A = [2, 2]
B = [3, 3]
i = 0
prod = 0
while i != len(A):
  prod = prod + A[i] * B[i]
  i = i + 1
print(prod)
```

Figure 7.20
Example program that computes the inner product.

7.9.1 Data Representation

Just as with tuples, we store arrays on the heap, which means that the garbage collector will need to inspect arrays. An immediate thought is to use the same representation for arrays that we use for tuples. However, we limit tuples to a length of fifty so that their length and pointer mask can fit into the 64-bit tag at the beginning of each tuple (section 7.2.3). We intend arrays to allow millions of elements, so we need more bits to store the length. However, because arrays are

```
class TypeCheckLarray(TypeCheckLtup):
  def type_check_exp(self, e, env):
    match e:
      case ast.List(es, Load()):
        ts = [self.type_check_exp(e, env) for e in es]
        elt_ty = ts[0]
        for (ty, elt) in zip(ts, es):
            self.check_type_equal(elt_ty, ty, elt)
        e.has_type = ListType(elt_ty)
        return e.has_type
      case Call(Name('len'), [tup]):
        tup_t = self.type_check_exp(tup, env)
        tup.has_type = tup_t
        match tup_t:
          case TupleType(ts):
            return IntType()
          case ListType(ty):
            return IntType()
          case _:
            raise Exception('len expected a tuple, not ' + repr(tup_t))
      case Subscript(tup, index, Load()):
        tup_ty = self.type_check_exp(tup, env)
        index_ty = self.type_check_exp(index, env)
        self.check_type_equal(index_ty, IntType(), index)
        match tup_ty:
          case TupleType(ts):
            match index:
              case Constant(i):
                return ts[i]
              case _:
                raise Exception('subscript required constant integer index')
          case ListType(ty):
            return ty
          case _:
            raise Exception('subscript expected a tuple, not ' + repr(tup_ty))
      case BinOp(left, Mult(), right):
        l = self.type_check_exp(left, env)
        self.check_type_equal(l, IntType(), left)
        r = self.type_check_exp(right, env)
        self.check_type_equal(r, IntType(), right)
        return IntType()
      case _:
        return super().type_check_exp(e, env)
```

Figure 7.21
Type checker for the $\mathcal{L}_{Array}$ language, part 1.

homogeneous, we need only 1 bit for the pointer mask instead of 1 bit per array element. Finally, the garbage collector must be able to distinguish between tuples and arrays, so we need to reserve one bit for that purpose. We arrive at the following layout for the 64-bit tag at the beginning of an array:

• The right-most bit is the forwarding bit, just as in a tuple. A 0 indicates that it is a forwarding pointer, and a 1 indicates that it is not.

```
def type_check_stmts(self, ss, env):
  if len(ss) == 0:
    return VoidType()
  match ss[0]:
    case Assign([Subscript(tup, index, Store())], value):
      tup_t = self.type_check_exp(tup, env)
      value_t = self.type_check_exp(value, env)
      index_ty = self.type_check_exp(index, env)
      self.check_type_equal(index_ty, IntType(), index)
      match tup_t:
        case ListType(ty):
          self.check_type_equal(ty, value_t, ss[0])
        case TupleType(ts):
          return self.type_check_stmts(ss, env)
        case _:
          raise Exception('type_check_stmts: '
            'expected tuple or list, not ' + repr(tup_t))
      return self.type_check_stmts(ss[1:], env)
    case _:
      return super().type_check_stmts(ss, env)
```

Figure 7.22
Type checker for the $\mathcal{L}_{\mathsf{Array}}$ language, part 2.

- The next bit to the left is the pointer mask. A 0 indicates that none of the elements are pointers, and a 1 indicates that all the elements are pointers.
- The next 60 bits store the length of the array.
- The bit at position 62 distinguishes between a tuple (0) and an array (1).
- The left-most bit is reserved as explained in chapter 11.

In the following subsections we provide hints regarding how to update the passes to handle arrays.

7.9.2 Overload Resolution

As noted previously, with the addition of arrays, several operators have become *overloaded*; that is, they can be applied to values of more than one type. In this case, the element access and length operators can be applied to both tuples and arrays. This kind of overloading is quite common in programming languages, so many compilers perform *overload resolution* to handle it. The idea is to translate each overloaded operator into different operators for the different types.

Implement a new pass named **resolve**. Translate the reading of an array element to **array_load** and the writing of an array element to **array_store**. Translate calls to **len** into **array_len**. When these operators are applied to tuples, leave them as is. The type checker for $\mathcal{L}_{\mathsf{Array}}$ adds a **has_type** field, which can be inspected to determine whether the operator is applied to a tuple or an array.

```
class InterpLarray(InterpLtup):
  def interp_exp(self, e, env):
    match e:
      case ast.List(es, Load()):
        return [self.interp_exp(e, env) for e in es]
      case BinOp(left, Mult(), right):
        l = self.interp_exp(left, env)
        r = self.interp_exp(right, env)
        return mul64(l, r)
      case Subscript(tup, index, Load()):
        t = self.interp_exp(tup, env)
        n = self.interp_exp(index, env)
        if n < len(t):
          return t[n]
        else:
          raise TrappedError('array index out of bounds')
      case _:
        return super().interp_exp(e, env)

  def interp_stmt(self, s, env, cont):
    match s:
      case Assign([Subscript(tup, index)], value):
        t = self.interp_exp(tup, env)
        n = self.interp_exp(index, env)
        if n < len(t):
          t[n] = self.interp_exp(value, env)
        else:
          raise TrappedError('array index out of bounds')
        return self.interp_stmts(cont, env)
      case _:
        return super().interp_stmt(s, env, cont)
```

Figure 7.23
Interpreter for $\mathcal{L}_{\mathsf{Array}}$.

7.9.3 Bounds Checking

Recall that the interpreter for $\mathcal{L}_{\mathsf{Array}}$ signals a TrappedError when there is an array access that is out of bounds. Therefore your compiler is obliged to also catch these errors during execution and halt, signaling an error. We recommend inserting a new pass named check_bounds that inserts code around each subscript operation to ensure that the index is greater than or equal to zero and less than the array's length. If not, the program should halt, for which we recommend using a new primitive operation named exit.

7.9.4 Expose Allocation

This pass should translate array creation into lower-level operations. In particular, the new AST node AllocateArray(*exp*, *type*) is analogous to the Allocate AST node for tuples. The *type* argument must be ListType(T), where T is the element type for the array. The AllocateArray AST node allocates an array of the length specified by the *exp* (of type `int`), but does not initialize the elements of the array. Generate code in this pass to initialize the elements analogous to the case for tuples.

7.9.5 Remove Complex Operands

Add cases in the `rco_atom` and `rco_exp` for `AllocateArray`. In particular, an `AllocateArray` node is complex, and its subexpression must be atomic.

7.9.6 Explicate Control

Add cases for `AllocateArray` to `explicate_tail` and `explicate_assign`.

7.9.7 Select Instructions

Generate instructions for `AllocateArray` similar to those for `Allocate` given in section 7.6 except that the tag at the front of the array should instead use the representation discussed in section 7.9.1.

Regarding `array_len`, extract the length from the tag.

The instructions generated for accessing an element of an array differ from those for a tuple (section 7.6) in that the index is not a constant so you need to generate instructions that compute the offset at runtime.

Compile the `exit` primitive into a call to the `exit` function of the C standard library, with an argument of 255.

Exercise 7.1 Implement a compiler for the $\mathcal{L}_{\text{Array}}$ language by extending your compiler for $\mathcal{L}_{\text{While}}$. Test your compiler on a half dozen new programs, including the one shown in figure 7.20 and also a program that multiplies two matrices. Note that although matrices are two-dimensional arrays, they can be encoded into one-dimensional arrays by laying out each row in the array, one after the next.

7.10 Further Reading

Appel (1990) describes many data representation approaches including the ones used in the compilation of Standard ML.

There are many alternatives to copying collectors (and their bigger siblings, the generational collectors) with regard to garbage collection, such as mark-and-sweep (McCarthy 1960) and reference counting (Collins 1960). The strengths of copying collectors are that allocation is fast (just a comparison and pointer increment), there is no fragmentation, cyclic garbage is collected, and the time complexity of collection depends only on the amount of live data and not on the amount of garbage (Wilson 1992). The main disadvantages of a two-space copying collector is that it uses a lot of extra space and takes a long time to perform the copy, though these problems are ameliorated in generational collectors. Object-oriented programs tend to allocate many small objects and generate a lot of garbage, so copying and generational collectors are a good fit (Dieckmann and Hölzle 1999). Garbage collection is an active research topic, especially concurrent garbage collection (Tene, Iyengar, and Wolf 2011). Researchers are continuously developing new techniques and revisiting old trade-offs (Blackburn, Cheng, and McKinley 2004;

Jones, Hosking, and Moss 2011; Shahriyar et al. 2013; Cutler and Morris 2015; Shidal et al. 2015; Österlund and Löwe 2016; Jacek and Moss 2019; Gamari and Dietz 2020). Researchers meet every year at the International Symposium on Memory Management to present these findings.

8 Functions

This chapter studies the compilation of a subset of Python in which only top-level function definitions are allowed. This kind of function appears in the C programming language, and it serves as an important stepping-stone to implementing lexically scoped functions in the form of **lambda** abstractions, which is the topic of chapter 9.

8.1 The $\mathcal{L}_{\mathsf{Fun}}$ Language

The concrete syntax and abstract syntax for function definitions and function application are shown in figures 8.1 and 8.2, with which we define the $\mathcal{L}_{\mathsf{Fun}}$ language. Programs in $\mathcal{L}_{\mathsf{Fun}}$ begin with zero or more function definitions. The function names from these definitions are in scope for the entire program, including all the function definitions, and therefore the ordering of function definitions does not matter. The abstract syntax for function parameters in figure 8.2 is a list of pairs, each of which consists of a parameter name and its type. This design differs from Python's **ast** module, which has a more complex structure for function parameters to handle keyword parameters, defaults, and so on. The type checker in **type_check_Lfun** converts the complex Python abstract syntax into the simpler syntax shown in figure 8.2. The fourth and sixth parameters of the **FunctionDef** constructor are for decorators and a type comment, neither of which are used by our compiler. We recommend replacing them with **None** in the **shrink** pass. The concrete syntax for function application is *exp(exp, ...)*, where the first expression must evaluate to a function and the remaining expressions are the arguments. The abstract syntax for function application is **Call**(*exp*, *exp**).

Functions are first-class in the sense that a function pointer is data and can be stored in memory or passed as a parameter to another function. Thus, there is a function type, written

Callable[[*type*$_1$,··· ,*type*$_n$], *type*$_R$]

for a function whose *n* parameters have the types *type*$_1$ through *type*$_n$ and whose return type is *type*$_R$. The main limitation of these functions (with respect to Python functions) is that they are not lexically scoped. That is, the only external entities that can be referenced from inside a function body are other globally defined functions. The syntax of $\mathcal{L}_{\mathsf{Fun}}$ prevents function definitions from being nested inside each other.

$$
\begin{array}{lll}
\textit{exp} & ::= & \textit{int} \mid \texttt{input\_int()} \mid -\textit{exp} \mid \textit{exp}+\textit{exp} \mid \textit{exp}-\textit{exp} \mid (\textit{exp}) \\
\textit{stmt} & ::= & \texttt{print}(\textit{exp}) \mid \textit{exp} \\
\hline
\textit{exp} & ::= & \textit{var} \\
\textit{stmt} & ::= & \textit{var}=\textit{exp} \\
\hline
\textit{cmp} & ::= & \texttt{==} \mid \texttt{!=} \mid \texttt{<} \mid \texttt{<=} \mid \texttt{>} \mid \texttt{>=} \\
\textit{exp} & ::= & \texttt{True} \mid \texttt{False} \mid \textit{exp}\ \texttt{and}\ \textit{exp} \mid \textit{exp}\ \texttt{or}\ \textit{exp} \mid \texttt{not}\ \textit{exp} \\
& \mid & \textit{exp}\ \textit{cmp}\ \textit{exp} \mid \textit{exp}\ \texttt{if}\ \textit{exp}\ \texttt{else}\ \textit{exp} \\
\textit{stmt} & ::= & \texttt{if}\ \textit{exp}\texttt{:}\ \textit{stmt}^{+}\ \texttt{else:}\ \textit{stmt}^{+} \\
\hline
\textit{stmt} & ::= & \texttt{while}\ \textit{exp}\texttt{:}\ \textit{stmt}^{+} \\
\hline
\textit{cmp} & ::= & \texttt{is} \\
\textit{exp} & ::= & \textit{exp},\ \dots\ ,\textit{exp} \mid \textit{exp}\texttt{[}\textit{int}\texttt{]} \mid \texttt{len}(\textit{exp}) \\
\hline
\textit{type} & ::= & \texttt{int} \mid \texttt{bool} \mid \texttt{void} \mid \texttt{tuple[}\textit{type}^{+}\texttt{]} \mid \texttt{Callable[[}\textit{type},\dots\texttt{]},\ \textit{type}\texttt{]} \\
\textit{exp} & ::= & \textit{exp}(\textit{exp},\dots) \\
\textit{stmt} & ::= & \texttt{return}\ \textit{exp} \\
\textit{def} & ::= & \texttt{def}\ \textit{var}(\textit{var}\texttt{:}\textit{type},\ \dots)\ \texttt{->}\ \textit{type}\texttt{:}\ \textit{stmt}^{+} \\
\mathcal{L}_{\mathsf{Fun}} & ::= & \textit{def}\ \dots\ \textit{stmt}\ \dots
\end{array}
$$

Figure 8.1
The concrete syntax of $\mathcal{L}_{\mathsf{Fun}}$, extending $\mathcal{L}_{\mathsf{Tup}}$ (figure 7.1).

$$
\begin{array}{lll}
\textit{exp} & ::= & \texttt{Constant}(\textit{int}) \mid \texttt{Call(Name('input\_int'),[])} \\
& \mid & \texttt{UnaryOp(USub(),}\textit{exp}\texttt{)} \mid \texttt{BinOp(}\textit{exp}\texttt{,Add(),}\textit{exp}\texttt{)} \\
& \mid & \texttt{BinOp(}\textit{exp}\texttt{,Sub(),}\textit{exp}\texttt{)} \\
\textit{stmt} & ::= & \texttt{Expr(Call(Name('print'),[}\textit{exp}\texttt{]))} \mid \texttt{Expr(}\textit{exp}\texttt{)} \\
\hline
\textit{exp} & ::= & \texttt{Name(}\textit{var}\texttt{)} \\
\textit{stmt} & ::= & \texttt{Assign([Name(}\textit{var}\texttt{)],}\ \textit{exp}\texttt{)} \\
\hline
\textit{boolop} & ::= & \texttt{And()} \mid \texttt{Or()} \\
\textit{cmp} & ::= & \texttt{Eq()} \mid \texttt{NotEq()} \mid \texttt{Lt()} \mid \texttt{LtE()} \mid \texttt{Gt()} \mid \texttt{GtE()} \\
\textit{bool} & ::= & \texttt{True} \mid \texttt{False} \\
\textit{exp} & ::= & \texttt{Constant(}\textit{bool}\texttt{)} \mid \texttt{BoolOp(}\textit{boolop}\texttt{,[}\textit{exp}\texttt{,}\textit{exp}\texttt{])} \\
& \mid & \texttt{UnaryOp(Not(),}\textit{exp}\texttt{)} \mid \texttt{Compare(}\textit{exp}\texttt{,[}\textit{cmp}\texttt{],[}\textit{exp}\texttt{])} \\
& \mid & \texttt{IfExp(}\textit{exp}\texttt{,}\textit{exp}\texttt{,}\textit{exp}\texttt{)} \\
\textit{stmt} & ::= & \texttt{If(}\textit{exp}\texttt{,}\ \textit{stmt}^{+}\texttt{,}\ \textit{stmt}^{+}\texttt{)} \\
\hline
\textit{stmt} & ::= & \texttt{While(}\textit{exp}\texttt{,}\ \textit{stmt}^{+}\texttt{,}\ \texttt{[])} \\
\hline
\textit{cmp} & ::= & \texttt{Is()} \\
\textit{exp} & ::= & \texttt{Tuple(}\textit{exp}^{+}\texttt{,Load())} \mid \texttt{Subscript(}\textit{exp}\texttt{,Constant(}\textit{int}\texttt{),Load())} \\
& \mid & \texttt{Call(Name('len'),[}\textit{exp}\texttt{])} \\
\hline
\textit{type} & ::= & \texttt{IntType()} \mid \texttt{BoolType()} \mid \texttt{VoidType()} \mid \texttt{TupleType[}\textit{type}^{+}\texttt{]} \\
& \mid & \texttt{FunctionType(}\textit{type}^{*}\texttt{,}\ \textit{type}\texttt{)} \\
\textit{exp} & ::= & \texttt{Call(}\textit{exp}\texttt{,}\ \textit{exp}^{*}\texttt{)} \\
\textit{stmt} & ::= & \texttt{Return(}\textit{exp}\texttt{)} \\
\textit{params} & ::= & (\textit{var}\texttt{,}\textit{type})^{*} \\
\textit{def} & ::= & \texttt{FunctionDef(}\textit{var}\texttt{,}\ \textit{params}\texttt{,}\ \textit{stmt}^{+}\texttt{,}\ \texttt{None,}\ \textit{type}\texttt{,}\ \texttt{None)} \\
\mathcal{L}_{\mathsf{Fun}} & ::= & \texttt{Module([}\textit{def}\ \dots\ \textit{stmt}\ \dots\texttt{])}
\end{array}
$$

Figure 8.2
The abstract syntax of $\mathcal{L}_{\mathsf{Fun}}$, extending $\mathcal{L}_{\mathsf{Tup}}$ (figure 7.2).

```
def map(f : Callable[[int], int], v : tuple[int,int]) -> tuple[int,int]:
  return f(v[0]), f(v[1])

def inc(x : int) -> int:
  return x + 1

print(map(inc, (0, 41))[1])
```

Figure 8.3
Example of using functions in $\mathcal{L}_{Fun}$.

The program shown in figure 8.3 is a representative example of defining and using functions in $\mathcal{L}_{Fun}$. We define a function `map` that applies some other function `f` to both elements of a tuple and returns a new tuple containing the results. We also define a function `inc`. The program applies `map` to `inc` and `(0, 41)`. The result is `(1, 42)`, from which we return 42.

The definitional interpreter for $\mathcal{L}_{Fun}$ is shown in figure 8.4. The case for the `Module` AST is responsible for setting up the mutual recursion between the top-level function definitions. We create a dictionary named `env` and fill it in by mapping each function name to a new `Function` value, each of which stores a reference to the `env`. (We define the class `Function` for this purpose.) To interpret a function call, we match the result of the function expression to obtain a function value. We then extend the function's environment with the mapping of parameters to argument values. Finally, we interpret the body of the function in this extended environment.

The type checker for $\mathcal{L}_{Fun}$ is shown in figure 8.5. (We omit the code that parses function parameters into the simpler abstract syntax.) Similarly to the interpreter, the case for the `Module` AST is responsible for setting up the mutual recursion between the top-level function definitions. We begin by creating a mapping `env` from every function name to its type. We then type check the program using this mapping. To check a function definition, we copy and extend the `env` with the parameters of the function. We then type check the body of the function and obtain the actual return type `rt`, which is either the type of the expression in a `return` statement or the `VoidType` if control reaches the end of the function without a `return` statement. (If there are multiple `return` statements, the types of their expressions must agree.) Finally, we check that the actual return type `rt` is equal to the declared return type `returns`. To check a function call, we match the type of the function expression to a function type and check that the types of the argument expressions are equal to the function's parameter types. The type of the call as a whole is the return type from the function type.

```
class InterpLfun(InterpLtup):
  def apply_fun(self, fun, args, e):
    match fun:
      case Function(name, xs, body, env):
        new_env = env.copy().update(zip(xs, args))
        return self.interp_stmts(body, new_env)
      case _:
        raise Exception('apply_fun: unexpected: ' + repr(fun))

  def interp_exp(self, e, env):
    match e:
      case Call(Name('input_int'), []):
        return super().interp_exp(e, env)
      case Call(func, args):
        f = self.interp_exp(func, env)
        vs = [self.interp_exp(arg, env) for arg in args]
        return self.apply_fun(f, vs, e)
      case _:
        return super().interp_exp(e, env)

  def interp_stmt(self, s, env, cont):
    match s:
      case Return(value):
        return self.interp_exp(value, env)
      case FunctionDef(name, params, bod, dl, returns, comment):
        if isinstance(params, ast.arguments):
            ps = [p.arg for p in params.args]
        else:
            ps = [x for (x,t) in params]
        env[name] = Function(name, ps, bod, env)
        return self.interp_stmts(cont, env)
      case _:
        return super().interp_stmt(s, env, cont)

  def interp(self, p):
    match p:
      case Module(ss):
        env = {}
        self.interp_stmts(ss, env)
        if 'main' in env.keys():
            self.apply_fun(env['main'], [], None)
      case _:
        raise Exception('interp: unexpected ' + repr(p))
```

Figure 8.4
Interpreter for the $\mathcal{L}_{\mathsf{Fun}}$ language.

```
class TypeCheckLfun(TypeCheckLtup):
  def type_check_exp(self, e, env):
    match e:
      case Call(Name('input_int'), []):
        return super().type_check_exp(e, env)
      case Call(func, args):
        func_t = self.type_check_exp(func, env)
        args_t = [self.type_check_exp(arg, env) for arg in args]
        match func_t:
          case FunctionType(params_t, return_t):
            for (arg_t, param_t) in zip(args_t, params_t):
                check_type_equal(param_t, arg_t, e)
            return return_t
          case _:
            raise Exception('type_check_exp: in call, unexpected ' +
                            repr(func_t))
      case _:
        return super().type_check_exp(e, env)

  def type_check_stmts(self, ss, env):
    if len(ss) == 0:
      return VoidType()
    match ss[0]:
      case FunctionDef(name, params, body, dl, returns, comment):
        new_env = env.copy().update(params)
        rt = self.type_check_stmts(body, new_env)
        check_type_equal(returns, rt, ss[0])
        return self.type_check_stmts(ss[1:], env)
      case Return(value):
        return self.type_check_exp(value, env)
      case _:
        return super().type_check_stmts(ss, env)

  def type_check(self, p):
    match p:
      case Module(body):
        env = {}
        for s in body:
          match s:
            case FunctionDef(name, params, bod, dl, returns, comment):
              if name in env:
                raise Exception('type_check: function ' +
                                repr(name) + ' defined twice')
              params_t = [t for (x,t) in params]
              env[name] = FunctionType(params_t, returns)
        self.type_check_stmts(body, env)
      case _:
        raise Exception('type_check: unexpected ' + repr(p))
```

Figure 8.5
Type checker for the $\mathcal{L}_{\text{Fun}}$ language.

8.2   Functions in x86

The x86 architecture provides a few features to support the implementation of
functions. We have already seen that there are labels in x86 so that one can refer
to the location of an instruction, as is needed for jump instructions. Labels can also
be used to mark the beginning of the instructions for a function. Going further, we
can obtain the address of a label by using the `leaq` instruction. For example, the
following puts the address of the `inc` label into the `rbx` register:

```
leaq inc(%rip), %rbx
```

Recall from section 7.6 that `inc(%rip)` is an example of instruction-pointer-relative
addressing.

   In section 2.2 we used the `callq` instruction to jump to functions whose locations
were given by a label, such as `read_int`. To support function calls in this chapter
we instead jump to functions whose location are given by an address in a register;
that is, we use *indirect function calls*. The x86 syntax for this is a `callq` instruction
that requires an asterisk before the register name.

```
callq *%rbx
```

8.2.1   Calling Conventions

The `callq` instruction provides partial support for implementing functions: it
pushes the return address on the stack and it jumps to the target. However, `callq`
does not handle

1. parameter passing,
2. pushing frames on the procedure call stack and popping them off, or
3. determining how registers are shared by different functions.

   Regarding parameter passing, recall that the x86-64 calling convention for Unix-
based systems uses the following six registers to pass arguments to a function, in
the given order:

```
rdi rsi rdx rcx r8 r9
```

If there are more than six arguments, then the calling convention mandates using
space on the frame of the caller for the rest of the arguments. However, to ease the
implementation of efficient tail calls (section 8.2.2), we arrange never to need more
than six arguments. The return value of the function is stored in register `rax`.

   Regarding frames and the procedure call stack, recall from section 2.2 that the
stack grows down and each function call uses a chunk of space on the stack called
a frame. The caller sets the stack pointer, register `rsp`, to the last data item in its
frame. The callee must not change anything in the caller's frame, that is, anything
that is at or above the stack pointer. The callee is free to use locations that are
below the stack pointer.

   Recall that we store variables of tuple type on the root stack. So, the prelude of
a function needs to move the root stack pointer `r15` up according to the number

Caller View	Callee View	Contents	Frame
8(%rbp)		return address	
0(%rbp)		old rbp	
-8(%rbp)		callee-saved 1	Caller
...		...	
$-8j$(%rbp)		callee-saved j	
$-8(j+1)$(%rbp)		local variable 1	
...		...	
$-8(j+k)$(%rbp)		local variable k	
	8(%rbp)	return address	
	0(%rbp)	old rbp	
	-8(%rbp)	callee-saved 1	Callee
	...	...	
	$-8n$(%rbp)	callee-saved n	
	$-8(n+1)$(%rbp)	local variable 1	
	...	...	
	$-8(n+m)$(%rbp)	local variable m	

Figure 8.6
Memory layout of caller and callee frames.

of variables of tuple type and the conclusion needs to move the root stack pointer back down. Also, the prelude must initialize to 0 this frame's slots in the root stack to signal to the garbage collector that those slots do not yet contain a valid pointer. Otherwise the garbage collector will interpret the garbage bits in those slots as memory addresses and try to traverse them, causing serious mayhem!

Regarding the sharing of registers between different functions, recall from section 4.1 that the registers are divided into two groups, the caller-saved registers and the callee-saved registers. The caller should assume that all the caller-saved registers are overwritten with arbitrary values by the callee. For that reason we recommend in section 4.1 that variables that are live during a function call should not be assigned to caller-saved registers.

On the flip side, if the callee wants to use a callee-saved register, the callee must save the contents of those registers on their stack frame and then put them back prior to returning to the caller. For that reason we recommend in section 4.1 that if the register allocator assigns a variable to a callee-saved register, then the prelude of the main function must save that register to the stack and the conclusion of main must restore it. This recommendation now generalizes to all functions.

Recall that the base pointer, register rbp, is used as a point of reference within a frame, so that each local variable can be accessed at a fixed offset from the base pointer (section 2.2). Figure 8.6 shows the layout of the caller and callee frames.

8.2.2 Efficient Tail Calls

In general, the amount of stack space used by a program is determined by the longest chain of nested function calls. That is, if function f_1 calls f_2, f_2 calls f_3, and so on to f_n, then the amount of stack space is linear in n. The depth n can grow quite large if functions are recursive. However, in some cases we can arrange to use only a constant amount of space for a long chain of nested function calls.

A *tail call* is a function call that happens as the last action in a function body. For example, in the following program, the recursive call to `tail_sum` is a tail call:

```
def tail_sum(n : int, r : int) -> int:
  if n == 0:
    return r
  else:
    return tail_sum(n - 1, n + r)

print(tail_sum(3, 0) + 36)
```

At a tail call, the frame of the caller is no longer needed, so we can pop the caller's frame before making the tail call. With this approach, a recursive function that makes only tail calls ends up using a constant amount of stack space.

Some care is needed with regard to argument passing in tail calls. As mentioned, for arguments beyond the sixth, the convention is to use space in the caller's frame for passing arguments. However, for a tail call we pop the caller's frame and can no longer use it. An alternative is to use space in the callee's frame for passing arguments. However, this option is also problematic because the caller and callee's frames overlap in memory. As we begin to copy the arguments from their sources in the caller's frame, the target locations in the callee's frame might collide with the sources for later arguments! We solve this problem by using the heap instead of the stack for passing more than six arguments (section 8.5).

As mentioned, for a tail call we pop the caller's frame prior to making the tail call. The instructions for popping a frame are the instructions that we usually place in the conclusion of a function. Thus, we also need to place such code immediately before each tail call. These instructions include restoring the callee-saved registers, so it is fortunate that the argument passing registers are all caller-saved registers.

One note remains regarding which instruction to use to make the tail call. When the callee is finished, it should not return to the current function but instead return to the function that called the current one. Thus, the return address that is already on the stack is the right one, and we should not use `callq` to make the tail call because that would overwrite the return address. Instead we simply use the `jmp` instruction. As with the indirect function call, we write an *indirect jump* with a register prefixed with an asterisk. We recommend using `rax` to hold the jump target because the conclusion can overwrite just about everything else.

```
jmp *%rax
```

8.3 Shrink $\mathcal{L}_{\mathsf{Fun}}$

The `shrink` pass performs a minor modification to ease the later passes. This pass introduces an explicit `main` function that gobbles up all the top-level statements of the module.

Module(*def ... stmt ...*)
⇒ Module(*def ... mainDef*)

where *mainDef* is

FunctionDef('main', [], int, None, *stmt* ... Return(Constant(0)), None)

8.4 Reveal Functions and the $\mathcal{L}_{\mathsf{FunRef}}$ Language

The syntax of $\mathcal{L}_{\mathsf{Fun}}$ is inconvenient for purposes of compilation in that it conflates the use of function names and local variables. This is a problem because we need to compile the use of a function name differently from the use of a local variable. In particular, we use `leaq` to convert the function name (a label in x86) to an address in a register. Thus, we create a new pass that changes function references from Name(f) to FunRef(f, n) where n is the arity of the function.[1] This pass is named `reveal_functions` and the output language is $\mathcal{L}_{\mathsf{FunRef}}$.

The `reveal_functions` pass should come before the `remove_complex_operands` pass because function references should be categorized as complex expressions.

8.5 Limit Functions

Recall that we wish to limit the number of function parameters to six so that we do not need to use the stack for argument passing, which makes it easier to implement efficient tail calls. However, because the input language $\mathcal{L}_{\mathsf{Fun}}$ supports arbitrary numbers of function arguments, we have some work to do! The `limit_functions` pass transforms functions and function calls that involve more than six arguments to pass the first five arguments as usual, but it packs the rest of the arguments into a tuple and passes it as the sixth argument.[2]

Each function definition with seven or more parameters is transformed as follows:

FunctionDef(f, [(x_1,T_1), ... ,(x_n,T_n)], T_r, None, *body*, None)
⇒
FunctionDef(f, [(x_1,T_1), ... ,(x_5,T_5),(tup,TupleType([T_6, ... ,T_n]))],
        T_r, None, *body'*, None)

where the *body* is transformed into *body'* by replacing the occurrences of each parameter x_i where $i > 5$ with the kth element of the tuple, where $k = i - 6$.

Name(x_i) ⇒ Subscript(tup, Constant(k), Load())

---

1. The arity is not needed in this chapter but is used in chapter 10.

2. The implementation this pass can be postponed to last because you can test the rest of the passes on functions with six or fewer parameters.

```
atm    ::=   Constant(int) | Name(var)
exp    ::=   atm | Call(Name('input_int'),[])
       |     UnaryOp(USub(),atm) | BinOp(atm,Add(),atm)
       |     BinOp(atm,Sub(),atm)
stmt   ::=   Expr(Call(Name('print'),[atm])) | Expr(exp)
       |     Assign([Name(var)], exp)
───────────────────────────────────────────────────────────────────
atm    ::=   Constant(bool)
exp    ::=   UnaryOp(Not(),exp) | Compare(atm,[cmp],[atm])
       |     IfExp(exp,exp,exp) | Begin(stmt*, exp)
stmt   ::=   If(exp, stmt*, stmt*)
───────────────────────────────────────────────────────────────────
stmt   ::=   While(exp, stmt⁺, [])
───────────────────────────────────────────────────────────────────
atm    ::=   GlobalValue(var)
exp    ::=   Subscript(atm,atm,Load()) | Call(Name('len'),[atm])
       |     Allocate(int,type)
stmt   ::=   Assign([Subscript(atm,atm,Store())], atm)
       |     Collect(int)
───────────────────────────────────────────────────────────────────
type   ::=   IntType() | BoolType() | VoidType() | TupleType[type⁺]
       |     FunctionType(type*, type)
exp    ::=   FunRef(label, int) | Call(atm, atm*)
stmt   ::=   Return(exp)
params ::=   (var,type)*
def    ::=   FunctionDef(var, params, stmt⁺, None, type, None)
𝓛ᵐᵒⁿ_FunRef ::= Module([def ... stmt ...])
```

Figure 8.7
$\mathcal{L}^{mon}_{\mathsf{FunRef}}$ is $\mathcal{L}_{\mathsf{FunRef}}$ in monadic normal form.

For function calls with too many arguments, the `limit_functions` pass transforms them in the following way:

$$\mathtt{Call}(e_0, [e_1, ..., e_n]) \quad \Rightarrow \quad \mathtt{Call}(e_0, [e_1, ..., e_5, \mathtt{Tuple}([e_6, ..., e_n])])$$

8.6   Remove Complex Operands

The primary decisions to make for this pass are whether to classify `FunRef` and `Call` as either atomic or complex expressions. Recall that an atomic expression ends up as an immediate argument of an x86 instruction. Function application translates to a sequence of instructions, so `Call` must be classified as a complex expression. On the other hand, the arguments of `Call` should be atomic expressions. Regarding `FunRef`, as discussed previously, the function label needs to be converted to an address using the `leaq` instruction. Thus, even though `FunRef` seems rather simple, it needs to be classified as a complex expression so that we generate an assignment statement with a left-hand side that can serve as the target of the `leaq`.

The output of this pass, $\mathcal{L}^{mon}_{\mathsf{FunRef}}$ (figure 8.7), extends $\mathcal{L}^{mon}_{\mathsf{Alloc}}$ (figure 7.11) with `FunRef` and `Call` in the grammar for expressions and augments programs to include a list of function definitions. Also, $\mathcal{L}^{mon}_{\mathsf{FunRef}}$ adds `Return` to the grammar for statements.

$$
\begin{array}{lll}
atm & ::= & \text{Constant}(int) \mid \text{Name}(var) \mid \text{Constant}(bool) \\
exp & ::= & atm \mid \text{Call}(\text{Name}('\text{input\_int}'),[\,]) \mid \text{UnaryOp}(\text{USub}(),atm) \\
& \mid & \text{BinOp}(atm,\text{Sub}(),atm) \mid \text{BinOp}(atm,\text{Add}(),atm) \\
& \mid & \text{Compare}(atm,[cmp],[atm]) \\
stmt & ::= & \text{Expr}(\text{Call}(\text{Name}('\text{print}'),[atm])) \mid \text{Expr}(exp) \\
& \mid & \text{Assign}([\text{Name}(var)],\ exp) \\
tail & ::= & \text{Return}(exp) \mid \text{Goto}(label) \\
& \mid & \text{If}(\text{Compare}(atm,[cmp],[atm]),\ [\text{Goto}(label)],\ [\text{Goto}(label)]) \\
\hline
atm & ::= & \text{GlobalValue}(var) \\
exp & ::= & \text{Subscript}(atm,atm,\text{Load}()) \mid \text{Allocate}(int,type) \\
& \mid & \text{Call}(\text{Name}('\text{len}'),[atm]) \\
stmt & ::= & \text{Collect}(int) \mid \text{Assign}([\text{Subscript}(atm,atm,\text{Store}())],\ atm) \\
\hline
exp & ::= & \textbf{FunRef}(label,\ int) \mid \textbf{Call}(atm,\ atm^*) \\
tail & ::= & \textbf{TailCall}(atm,\ atm^*) \\
params & ::= & [(var,type),\dots] \\
block & ::= & label\!:\!stmt^*\ tail \\
def & ::= & \textbf{FunctionDef}(label,\ params,\ \{block,\dots\},\ \text{None},\ type,\ \text{None}) \\
\mathcal{C}_{\text{Fun}} & ::= & \textbf{CProgramDefs}([def,\dots]) \\
\end{array}
$$

Figure 8.8
The abstract syntax of $\mathcal{C}_{\text{Fun}}$, extending $\mathcal{C}_{\text{Tup}}$ (figure 7.12).

8.7   Explicate Control and the $\mathcal{C}_{\text{Fun}}$ Language

Figure 8.8 defines the abstract syntax for $\mathcal{C}_{\text{Fun}}$, the output of `explicate_control`. The auxiliary functions for assignment should be updated with cases for `Call` and `FunRef` and the function for predicate context should be updated for `Call` but not `FunRef`. (A `FunRef` cannot be a Boolean.) In assignment and predicate contexts, `Apply` becomes `Call`. We recommend defining a new auxiliary function for processing function definitions. This code is similar to the case for `Program` in $\mathcal{L}_{\text{Tup}}$. The top-level `explicate_control` function that handles the `ProgramDefs` form of $\mathcal{L}_{\text{Fun}}$ can then apply this new function to all the function definitions.

The translation of `Return` statements requires a new auxiliary function to handle expressions in tail context, called `explicate_tail`. The function should take an expression and the dictionary of basic blocks and produce a list of statements in the $\mathcal{C}_{\text{Fun}}$ language. The `explicate_tail` function should include cases for `Begin`, `IfExp`, and `Call`, and a default case for other kinds of expressions. The default case should produce a `Return` statement. The case for `Call` should change it into `TailCall`. The other cases should recursively process their subexpressions and statements, choosing the appropriate explicate functions for the various contexts.

$$
\begin{array}{rcl}
\textit{reg} & ::= & \texttt{rsp}\mid\texttt{rbp}\mid\texttt{rax}\mid\texttt{rbx}\mid\texttt{rcx}\mid\texttt{rdx}\mid\texttt{rsi}\mid\texttt{rdi}\mid\\
 & & \texttt{r8}\mid\texttt{r9}\mid\texttt{r10}\mid\texttt{r11}\mid\texttt{r12}\mid\texttt{r13}\mid\texttt{r14}\mid\texttt{r15}\\
\textit{arg} & ::= & \texttt{\$}\textit{int}\mid\texttt{\%}\textit{reg}\mid\textit{int}\,(\texttt{\%}\textit{reg})\\
\textit{instr} & ::= & \texttt{addq}\,\textit{arg},\textit{arg}\mid\texttt{subq}\,\textit{arg},\textit{arg}\mid\texttt{negq}\,\textit{arg}\mid\texttt{movq}\,\textit{arg},\textit{arg}\mid\\
 & & \texttt{pushq}\,\textit{arg}\mid\texttt{popq}\,\textit{arg}\mid\texttt{callq}\,\textit{label}\mid\texttt{retq}\mid\texttt{jmp}\,\textit{label}\mid\\
 & & \textit{label}:\textit{instr}
\end{array}
$$

$$
\begin{array}{rcl}
\textit{bytereg} & ::= & \texttt{ah}\mid\texttt{al}\mid\texttt{bh}\mid\texttt{bl}\mid\texttt{ch}\mid\texttt{cl}\mid\texttt{dh}\mid\texttt{dl}\\
\textit{arg} & ::= & \texttt{\%}\textit{bytereg}\\
\textit{cc} & ::= & \texttt{e}\mid\texttt{ne}\mid\texttt{l}\mid\texttt{le}\mid\texttt{g}\mid\texttt{ge}\\
\textit{instr} & ::= & \texttt{xorq}\,\textit{arg},\,\textit{arg}\mid\texttt{cmpq}\,\textit{arg},\,\textit{arg}\mid\texttt{set}\textit{cc}\,\textit{arg}\mid\texttt{movzbq}\,\textit{arg},\,\textit{arg}\\
 & \mid & \texttt{j}\textit{cc}\,\textit{label}
\end{array}
$$

$$
\begin{array}{rcl}
\textit{arg} & ::= & \textit{label}\,(\texttt{\%rip})\\
\textit{instr} & ::= & \texttt{callq}\,\texttt{*}\textit{arg}\mid\texttt{tailjmp}\,\textit{arg}\mid\texttt{leaq}\,\textit{arg},\texttt{\%}\textit{reg}\\
\textit{block} & ::= & \textit{instr}^{+}\\
\textit{def} & ::= & \texttt{.globl}\,\texttt{.align}\,8\,\textit{label}\,(\textit{label}:\textit{block})^{*}\\
\text{x86}^{\text{Def}}_{\text{callq*}} & ::= & \textit{def}^{*}
\end{array}
$$

Figure 8.9
The concrete syntax of $\text{x86}^{\text{Def}}_{\text{callq*}}$ (extends $\text{x86}_{\text{Global}}$ of figure 7.13).

$$
\begin{array}{rcl}
\textit{arg} & ::= & \texttt{Constant}(\textit{int})\mid\texttt{Reg}(\textit{reg})\mid\texttt{Deref}(\textit{reg},\textit{int})\mid\texttt{ByteReg}(\textit{reg})\\
 & \mid & \texttt{Global}(\textit{label})\mid\textbf{\texttt{FunRef}}(\textit{label},\ \textit{int})\\
\textit{instr} & ::= & \dots\mid\textbf{\texttt{IndirectCallq}}(\textit{arg},\ \textit{int})\mid\textbf{\texttt{TailJmp}}(\textit{arg},\ \textit{int})\\
 & \mid & \textbf{\texttt{Instr}}(\texttt{'leaq'},[\textit{arg},\texttt{Reg}(\textit{reg})])\\
\textit{block} & ::= & \textit{label}:\textit{instr}^{*}\\
\textit{def} & ::= & \texttt{FunctionDef}(\textit{label},\,[\,],\,\{\textit{block},\dots\},\,\_,\,\textit{type},\,\_)\\
\text{x86}^{\text{Def}}_{\text{callq*}} & ::= & \texttt{X86ProgramDefs}([\textit{def},\dots])
\end{array}
$$

Figure 8.10
The abstract syntax of $\text{x86}^{\text{Def}}_{\text{callq*}}$ (extends $\text{x86}_{\text{Global}}$ of figure 7.14).

8.8　Select Instructions and the $\text{x86}^{\text{Def}}_{\text{callq*}}$ Language

The output of select instructions is a program in the $\text{x86}^{\text{Def}}_{\text{callq*}}$ language; the definition of its concrete syntax is shown in figure 8.9, and the definition of its abstract syntax is shown in figure 8.10. We use the `align` directive on the labels of function definitions to make sure the bottom three bits are zero, which we put to use in chapter 10. We discuss the new instructions as needed in this section.

An assignment of a function reference to a variable becomes a load-effective-address instruction as follows, where lhs' is the translation of lhs from atm in C_{Fun} to arg in $\text{x86}^{\text{Var,Def}}_{\text{callq*}}$. The FunRef becomes a Global AST node, whose concrete syntax is instruction-pointer-relative addressing.

$$lhs = \text{FunRef}(f\ n)\,;\qquad\Rightarrow\qquad \text{leaq}\ f(\text{\%rip}),\ lhs'$$

Regarding function definitions, we need to remove the parameters and instead perform parameter passing using the conventions discussed in section 8.2. That is, the arguments are passed in registers. We recommend turning the parameters into local variables and generating instructions at the beginning of the function to move from the argument-passing registers (section 8.2.1) to these local variables.

$$\text{FunctionDef}(f,\ [(x_1, T_1),\ \dots\,],\ B,\ \_,\ T_r,\ \_)$$
$$\Rightarrow$$
$$\text{FunctionDef}(f,\ [],\ B',\ \_,\ \text{int},\ \_)$$

The basic blocks B' are the same as B except that the **start** block is modified to add the instructions for moving from the argument registers to the parameter variables. So the **start** block of B shown on the left of the following is changed to the code on the right:

<pre>
                                  f start:
                                      movq %rdi, x₁
              start: movq %rsi, x₂
                  instr₁   ...
                  ...   ⇒   instr₁
                  instrₙ   ...
                                      instrₙ
</pre>

Recall that we use the label **start** for the initial block of a program, and in section 2.5 we recommend labeling the conclusion of the program with **conclusion**, so that $\text{Return}(Arg)$ can be compiled to an assignment to **rax** followed by a jump to **conclusion**. With the addition of function definitions, there is a start block and conclusion for each function, but their labels need to be unique. We recommend prepending the function's name to **start** and **conclusion**, respectively, to obtain unique labels.

By changing the parameters to local variables, we are giving the register allocator control over which registers or stack locations to use for them. If you implement the move-biasing challenge (section 4.7), the register allocator will try to assign the parameter variables to the corresponding argument register, in which case the **patch_instructions** pass will remove the **movq** instruction. This happens in the example translation given in figure 8.12 in section 8.12, in the **add** function. Also, note that the register allocator will perform liveness analysis on this sequence of move instructions and build the interference graph. So, for example, x_1 will be marked as interfering with **rsi**, and that will prevent the mapping of x_1 to **rsi**, which is good because otherwise the first **movq** would overwrite the argument in **rsi** that is needed for x_2.

Next, consider the compilation of function calls. In the mirror image of the handling of parameters in function definitions, the arguments are moved to the argument-passing registers. Note that the function is not given as a label, but its address is produced by the argument arg_0. So, we translate the call into an indirect function call. The return value from the function is stored in `rax`, so it needs to be moved into the *lhs*.

lhs = Call(arg_0, [arg_1 arg_2 ...])
$\Rightarrow$
movq arg_1, %rdi
movq arg_2, %rsi
$\vdots$
callq *arg_0
movq %rax, lhs

The `IndirectCallq` AST node includes an integer for the arity of the function, that is, the number of parameters. That information is useful in the `uncover_live` pass for determining which argument-passing registers are potentially read during the call.

For tail calls, the parameter passing is the same as non-tail calls: generate instructions to move the arguments into the argument-passing registers. After that we need to pop the frame from the procedure call stack. However, we do not yet know how big the frame is; that gets determined during register allocation. So, instead of generating those instructions here, we invent a new instruction that means "pop the frame and then do an indirect jump," which we name `TailJmp`. The abstract syntax for this instruction includes an argument that specifies where to jump and an integer that represents the arity of the function being called.

8.9   Register Allocation

The addition of functions requires some changes to all three aspects of register allocation, which we discuss in the following subsections.

8.9.1   Liveness Analysis
The `IndirectCallq` instruction should be treated like `Callq` regarding its written locations W, in that they should include all the caller-saved registers. Recall that the reason for that is to force variables that are live across a function call to be assigned to callee-saved registers or to be spilled to the stack.

Regarding the set of read locations R, the arity fields of `TailJmp` and `IndirectCallq` determine how many of the argument-passing registers should be considered as read by those instructions. Also, the target field of `TailJmp` and `IndirectCallq` should be included in the set of read locations R.

8.9.2   Build Interference Graph
With the addition of function definitions, we compute a separate interference graph for each function (not just one for the whole program).

Recall that in section 7.7 we discussed the need to spill tuple-typed variables that are live during a call to `collect`, the garbage collector. With the addition of functions to our language, we need to revisit this issue. Functions that perform allocation contain calls to the collector. Thus, we should not only spill a tuple-typed variable when it is live during a call to `collect`, but we should spill the variable if it is live during a call to any user-defined function. Thus, in the `build_interference` pass, we recommend adding interference edges between call-live tuple-typed variables and the callee-saved registers (in addition to creating edges between call-live variables and the caller-saved registers).

8.9.3 Allocate Registers

The primary change to the `allocate_registers` pass is adding an auxiliary function for handling definitions (the *def* nonterminal shown in figure 8.10) with one case for function definitions. The logic is the same as described in chapter 4 except that now register allocation is performed many times, once for each function definition, instead of just once for the whole program.

8.10 Patch Instructions

In `patch_instructions`, you should deal with the x86 idiosyncrasy that the destination argument of `leaq` must be a register. Additionally, you should ensure that the argument of `TailJmp` is *rax*, our reserved register—because we trample many other registers before the tail call, as explained in the next section.

8.11 Generate Prelude and Conclusion

Now that register allocation is complete, we can translate the `TailJmp` into a sequence of instructions. A naive translation of `TailJmp` would simply be `jmp *arg`. However, before the jump we need to pop the current frame to achieve efficient tail calls. This sequence of instructions is the same as the code for the conclusion of a function, except that the `retq` is replaced with `jmp *arg`.

Regarding function definitions, we generate a prelude and conclusion for each one. This code is similar to the prelude and conclusion generated for the `main` function presented in chapter 7. To review, the prelude of every function should carry out the following steps:

1. Push `rbp` to the stack and set `rbp` to current stack pointer.
2. Push to the stack all the callee-saved registers that were used for register allocation.
3. Move the stack pointer `rsp` down to make room for the regular spills (aligned to 16 bytes).
4. Move the root stack pointer `r15` up by the size of the root-stack frame for this function, which depends on the number of spilled tuple-typed variables.
5. Initialize to zero all new entries in the root-stack frame.
6. Jump to the start block.

The prelude of the `main` function has an additional task: call the `initialize` function to set up the garbage collector, and then move the value of the global

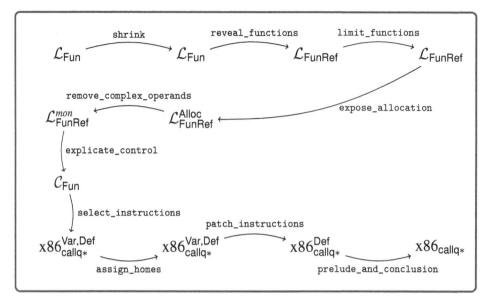

Figure 8.11
Diagram of the passes for $\mathcal{L}_{\text{Fun}}$, a language with functions.

`rootstack_begin` in `r15`. This initialization should happen before step 4, which depends on `r15`.

The conclusion of every function should do the following:

1. Move the stack pointer back up past the regular spills.
2. Restore the callee-saved registers by popping them from the stack.
3. Move the root stack pointer back down by the size of the root-stack frame for this function.
4. Restore `rbp` by popping it from the stack.
5. Return to the caller with the `retq` instruction.

The output of this pass is $x86_{\text{callq}*}$, which differs from $x86_{\text{callq}*}^{\text{Def}}$ in that there is no longer an AST node for function definitions. Instead, a program is just a dictionary of basic blocks, as in $x86_{\text{Global}}$. So we have the following grammar rule:

$$x86_{\text{callq}*} ::= \text{X86Program}(\{label : instr^*, \dots \})$$

Figure 8.11 gives an overview of the passes for compiling $\mathcal{L}_{\text{Fun}}$ to x86.

Exercise 8.1 Expand your compiler to handle $\mathcal{L}_{\text{Fun}}$ as outlined in this chapter. Create eight new programs that use functions including examples that pass functions and return functions from other functions, recursive functions, functions that create tuples, and functions that make tail calls. Test your compiler on these new programs and all your previously created test programs.

8.12 An Example Translation

Figure 8.12 shows an example translation of a simple function in $\mathcal{L}_{\mathsf{Fun}}$ to x86. The figure includes the results of `explicate_control` and `select_instructions`.

```
                                        def add() -> int:
                                          addstart:
                                            movq %rdi, x
 def add(x:int, y:int) -> int:                movq %rsi, y
     return x + y                           movq x, %rax
 print(add(40, 2))                          addq y, %rax
                                            jmp addconclusion
 ⇓                                      def main() -> int:
                                          mainstart:
 def add(x:int, y:int) -> int:      ⇒        leaq add, fun.0
   addstart:                                 movq $40, %rdi
     return x + y                            movq $2, %rsi
 def main() -> int:                          callq *fun.0
   mainstart:                                movq %rax, tmp.1
     fun.0 = add                             movq tmp.1, %rdi
     tmp.1 = fun.0(40, 2)                     callq print_int
     print(tmp.1)                            movq $0, %rax
     return 0                                jmp mainconclusion

                                        ⇓

                                   .globl main
                                   .align 8
                                 main:
                                   pushq %rbp
                                   movq %rsp, %rbp
    .align 8                       subq $0, %rsp
 add:                              movq $65536, %rdi
   pushq %rbp                      movq $65536, %rsi
   movq %rsp, %rbp                 callq initialize
   subq $0, %rsp                   movq rootstack_begin(%rip), %r15
   jmp addstart                    jmp mainstart
 addstart:                       mainstart:
   movq %rdi, %rdx                 leaq add(%rip), %rcx
   movq %rsi, %rcx                 movq $40, %rdi
   movq %rdx, %rax                 movq $2, %rsi
   addq %rcx, %rax                 callq *%rcx
   jmp addconclusion               movq %rax, %rcx
 addconclusion:                    movq %rcx, %rdi
   subq $0, %r15                    callq print_int
   addq $0, %rsp                   movq $0, %rax
   popq %rbp                       jmp mainconclusion
   retq                          mainconclusion:
                                   subq $0, %r15
                                   addq $0, %rsp
                                   popq %rbp
                                   retq
```

Figure 8.12
Example compilation of a simple function to x86.

9 Lexically Scoped Functions

This chapter studies lexically scoped functions. Lexical scoping means that a function's body may refer to variables whose binding site is outside of the function, in an enclosing scope. Consider the example shown in figure 9.1 written in $\mathcal{L}_\lambda$, which extends $\mathcal{L}_{\mathsf{Fun}}$ with the lambda form for creating lexically scoped functions. The body of the lambda refers to three variables: x, y, and z. The binding sites for x and y are outside of the lambda. Variable y is a local variable of function f, and x is a parameter of function f. Note that function f returns the lambda as its result value. The main expression of the program includes two calls to f with different arguments for x: first 5 and then 3. The functions returned from f are bound to variables g and h. Even though these two functions were created by the same lambda, they are really different functions because they use different values for x. Applying g to 11 produces 20 whereas applying h to 15 produces 22, so the result of the program is 42.

The approach that we take for implementing lexically scoped functions is to compile them into top-level function definitions, translating from $\mathcal{L}_\lambda$ into $\mathcal{L}_{\mathsf{Fun}}$. However, the compiler must give special treatment to variable occurrences such as x and y in the body of the lambda shown in figure 9.1. After all, an $\mathcal{L}_{\mathsf{Fun}}$ function may not refer to variables defined outside of it. To identify such variable occurrences, we review the standard notion of free variable.

Definition 9.1 A variable is *free in expression* e if the variable occurs inside e but does not have an enclosing definition that is also in e.

```
def f(x : int) -> Callable[[int], int]:
  y = 4
  return lambda z: x + y + z

g = f(5)
h = f(3)
print(g(11) + h(15))
```

Figure 9.1
Example of a lexically scoped function.

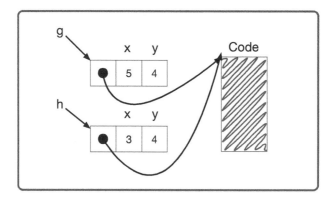

Figure 9.2
Flat closure representations for the two functions produced by the `lambda` in figure 9.1.

For example, in the expression `x + y + z` the variables `x`, `y`, and `z` are all free. On the other hand, only `x` and `y` are free in the following expression, because `z` is defined by the `lambda`

```
lambda z: x + y + z
```

Thus the free variables of a `lambda` are the ones that need special treatment. We need to transport at runtime the values of those variables from the point where the `lambda` was created to the point where the `lambda` is applied. An efficient solution to the problem, due to Cardelli (1983), is to bundle the values of the free variables together with a function pointer into a tuple, an arrangement called a *flat closure* (which we shorten to just *closure*). By design, we have all the ingredients to make closures: chapter 7 gave us tuples, and chapter 8 gave us function pointers. The function pointer resides at index 0, and the values for the free variables fill in the rest of the tuple.

Let us revisit the example shown in figure 9.1 to see how closures work. It is a three-step dance. The program calls function `f`, which creates a closure for the `lambda`. The closure is a tuple whose first element is a pointer to the top-level function that we will generate for the `lambda`; the second element is the value of `x`, which is 5; and the third element is 4, the value of `y`. The closure does not contain an element for `z` because `z` is not a free variable of the `lambda`. Creating the closure is step 1 of the dance. The closure is returned from `f` and bound to `g`, as shown in figure 9.2. The second call to `f` creates another closure, this time with 3 in the second slot (for `x`). This closure is also returned from `f` but bound to `h`, which is also shown in figure 9.2.

Continuing with the example, consider the application of `g` to 11 shown in figure 9.1. To apply a closure, we obtain the function pointer from the first element of the closure and call it, passing in the closure itself and then the regular arguments, in this case 11. This technique for applying a closure is step 2 of the dance. But doesn't this `lambda` take only one argument, for parameter `z`? The third and final step of the dance is generating a top-level function for a `lambda`. We add an additional parameter for the closure and insert an initialization at the beginning

$$
\begin{array}{lll}
exp & ::= & int \mid \texttt{input\_int()} \mid -exp \mid exp + exp \mid exp - exp \mid (exp) \\
stmt & ::= & \texttt{print}(exp) \mid exp \\
\hline
exp & ::= & var \\
stmt & ::= & var = exp \\
\hline
cmp & ::= & \texttt{==} \mid \texttt{!=} \mid \texttt{<} \mid \texttt{<=} \mid \texttt{>} \mid \texttt{>=} \\
exp & ::= & \texttt{True} \mid \texttt{False} \mid exp \texttt{ and } exp \mid exp \texttt{ or } exp \mid \texttt{not } exp \\
& \mid & exp \; cmp \; exp \mid exp \texttt{ if } exp \texttt{ else } exp \\
stmt & ::= & \texttt{if } exp\texttt{: } stmt^{+} \texttt{ else: } stmt^{+} \\
\hline
stmt & ::= & \texttt{while } exp\texttt{: } stmt^{+} \\
\hline
cmp & ::= & \texttt{is} \\
exp & ::= & exp, \ldots, exp \mid exp[int] \mid \texttt{len}(exp) \\
type & ::= & \texttt{int} \mid \texttt{bool} \mid \texttt{void} \mid \texttt{tuple}[type^{+}] \mid \texttt{Callable}[[type, \ldots], \; type] \\
exp & ::= & exp(exp, \ldots) \\
stmt & ::= & \texttt{return } exp \\
def & ::= & \texttt{def } var(var\texttt{:}type, \ldots) \texttt{ -> } type\texttt{: } stmt^{+} \\
\hline
exp & ::= & \texttt{lambda } var, \; \ldots \texttt{ : } exp \mid \texttt{arity}(exp) \\
stmt & ::= & var \texttt{ : } type \texttt{ = } exp \\
\mathcal{L}_{\mathsf{Fun}} & ::= & def \ldots stmt \ldots
\end{array}
$$

Figure 9.3
The concrete syntax of $\mathcal{L}_{\lambda}$, extending $\mathcal{L}_{\mathsf{Fun}}$ (figure 8.1) with `lambda`.

of the function for each free variable, to bind those variables to the appropriate elements from the closure parameter. This three-step dance is known as *closure conversion*. We discuss the details of closure conversion in section 9.5 and show the code generated from the example in section 9.5.1. First, we define the syntax and semantics of $\mathcal{L}_{\lambda}$ in section 9.1.

9.1   The $\mathcal{L}_{\lambda}$ Language

The definitions of the concrete syntax and abstract syntax for $\mathcal{L}_{\lambda}$, a language with anonymous functions and lexical scoping, are shown in figures 9.3 and 9.4. They add the `lambda` form to the grammar for $\mathcal{L}_{\mathsf{Fun}}$, which already has syntax for function application. The syntax also includes an assignment statement that includes a type annotation for the variable on the left-hand side, which facilitates the type checking of `lambda` expressions that we discuss later in this section. The `arity` operation returns the number of parameters of a given function, an operation that we need for the translation of dynamic typing that is discussed in chapter 10. The `arity` operation is not in Python, but the same functionality is available in a more complex form. We include `arity` in the $\mathcal{L}_{\lambda}$ source language to enable testing.

Figure 9.5 shows the definitional interpreter for $\mathcal{L}_{\lambda}$. The case for Lambda saves the current environment inside the returned function value. Recall that during function application, the environment stored in the function value, extended with the mapping of parameters to argument values, is used to interpret the body of the function.

```
exp     ::=   Constant(int) | Call(Name('input_int'),[])
        |     UnaryOp(USub(),exp) | BinOp(exp,Add(),exp)
        |     BinOp(exp,Sub(),exp)
stmt    ::=   Expr(Call(Name('print'),[exp])) | Expr(exp)
```
```
exp     ::=   Name(var)
stmt    ::=   Assign([Name(var)], exp)
```
```
boolop  ::=   And() | Or()
cmp     ::=   Eq() | NotEq() | Lt() | LtE() | Gt() | GtE()
bool    ::=   True | False
exp     ::=   Constant(bool) | BoolOp(boolop,[exp,exp])
        |     UnaryOp(Not(),exp) | Compare(exp,[cmp],[exp])
        |     IfExp(exp,exp,exp)
stmt    ::=   If(exp, stmt⁺, stmt⁺)
```
```
stmt    ::=   While(exp, stmt⁺, [])
```
```
cmp     ::=   Is()
exp     ::=   Tuple(exp⁺,Load()) | Subscript(exp,Constant(int),Load())
        |     Call(Name('len'),[exp])
```
```
type    ::=   IntType() | BoolType() | VoidType() | TupleType[type⁺]
        |     FunctionType(type*, type)
exp     ::=   Call(exp, exp*)
stmt    ::=   Return(exp)
params  ::=   (var,type)*
def     ::=   FunctionDef(var, params, stmt⁺, None, type, None)
```
```
exp     ::=   Lambda(var*, exp) | Call(Name('arity'), [exp])
stmt    ::=   AnnAssign(var, type, exp, 0)
ℒλ      ::=   Module([def ... stmt ...])
```

Figure 9.4
The abstract syntax of $\mathcal{L}_\lambda$, extending $\mathcal{L}_{\mathsf{Fun}}$ (figure 8.2).

Figures 9.6 and 9.7 define the type checker for $\mathcal{L}_\lambda$, which is more complex than one might expect. The reason for the added complexity is that the syntax of **lambda** does not include type annotations for the parameters or return type. Instead they must be inferred. There are many approaches to type inference from which to choose, of varying degrees of complexity. We choose one of the simpler approaches, bidirectional type inference (Pierce and Turner 2000; Dunfield and Krishnaswami 2021), because the focus of this book is compilation, not type inference.

The main idea of bidirectional type inference is to add an auxiliary function, here named **check_exp**, that takes an expected type and checks whether the given expression is of that type. Thus, in **check_exp**, type information flows in a top-down manner with respect to the AST, in contrast to the regular **type_check_exp** function, where type information flows in a primarily bottom-up manner. The idea then is to use **check_exp** in all the places where we already know what the type of an expression should be, such as in the **return** statement of a top-level function definition or on the right-hand side of an annotated assignment statement.

```
class InterpLlambda(InterpLfun):
  def arity(self, v):
    match v:
      case Function(name, params, body, env):
        return len(params)
      case _:
        raise Exception('Llambda arity unexpected ' + repr(v))

  def interp_exp(self, e, env):
    match e:
      case Call(Name('arity'), [fun]):
        f = self.interp_exp(fun, env)
        return self.arity(f)
      case Lambda(params, body):
        return Function('lambda', params, [Return(body)], env)
      case _:
        return super().interp_exp(e, env)

  def interp_stmt(self, s, env, cont):
    match s:
      case AnnAssign(lhs, typ, value, simple):
        env[lhs.id] = self.interp_exp(value, env)
        return self.interp_stmts(cont, env)
      case Pass():
        return self.interp_stmts(cont, env)
      case _:
        return super().interp_stmt(s, env, cont)
```

Figure 9.5
Interpreter for $\mathcal{L}_\lambda$.

With regard to `lambda`, it is straightforward to check a `lambda` inside `check_exp` because the expected type provides the parameter types and the return type. On the other hand, inside `type_check_exp` we disallow `lambda`, which means that we do not allow `lambda` in contexts in which we don't already know its type. This restriction does not incur a loss of expressiveness for $\mathcal{L}_\lambda$ because it is straightforward to modify a program to sidestep the restriction, for example, by using an annotated assignment statement to assign the `lambda` to a temporary variable.

Note that for the `Name` and `Lambda` AST nodes, the type checker records their type in a `has_type` field. This type information is used further on in this chapter.

```
class TypeCheckLlambda(TypeCheckLfun):
  def type_check_exp(self, e, env):
    match e:
      case Name(id):
        e.has_type = env[id]
        return env[id]
      case Lambda(params, body):
        raise Exception('cannot synthesize a type for a lambda')
      case Call(Name('arity'), [func]):
        func_t = self.type_check_exp(func, env)
        match func_t:
          case FunctionType(params_t, return_t):
            return IntType()
          case _:
            raise Exception('in arity, unexpected ' + repr(func_t))
      case _:
        return super().type_check_exp(e, env)

  def check_exp(self, e, ty, env):
    match e:
      case Lambda(params, body):
        e.has_type = ty
        match ty:
          case FunctionType(params_t, return_t):
            new_env = env.copy().update(zip(params, params_t))
            self.check_exp(body, return_t, new_env)
          case _:
            raise Exception('lambda does not have type ' + str(ty))
      case Call(func, args):
        func_t = self.type_check_exp(func, env)
        match func_t:
          case FunctionType(params_t, return_t):
            for (arg, param_t) in zip(args, params_t):
                self.check_exp(arg, param_t, env)
            self.check_type_equal(return_t, ty, e)
          case _:
            raise Exception('type_check_exp: in call, unexpected ' + \
                            repr(func_t))
      case _:
        t = self.type_check_exp(e, env)
        self.check_type_equal(t, ty, e)
```

Figure 9.6
Type checking $\mathcal{L}_\lambda$, part 1.

```
    def check_stmts(self, ss, return_ty, env):
      if len(ss) == 0:
        return
      match ss[0]:
        case FunctionDef(name, params, body, dl, returns, comment):
          new_env = env.copy().update(params)
          rt = self.check_stmts(body, returns, new_env)
          self.check_stmts(ss[1:], return_ty, env)
        case Return(value):
          self.check_exp(value, return_ty, env)
        case Assign([Name(id)], value):
          if id in env:
            self.check_exp(value, env[id], env)
          else:
            env[id] = self.type_check_exp(value, env)
          self.check_stmts(ss[1:], return_ty, env)
        case Assign([Subscript(tup, Constant(index), Store())], value):
          tup_t = self.type_check_exp(tup, env)
          match tup_t:
            case TupleType(ts):
              self.check_exp(value, ts[index], env)
            case _:
              raise Exception('expected a tuple, not ' + repr(tup_t))
          self.check_stmts(ss[1:], return_ty, env)
        case AnnAssign(Name(id), ty_annot, value, simple):
          ss[0].annotation = ty_annot
          if id in env:
              self.check_type_equal(env[id], ty_annot)
          else:
              env[id] = ty_annot
          self.check_exp(value, ty_annot, env)
          self.check_stmts(ss[1:], return_ty, env)
        case _:
          self.type_check_stmts(ss, env)

    def type_check(self, p):
      match p:
        case Module(body):
          env = {}
          for s in body:
              match s:
                case FunctionDef(name, params, bod, dl, returns, comment):
                  params_t = [t for (x,t) in params]
                  env[name] = FunctionType(params_t, returns)
          self.check_stmts(body, int, env)
```

Figure 9.7
Type checking the lambda's in $\mathcal{L}_\lambda$, part 2.

9.2 Assignment and Lexically Scoped Functions

The combination of lexically scoped functions and assignment to variables raises a
challenge with the flat-closure approach to implementing lexically scoped functions.
Consider the following example in which function f has a free variable x that is
changed after f is created but before the call to f.

```
def g(z : int) -> int:
  x = 0
  y = 0
  f : Callable[[int],int] = lambda a: a + x + z
  x = 10
  y = 12
  return f(y)

print(g(20))
```

   The correct output for this example is 42 because the call to f is required to
use the current value of x (which is 10). Unfortunately, the closure conversion pass
(section 9.5) generates code for the lambda that copies the old value of x into a
closure. Thus, if we naively applied closure conversion, the output of this program
would be 32.
   A first attempt at solving this problem would be to save a pointer to x in the closure and change the occurrences of x inside the lambda to dereference the pointer.
Of course, this would require assigning x to the stack and not to a register. However, the problem goes a bit deeper. Consider the following example that returns a
function that refers to a local variable of the enclosing function:

```
def f():
  x = 0
  g = lambda: x
  x = 42
  return g

print(f()())
```

In this example, the lifetime of x extends beyond the lifetime of the call to f. Thus,
if we were to store x on the stack frame for the call to f, it would be gone by the
time we called g, leaving us with dangling pointers for x. This example demonstrates
that when a variable occurs free inside a function, its lifetime becomes indefinite.
Thus, the value of the variable needs to live on the heap. The verb *box* is often
used for allocating a single value on the heap, producing a pointer, and *unbox* for
dereferencing the pointer. We introduce a new pass named convert_assignments
to address this challenge. But before diving into that, we have one more problem
to discuss.

9.3 Uniquify Variables

With the addition of `lambda` we have a complication to deal with: name shadowing.
Consider the following program with a function `f` that has a parameter `x`. Inside
`f` there are two `lambda` expressions. The first `lambda` has a parameter that is also
named `x`.

```
def f(x:int, y:int) -> Callable[[int], int]:
  g : Callable[[int],int] = (lambda x: x + y)
  h : Callable[[int],int] = (lambda y: x + y)
  x = input_int()
  return g

print(f(0, 10)(32))
```

Many of our compiler passes rely on being able to connect variable uses with
their definitions using just the name of the variable. However, in the example above,
the name of the variable does not uniquely determine its definition. To solve this
problem we recommend implementing a pass named `uniquify` that renames every
variable in the program to make sure that they are all unique.

The following shows the result of `uniquify` for the example above. The `x` parameter of function `f` is renamed to `x_0`, and the `x` parameter of the first `lambda` is
renamed to `x_4`.

```
def f(x_0:int, y_1:int) -> Callable[[int], int] :
  g_2 : Callable[[int], int] = (lambda x_4: x_4 + y_1)
  h_3 : Callable[[int], int] = (lambda y_5: x_0 + y_5)
  x_0 = input_int()
  return g_2

def main() -> int :
  print(f(0, 10)(32))
  return 0
```

9.4 Assignment Conversion

The purpose of the `convert_assignments` pass is to address the challenge regarding the interaction between variable assignments and closure conversion. First we
identify which variables need to be boxed, and then we transform the program to
box those variables. In general, boxing introduces runtime overhead that we would
like to avoid, so we should box as few variables as possible. We recommend boxing
the variables in the intersection of the following two sets of variables:

1. The variables that are free in a `lambda`.
2. The variables that appear on the left-hand side of an assignment.

The first condition is a must but the second condition is conservative. It is possible
to develop a more liberal condition using static program analysis.

Consider again the first example from section 9.2:

```
def g(z : int) -> int:
  x = 0
  y = 0
  f : Callable[[int],int] = lambda a: a + x + z
  x = 10
  y = 12
  return f(y)

print(g(20))
```

The variables x and y appear on the left-hand side of assignments. The variables x and z occur free inside the lambda. Thus, variable x needs to be boxed but not y or z. The boxing of x consists of three transformations: initialize x with a tuple whose element is uninitialized, replace reads from x with tuple reads, and replace each assignment to x with a tuple write. The output of convert_assignments for this example is as follows:

```
def g(z : int)-> int:
  x = (uninitialized(int),)
  x[0] = 0
  y = 0
  f : Callable[[int], int] = (lambda a: a + x[0] + z)
  x[0] = 10
  y = 12
  return f(y)

def main() -> int:
  print(g(20))
  return 0
```

To compute the free variables of all the lambda expressions, we recommend defining the following two auxiliary functions:

1. free_variables computes the free variables of an expression, and
2. free_in_lambda collects all the variables that are free in any of the lambda expressions, using free_variables in the case for each lambda.

To compute the variables that are assigned to, we recommend defining an auxiliary function named assigned_vars_stmt that returns the set of variables that occur in the left-hand side of an assignment statement and otherwise returns the empty set.

Let *AF* be the intersection of the set of variables that are free in a lambda and that are assigned to in the enclosing function definition.

Next we discuss the convert_assignments pass. In the case for Name(x), if x is in *AF*, then unbox it by translating Name(x) to a tuple read.

```
Name(x)
⇒
Subscript(Name(x), Constant(0), Load())
```

In the case for assignment, recursively process the right-hand side *rhs* to obtain *rhs'*. If the left-hand side *x* is in *AF*, translate the assignment into a tuple write as follows:

```
Assign([Name(x)],rhs)
⇒
Assign([Subscript(Name(x), Constant(0), Store())], rhs')
```

To translate a function definition, we first compute *AF*, the intersection of the variables that are free in a `lambda` and that are assigned to. We then apply assignment conversion to the body of the function definition. Finally, we box the parameters of this function definition that are in *AF*. For example, the parameter x of the following function g needs to be boxed:

```
def g(x : int) -> int:
  f : Callable[[int],int] = lambda a: a + x
  x = 10
  return f(32)
```

We box parameter x by creating a local variable named x that is initialized to a tuple whose contents is the value of the parameter, which is renamed to x_0.

```
def g(x_0 : int)-> int:
  x = (x_0,)
  f : Callable[[int], int] = (lambda a: a + x[0])
  x[0] = 10
  return f(32)
```

9.5 Closure Conversion

The compiling of lexically scoped functions into top-level function definitions and flat closures is accomplished in the pass `convert_to_closures` that comes after `reveal_functions` and before `limit_functions`.

As usual, we implement the pass as a recursive function over the AST. The interesting cases are for `lambda` and function application. We transform a `lambda` expression into an expression that creates a closure, that is, a tuple for which the first element is a function pointer and the rest of the elements are the values of the free variables of the `lambda`. However, we use the `Closure` AST node instead of using a tuple so that we can record the arity. In the generated code that follows, *fvs* is the list of free variables of the lambda and *name* is a unique symbol generated to identify the lambda.

```
Lambda([x₁, ...,xₙ] , body)
⇒
Closure(n, [FunRef(name, n), fvs₁, ... , fvsₘ])
```

In addition to transforming each `Lambda` AST node into a tuple, we create a top-level function definition for each `Lambda`, as shown next.

```
def name(clos : closTy, x₁:T₁′, ... , xₙ:Tₙ′) -> rt′:
    fvs₁ = clos[1]
    ...
    fvsₘ = clos[m]
    body′
```

The `clos` parameter refers to the closure. The type *closTy* is a tuple type for which the first element type is `Bottom()` and the rest of the element types are the types of the free variables in the lambda. We use `Bottom()` because it is nontrivial to give a type to the function in the closure's type.[1] The `has_type` field of the `Lambda` AST node is of the form `FunctionType([x₁ : T₁, ..., xₙ : Tₙ], rt)`. Translate the parameter types $T_1, \ldots, T_n$ and return type *rt* to obtain $T_1', \ldots, T_n'$ and *rt′*. The free variables become local variables that are initialized with their values in the closure.

Closure conversion turns every function into a tuple, so the type annotations in the program must also be translated. We recommend defining an auxiliary recursive function for this purpose. Function types should be translated as follows:

`FunctionType([T₁, ..., Tₙ], Tᵣ)`
⇒
`TupleType([FunctionType([TupleType([]), T₁′, ..., Tₙ′], Tᵣ′)])`

This type indicates that the first thing in the tuple is a function. The first parameter of the function is a tuple (a closure) and the rest of the parameters are the ones from the original function, with types $T_1', \ldots, T_n'$. The type for the closure omits the types of the free variables because (1) those types are not available in this context, and (2) we do not need them in the code that is generated for function application. So this type describes only the first component of the closure tuple. At runtime the tuple may have more components, but we ignore them at this point.

We transform function application into code that retrieves the function from the closure and then calls the function, passing the closure as the first argument. We place *e′* in a temporary variable to avoid code duplication.

`Call(e, [e₁, ..., eₙ])`
⇒
`Begin([Assign([tmp], e′)],`
`    Call(Subscript(Name(tmp), Constant(0)),`
`        [tmp, e₁′, ..., eₙ′]))`

There is also the question of what to do with references to top-level function definitions. To maintain a uniform translation of function application, we turn function references into closures.

`FunRef(f, n)`   ⇒   `Closure(n, [FunRef(f n)])`

---

1. To give an accurate type to a closure, we would need to add existential types to the type checker (Minamide, Morrisett, and Harper 1996).

```
def f(x: int) -> Callable[[int],int]:
  y = 4
  return lambda z: x + y + z

g = f(5)
h = f(3)
print(g(11) + h(15))

⇒

def lambda_0(fvs_1: tuple[bot,int,tuple[int]], z: int) -> int:
  x = fvs_1[1]
  y = fvs_1[2]
  return (x + y[0] + z)

def f(fvs_2: tuple[bot], x: int) -> tuple[Callable[[tuple[]],int],int]]:
  y = (uninitialized(int),)
  y[0] = 4
  return closure{1}({lambda_0}, x, y)

def main() -> int:
  g = (begin: clos_3 = closure{1}({f})
               clos_3[0](clos_3, 5))
  h = (begin: clos_4 = closure{1}({f})
               clos_4[0](clos_4, 3))
  print((begin: clos_5 = g
                 clos_5[0](clos_5, 11))
       + (begin: clos_6 = h
                  clos_6[0](clos_6, 15)))
  return 0
```

Figure 9.8
Example of closure conversion.

We no longer need the annotated assignment statement **AnnAssign** to support the type checking of **lambda** expressions, so we translate it to a regular **Assign** statement.

The top-level function definitions need to be updated to take an extra closure parameter, but that parameter is ignored in the body of those functions.

9.5.1 An Example Translation

Figure 9.8 shows the result of **reveal_functions** and **convert_to_closures** for the example program demonstrating lexical scoping that we discussed at the beginning of this chapter.

Exercise 9.1 Expand your compiler to handle $\mathcal{L}_\lambda$ as outlined in this chapter. Create five new programs that use **lambda** functions and make use of lexical scoping. Test your compiler on these new programs and all your previously created test programs.

```
atm    ::=  Constant(int) | Name(var) | Constant(bool)
exp    ::=  atm | Call(Name('input_int'),[]) | UnaryOp(USub(),atm)
       |    BinOp(atm,Sub(),atm) | BinOp(atm,Add(),atm)
       |    Compare(atm,[cmp],[atm])
stmt   ::=  Expr(Call(Name('print'),[atm])) | Expr(exp)
       |    Assign([Name(var)], exp)
tail   ::=  Return(exp) | Goto(label)
       |    If(Compare(atm,[cmp],[atm]), [Goto(label)], [Goto(label)])
atm    ::=  GlobalValue(var)
exp    ::=  Subscript(atm,atm,Load()) | Allocate(int,type)
       |    Call(Name('len'),[atm])
stmt   ::=  Collect(int) | Assign([Subscript(atm,atm,Store())], atm)
exp     ::=  FunRef(label, int) | Call(atm, atm*)
tail    ::=  TailCall(atm, atm*)
params  ::=  [(var,type), ...]
block   ::=  label:stmt* tail
def     ::=  FunctionDef(label, params, {block, ...}, None, type, None)
exp    ::=  Uninitialized(type) | AllocateClosure(len,type,arity)
       |    Call(Name('arity'), [atm]) | UncheckedCast(exp,type)
C_Clos ::=  CProgramDefs([def, ...])
```

Figure 9.9
The abstract syntax of C_{Clos}, extending C_{Fun} (figure 8.8).

9.6 Expose Allocation

Compile the Closure(*arity*, *exp**) form into code that allocates and initializes a tuple, similar to the translation of the tuple creation in section 7.3. The main difference is replacing the use of Allocate(*len*, *type*) with AllocateClosure(*len*, *type*, *arity*). The result type of the translation of Closure(*arity*, *exp**) should be a tuple type, but only a single element tuple type. The types of the tuple elements that correspond to the free variables of the closure should not appear in the tuple type. The new AST class UncheckedCast can be used to adjust the result type.

9.7 Explicate Control and C_{Clos}

The output language of explicate_control is C_{Clos}; the definition of its abstract syntax is shown in figure 9.9. The differences with respect to C_{Fun} are the additions of Uninitialized, AllocateClosure, and arity to the grammar for *exp*. The handling of them in the explicate_control pass is similar to the handling of other expressions such as primitive operators.

9.8   Select Instructions

Compile `AllocateClosure(len, type, arity)` in almost the same way as the `Allocate(len, type)` form (section 7.6). The only difference is that you should place the *arity* in the tag that is stored at position 0 of the tuple. Recall that in section 7.6 a portion of the 64-bit tag was not used. We store the arity in the 5 bits starting at position 58.

Compile a call to the `arity` operator to a sequence of instructions that access the tag from position 0 of the tuple (representing a closure) and extract the 5 bits starting at position 58 from the tag.

Figure 9.10 provides an overview of the passes needed for the compilation of $\mathcal{L}_\lambda$.

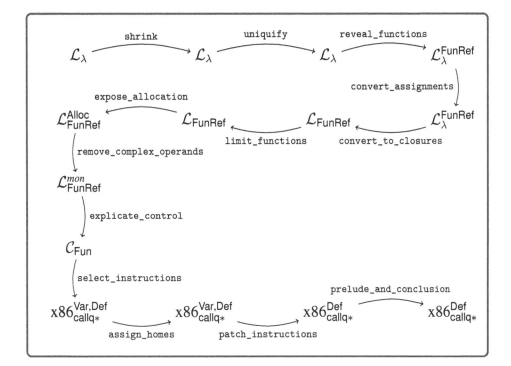

Figure 9.10
Diagram of the passes for $\mathcal{L}_\lambda$, a language with lexically scoped functions.

9.9   Challenge: Optimize Closures

In this chapter we compile lexically scoped functions into a relatively efficient representation: flat closures. However, even this representation comes with some overhead. For example, consider the following program with a function `tail_sum` that does not have any free variables and where all the uses of `tail_sum` are in applications in which we know that only `tail_sum` is being applied (and not any other functions):

```
def tail_sum(n : int, s : int) -> int:
   if n == 0:
      return s
   else:
      return tail_sum(n - 1, n + s)

print(tail_sum(3, 0) + 36)
```

As described in this chapter, we uniformly apply closure conversion to all functions, obtaining the following output for this program:

```
def tail_sum(fvs_3:bot,n_0:int,s_1:int) -> int :
  if n_0 == 0:
    return s_1
  else:
    return (begin: clos_2 = (tail_sum,)
                 clos_2[0](clos_2, n_0 - 1, n_0 + s_1))
def main() -> int :
  print((begin: clos_4 = (tail_sum,)
               clos_4[0](clos_4, 3, 0)) + 36)
  return 0
```

If this program were compiled according to the previous chapter, there would be no allocation and the calls to `tail_sum` would be direct calls. In contrast, the program presented here allocates memory for each closure and the calls to `tail_sum` are indirect. These two differences incur considerable overhead in a program such as this, in which the allocations and indirect calls occur inside a tight loop.

One might think that this problem is trivial to solve: can't we just recognize calls of the form `Call(FunRef(f, n), args)` and compile them to direct calls instead of treating it like a call to a closure? We would also drop the new `fvs` parameter of `tail_sum`. However, this problem is not so trivial, because a global function may *escape* and become involved in applications that also involve closures. Consider the following example in which the application `f(41)` needs to be compiled into a closure application because the `lambda` may flow into `f`, but the `inc` function might also flow into `f`:

```
def add1(x : int) -> int:
  return x + 1

y = input_int()
g : Callable[[int], int] = lambda x: x - y
f = add1 if input_int() == 0 else g
print(f(41))
```

If a global function name is used in any way other than as the operator in a direct call, then we say that the function *escapes*. If a global function does not escape, then we do not need to perform closure conversion on the function.

Exercise 9.2 Implement an auxiliary function for detecting which global functions escape. Using that function, implement an improved version of closure conversion that does not apply closure conversion to global functions that do not escape but instead compiles them as regular functions. Create several new test cases that check whether your compiler properly detects whether global functions escape or not.

So far we have reduced the overhead of calling global functions, but it would also be nice to reduce the overhead of calling a lambda when we can determine at compile time which lambda will be called. We refer to such calls as *known calls*. Consider the following example in which a lambda is bound to f and then applied.

```
y = input_int()
f : Callable[[int],int] = lambda x: x + y
print(f(21))
```

Closure conversion compiles the application f(21) into an indirect call, as follows:

```
def lambda_3(fvs_4:tuple[bot,tuple[int]], x_2:int) -> int:
  y_1 = fvs_4[1]
  return x_2 + y_1[0]

def main() -> int:
  y_1 = (777,)
  y_1[0] = input_int()
  f_0 = (lambda_3, y_1)
  print((let clos_5 = f_0 in clos_5[0](clos_5, 21)))
  return 0
```

However, we can instead compile the application f(21) into a direct call, as follows:

```
def main() -> int:
  y_1 = (777,)
  y_1[0] = input_int()
  f_0 = (lambda_3, y_1)
  print(lambda_3(f_0, 21))
  return 0
```

The problem of determining which lambda will be called from a particular application is quite challenging in general and the topic of considerable research (Shivers

1988; Gilray et al. 2016). For the following exercise we recommend that you compile an application to a direct call when the operator is a variable and the previous assignment to the variable is a closure. This can be accomplished by maintaining an environment that maps variables to function names. Extend the environment whenever you encounter a closure on the right-hand side of an assignment, mapping the variable to the name of the global function for the closure. This pass should come after closure conversion.

Exercise 9.3 Implement a compiler pass, named `optimize_known_calls`, that compiles known calls into direct calls. Verify that your compiler is successful in this regard on several example programs.

These exercises only scratch the surface of closure optimization. A good next step for the interested reader is to look at the work of Keep, Hearn, and Dybvig (2012).

9.10   Further Reading

The notion of lexically scoped functions predates modern computers by about a decade. They were invented by Church (1932), who proposed the lambda calculus as a foundation for logic. Anonymous functions were included in the LISP (McCarthy 1960) programming language but were initially dynamically scoped. The Scheme dialect of LISP adopted lexical scoping, and Steele (1978) demonstrated how to efficiently compile Scheme programs. However, environments were represented as linked lists, so variable look-up was linear in the size of the environment. Appel (1991) gives a detailed description of several closure representations. In this chapter we represent environments using flat closures, which were invented by Cardelli (1983, 1984) for the purpose of compiling the ML language (Gordon et al. 1978; Milner, Tofte, and Harper 1990). With flat closures, variable look-up is constant time but the time to create a closure is proportional to the number of its free variables. Flat closures were reinvented by Dybvig (1987b) in his PhD thesis and used in Chez Scheme version 1 (Dybvig 2006).

10 Dynamic Typing

In this chapter we learn how to compile $\mathcal{L}_{\mathsf{Dyn}}$, a dynamically typed language that is a subset of Python. The focus on dynamic typing is in contrast to the previous chapters, which have studied the compilation of statically typed languages. In dynamically typed languages such as $\mathcal{L}_{\mathsf{Dyn}}$, a particular expression may produce a value of a different type each time it is executed. Consider the following example with a conditional `if` expression that may return a Boolean or an integer depending on the input to the program:

```
not (False if input_int() == 1 else 0)
```

Languages that allow expressions to produce different kinds of values are called *polymorphic*, a word composed of the Greek roots *poly*, meaning *many*, and *morph*, meaning *form*. There are several kinds of polymorphism in programming languages, such as subtype polymorphism and parametric polymorphism (aka generics) (Cardelli and Wegner 1985). The kind of polymorphism that we study in this chapter does not have a special name; it is the kind that arises in dynamically typed languages.

Another characteristic of dynamically typed languages is that their primitive operations, such as `not`, are often defined to operate on many different types of values. In fact, in Python, the `not` operator produces a result for any kind of value: given `False` it returns `True`, and given anything else it returns `False`.

Furthermore, even when primitive operations restrict their inputs to values of a certain type, this restriction is enforced at runtime instead of during compilation. For example, the tuple read operation `True[0]` results in a runtime error because the first argument must be a tuple, not a Boolean.

10.1 The $\mathcal{L}_{\mathsf{Dyn}}$ Language

The definitions of the concrete and abstract syntax of $\mathcal{L}_{\mathsf{Dyn}}$ are shown in figures 10.1 and 10.2. There is no type checker for $\mathcal{L}_{\mathsf{Dyn}}$ because it checks types only at runtime.

The definitional interpreter for $\mathcal{L}_{\mathsf{Dyn}}$ is presented in figures 10.3 and 10.4, and definitions of its auxiliary functions are shown in figure 10.5. Consider the match case for `Constant(n)`. Instead of simply returning the integer `n` (as in the interpreter for $\mathcal{L}_{\mathsf{Var}}$ in figure 2.4), the interpreter for $\mathcal{L}_{\mathsf{Dyn}}$ creates a *tagged value* that combines an underlying value with a tag that identifies what

$$
\begin{array}{rcl}
cmp & ::= & \texttt{==} \mid \texttt{!=} \mid \texttt{<} \mid \texttt{<=} \mid \texttt{>} \mid \texttt{>=} \mid \texttt{is} \\
exp & ::= & int \mid \texttt{input\_int()} \mid -exp \mid exp+exp \mid exp-exp \mid (exp) \\
 & \mid & var \mid \texttt{True} \mid \texttt{False} \mid exp\ \texttt{and}\ exp \mid exp\ \texttt{or}\ exp \mid \texttt{not}\ exp \\
 & \mid & exp\ cmp\ exp \mid exp\ \texttt{if}\ exp\ \texttt{else}\ exp \\
 & \mid & exp,\dots,exp \mid exp\,[exp] \mid \texttt{len}(exp) \\
 & \mid & exp(exp,\dots) \mid \texttt{lambda}\ var,\ \dots : exp \\
stmt & ::= & \texttt{print}(exp) \mid exp \mid var=exp \\
 & \mid & \texttt{if}\ exp\colon\ stmt^{+}\ \texttt{else}\colon\ stmt^{+} \mid \texttt{while}\ exp\colon\ stmt^{+} \\
 & \mid & \texttt{return}\ exp \\
def & ::= & \texttt{def}\ var(var,\dots)\colon\ stmt^{+} \\
\mathcal{L}_{\mathsf{Dyn}} & ::= & def \dots stmt \dots
\end{array}
$$

Figure 10.1
Syntax of $\mathcal{L}_{\mathsf{Dyn}}$, an untyped language (a subset of Python).

$$
\begin{array}{rcl}
boolop & ::= & \texttt{And()} \mid \texttt{Or()} \\
cmp & ::= & \texttt{Eq()} \mid \texttt{NotEq()} \mid \texttt{Lt()} \mid \texttt{LtE()} \mid \texttt{Gt()} \mid \texttt{GtE()} \mid \texttt{Is()} \\
bool & ::= & \texttt{True} \mid \texttt{False} \\
exp & ::= & \texttt{Constant}(int) \mid \texttt{Call(Name('input\_int'),[])} \\
 & \mid & \texttt{UnaryOp(USub(),}exp\texttt{)} \\
 & \mid & \texttt{BinOp(}exp\texttt{,Add(),}exp\texttt{)} \mid \texttt{BinOp(}exp\texttt{,Sub(),}exp\texttt{)} \\
 & \mid & \texttt{Name(}var\texttt{)} \mid \texttt{Constant(}bool\texttt{)} \mid \texttt{BoolOp(}boolop\texttt{,[}exp\texttt{,}exp\texttt{])} \\
 & \mid & \texttt{Compare(}exp\texttt{,[}cmp\texttt{],[}exp\texttt{])} \mid \texttt{IfExp(}exp\texttt{,}exp\texttt{,}exp\texttt{)} \\
 & \mid & \texttt{Tuple(}exp^{+}\texttt{,Load())} \mid \texttt{Subscript(}exp\texttt{,}exp\texttt{,Load())} \\
 & \mid & \texttt{Call(Name('len'),[}exp\texttt{])} \\
 & \mid & \texttt{Call(}exp\texttt{,\ }exp^{*}\texttt{)} \mid \texttt{Lambda(}var^{*}\texttt{,\ }exp\texttt{)} \\
stmt & ::= & \texttt{Expr(Call(Name('print'),[}exp\texttt{]))} \mid \texttt{Expr(}exp\texttt{)} \\
 & \mid & \texttt{Assign([Name(}var\texttt{)],\ }exp\texttt{)} \\
 & \mid & \texttt{If(}exp\texttt{,\ }stmt^{+}\texttt{,\ }stmt^{+}\texttt{)} \mid \texttt{While(}exp\texttt{,\ }stmt^{+}\texttt{,\ [])} \\
 & \mid & \texttt{Return(}exp\texttt{)} \\
params & ::= & \texttt{(}var\texttt{,AnyType())}^{*} \\
def & ::= & \texttt{FunctionDef(}var\texttt{,\ }params\texttt{,\ }stmt^{+}\texttt{,\ None,\ AnyType(),\ None)} \\
\mathcal{L}_{\mathsf{Dyn}} & ::= & \texttt{Module([}def \dots stmt \dots\texttt{])}
\end{array}
$$

Figure 10.2
The abstract syntax of $\mathcal{L}_{\mathsf{Dyn}}$.

kind of value it is. We define the following class to represent tagged values:

```python
@dataclass(eq=True)
class Tagged(Value):
  value : Value
  tag : str
  def __str__(self):
    return str(self.value)
```

The tags are `'int'`, `'bool'`, `'none'`, `'tuple'`, and `'function'`. Tags are closely related to types but do not always capture all the information that a type does.

```
class InterpLdyn(InterpLlambda):
  def interp_exp(self, e, env):
    match e:
      case Constant(n):
        return self.tag(super().interp_exp(e, env))
      case Tuple(es, Load()):
        return self.tag(super().interp_exp(e, env))
      case Lambda(params, body):
        return self.tag(super().interp_exp(e, env))
      case Call(Name('input_int'), []):
        return self.tag(super().interp_exp(e, env))
      case BinOp(left, Add(), right):
        l = self.interp_exp(left, env); r = self.interp_exp(right, env)
        return self.tag(self.untag(l, 'int', e) + self.untag(r, 'int', e))
      case BinOp(left, Sub(), right):
        l = self.interp_exp(left, env); r = self.interp_exp(right, env)
        return self.tag(self.untag(l, 'int', e) - self.untag(r, 'int', e))
      case UnaryOp(USub(), e1):
        v = self.interp_exp(e1, env)
        return self.tag(- self.untag(v, 'int', e))
      case IfExp(test, body, orelse):
        v = self.interp_exp(test, env)
        if self.untag(v, 'bool', e):
          return self.interp_exp(body, env)
        else:
          return self.interp_exp(orelse, env)
      case UnaryOp(Not(), e1):
        v = self.interp_exp(e1, env)
        return self.tag(not self.untag(v, 'bool', e))
      case BoolOp(And(), values):
        left = values[0]; right = values[1]
        l = self.interp_exp(left, env)
        if self.untag(l, 'bool', e):
          return self.interp_exp(right, env)
        else:
          return self.tag(False)
      case BoolOp(Or(), values):
        left = values[0]; right = values[1]
        l = self.interp_exp(left, env)
        if self.untag(l, 'bool', e):
          return self.tag(True)
        else:
          return self.interp_exp(right, env)
```

Figure 10.3
Interpreter for the $\mathcal{L}_{\mathsf{Dyn}}$ language, part 1.

For example, a tuple of type `TupleType([AnyType(),AnyType()])` is tagged with `'tuple'` and a function of type `FunctionType([AnyType(), AnyType()], AnyType())` is tagged with `'function'`.

Next consider the match case for accessing the element of a tuple. The `untag` auxiliary function (figure 10.5) is used to ensure that the first argument is a tuple and the second is an integer. If they are not, an exception is raised. The compiled code must also signal an error by exiting with return code 255. A exception is also raised if the index is not less than the length of the tuple or if it is negative.

```
# interp_exp continued
    case Compare(left, [cmp], [right]):
      l = self.interp_exp(left, env)
      r = self.interp_exp(right, env)
      if l.tag == r.tag:
        return self.tag(self.interp_cmp(cmp)(l.value, r.value))
      else:
        raise Exception('interp Compare unexpected '
                        + repr(l) + ' ' + repr(r))
    case Subscript(tup, index, Load()):
      t = self.interp_exp(tup, env)
      n = self.interp_exp(index, env)
      return self.untag(t, 'tuple', e)[self.untag(n, 'int', e)]
    case Call(Name('len'), [tup]):
      t = self.interp_exp(tup, env)
      return self.tag(len(self.untag(t, 'tuple', e)))
    case _:
      return self.tag(super().interp_exp(e, env))

def interp_stmt(self, s, env, cont):
  match s:
    case If(test, body, orelse):
      v = self.interp_exp(test, env)
      match self.untag(v, 'bool', s):
        case True:
          return self.interp_stmts(body + cont, env)
        case False:
          return self.interp_stmts(orelse + cont, env)
    case While(test, body, []):
      v = self.interp_exp(test, env)
      if self.untag(v, 'bool', test):
          self.interp_stmts(body + [s] + cont, env)
      else:
        return self.interp_stmts(cont, env)
    case Assign([Subscript(tup, index)], value):
      tup = self.interp_exp(tup, env)
      index = self.interp_exp(index, env)
      tup_v = self.untag(tup, 'tuple', s)
      index_v = self.untag(index, 'int', s)
      tup_v[index_v] = self.interp_exp(value, env)
      return self.interp_stmts(cont, env)
    case FunctionDef(name, params, bod, dl, returns, comment):
      if isinstance(params, ast.arguments):
          ps = [p.arg for p in params.args]
      else:
          ps = [x for (x,t) in params]
      env[name] = self.tag(Function(name, ps, bod, env))
      return self.interp_stmts(cont, env)
    case _:
      return super().interp_stmt(s, env, cont)
```

Figure 10.4
Interpreter for the $\mathcal{L}_{Dyn}$ language, part 2.

```
class InterpLdyn(InterpLlambda):
  def tag(self, v):
    if v is True or v is False:
      return Tagged(v, 'bool')
    elif isinstance(v, int):
      return Tagged(v, 'int')
    elif isinstance(v, Function):
      return Tagged(v, 'function')
    elif isinstance(v, tuple):
      return Tagged(v, 'tuple')
    elif isinstance(v, type(None)):
      return Tagged(v, 'none')
    else:
      raise Exception('tag: unexpected ' + repr(v))

  def untag(self, v, expected_tag, ast):
    match v:
      case Tagged(val, tag) if tag == expected_tag:
        return val
      case _:
        raise TrappedError('expected Tagged value with '
                           + expected_tag + ', not ' + ' ' + repr(v))

  def apply_fun(self, fun, args, e):
    f = self.untag(fun, 'function', e)
    return super().apply_fun(f, args, e)
```

Figure 10.5
Auxiliary functions for the $\mathcal{L}_{Dyn}$ interpreter.

10.2   Representation of Tagged Values

The interpreter for $\mathcal{L}_{Dyn}$ introduced a new kind of value: the tagged value. To compile $\mathcal{L}_{Dyn}$ to x86 we must decide how to represent tagged values at the bit level. Because almost every operation in $\mathcal{L}_{Dyn}$ involves manipulating tagged values, the representation must be efficient. Recall that all our values are 64 bits. We shall steal the right-most 3 bits to encode the tag. We use 001 to identify integers, 100 for Booleans, 010 for tuples, 011 for procedures, and 101 for the void value, **None**. We define the following auxiliary function for mapping types to tag codes:

$$tagof(\text{IntType}()) = 001$$

$$tagof(\text{BoolType}()) = 100$$

$$tagof(\text{TupleType}(\text{ts})) = 010$$

$$tagof(\text{FunctionType}(\text{ps, rt})) = 011$$

$$tagof(\text{type}(\text{None})) = 101$$

This stealing of 3 bits comes at some price: integers are now restricted to the range -2^{60} to $2^{60} - 1$. The stealing does not adversely affect tuples and procedures because those values are addresses, and our addresses are 8-byte aligned so the rightmost 3 bits are unused; they are always 000. Thus, we do not lose information by overwriting the rightmost 3 bits with the tag, and we can simply zero out the tag to recover the original address.

To make tagged values into first-class entities, we can give them a type called `AnyType` and define operations such as `Inject` and `Project` for creating and using them, yielding the statically typed $\mathcal{L}_{\mathsf{Any}}$ intermediate language. We describe how to compile $\mathcal{L}_{\mathsf{Dyn}}$ to $\mathcal{L}_{\mathsf{Any}}$ in section 10.4; in the next section we describe the $\mathcal{L}_{\mathsf{Any}}$ language in greater detail.

10.3 The $\mathcal{L}_{\mathsf{Any}}$ Language

The definition of the abstract syntax of $\mathcal{L}_{\mathsf{Any}}$ is given in figure 10.6. The `Inject(e, T)` form converts the value produced by expression e of type T into a tagged value. The `Project(e, T)` form either converts the tagged value produced by expression e into a value of type T or halts the program if the type tag does not match T. Note that in both `Inject` and `Project`, the type T is restricted to be a flat type (the nonterminal *ftype*) which simplifies the implementation and complies with the needs for compiling $\mathcal{L}_{\mathsf{Dyn}}$.

The operators `any_tuple_load` and `any_len` adapt the tuple operations so that they can be applied to a value of type `AnyType`. They also generalize the tuple operations in that the index is not restricted to a literal integer in the grammar but is allowed to be any expression.

The type checker for $\mathcal{L}_{\mathsf{Any}}$ is shown in figure 10.7. The interpreter for $\mathcal{L}_{\mathsf{Any}}$ is shown in figure 10.8 and its auxiliary functions are shown in figure 10.9.

exp	::=	Constant(*int*) | Call(Name('input_int'),[])
	|	UnaryOp(USub(),*exp*) | BinOp(*exp*,Add(),*exp*)
	|	BinOp(*exp*,Sub(),*exp*)
stmt	::=	Expr(Call(Name('print'),[*exp*])) | Expr(*exp*)
exp	::=	Name(*var*)
stmt	::=	Assign([Name(*var*)], *exp*)
boolop	::=	And() | Or()
cmp	::=	Eq() | NotEq() | Lt() | LtE() | Gt() | GtE()
bool	::=	True | False
exp	::=	Constant(*bool*) | BoolOp(*boolop*,[*exp*,*exp*])
	|	UnaryOp(Not(),*exp*) | Compare(*exp*,[*cmp*],[*exp*])
	|	IfExp(*exp*,*exp*,*exp*)
stmt	::=	If(*exp*, *stmt*$^+$, *stmt*$^+$)
stmt	::=	While(*exp*, *stmt*$^+$, [])
cmp	::=	Is()
exp	::=	Tuple(*exp*$^+$,Load()) | Subscript(*exp*,Constant(*int*),Load())
	|	Call(Name('len'),[*exp*])
type	::=	IntType() | BoolType() | VoidType() | TupleType[*type*$^+$]
	|	FunctionType(*type**, *type*)
exp	::=	Call(*exp*, *exp**)
stmt	::=	Return(*exp*)
params	::=	(*var*,*type*)*
def	::=	FunctionDef(*var*, *params*, *stmt*$^+$, None, *type*, None)
exp	::=	Lambda(*var**, *exp*) | Call(Name('arity'), [*exp*])
stmt	::=	AnnAssign(*var*, *type*, *exp*, 0)
type	::=	**AnyType()**
ftype	::=	**IntType() | BoolType() | VoidType() | TupleType[AnyType()$^+$]**
	|	**FunctionType(AnyType()*, AnyType())**
exp	::=	**Inject(*exp*, *ftype*) | Project(*exp*, *ftype*)**
	|	**Call(Name('any_tuple_load'), [*exp*, *exp*])**
	|	**Call(Name('any_len'), [*exp*])**
	|	**Call(Name('arity'), [*exp*])**
	|	**Call(Name('make_any'), [*exp*, Constant(*int*)])**
$\mathcal{L}_{\text{Any}}$	::=	**Module([*def* ... *stmt* ...])**

Figure 10.6
The abstract syntax of $\mathcal{L}_{\text{Any}}$, extending $\mathcal{L}_\lambda$ (figure 9.4).

```
class TypeCheckLany(TypeCheckLlambda):
  def type_check_exp(self, e, env):
    match e:
      case Inject(value, typ):
        self.check_exp(value, typ, env)
        return AnyType()
      case Project(value, typ):
        self.check_exp(value, AnyType(), env)
        return typ
      case Call(Name('any_tuple_load'), [tup, index]):
        self.check_exp(tup, AnyType(), env)
        self.check_exp(index, IntType(), env)
        return AnyType()
      case Call(Name('any_len'), [tup]):
        self.check_exp(tup, AnyType(), env)
        return IntType()
      case Call(Name('arity'), [fun]):
        ty = self.type_check_exp(fun, env)
        match ty:
          case FunctionType(ps, rt):
            return IntType()
          case TupleType([FunctionType(ps,rs)]):
            return IntType()
          case _:
            raise Exception('type check arity unexpected ' + repr(ty))
      case Call(Name('make_any'), [value, tag]):
        self.type_check_exp(value, env)
        self.check_exp(tag, IntType(), env)
        return AnyType()
      case AnnLambda(params, returns, body):
        new_env = {x:t for (x,t) in env.items()}
        for (x,t) in params:
          new_env[x] = t
        return_t = self.type_check_exp(body, new_env)
        self.check_type_equal(returns, return_t, e)
        return FunctionType([t for (x,t) in params], return_t)
      case _:
        return super().type_check_exp(e, env)
```

Figure 10.7
Type checker for the $\mathcal{L}_{\mathsf{Any}}$ language.

```
class InterpLany(InterpLlambda):
  def interp_exp(self, e, env):
    match e:
      case Inject(value, typ):
        return Tagged(self.interp_exp(value, env), self.type_to_tag(typ))
      case Project(value, typ):
        match self.interp_exp(value, env):
          case Tagged(val, tag) if self.type_to_tag(typ) == tag:
            return val
          case _:
            raise Exception('failed project to ' + self.type_to_tag(typ))
      case Call(Name('any_tuple_load'), [tup, index]):
        match self.interp_exp(tup, env):
          case Tagged(v, tag):
            return v[self.interp_exp(index, env)]
          case _:
            raise Exception('in any_tuple_load untagged value')
      case Call(Name('any_len'), [value]):
        match self.interp_exp(value, env):
          case Tagged(value, tag):
            return len(value)
          case _:
            raise Exception('interp any_len untagged value')
      case Call(Name('arity'), [fun]):
        return self.arity(self.interp_exp(fun, env))
      case _:
        return super().interp_exp(e, env)
```

Figure 10.8
Interpreter for $\mathcal{L}_{\text{Any}}$.

```
class InterpLany(InterpLlambda):
  def type_to_tag(self, typ):
    match typ:
      case FunctionType(params, rt):
        return 'function'
      case TupleType(fields):
        return 'tuple'
      case IntType():
        return 'int'
      case BoolType():
        return 'bool'
      case _:
        raise Exception('type_to_tag unexpected ' + repr(typ))
  def arity(self, v):
    match v:
      case Function(name, params, body, env):
        return len(params)
      case _:
        raise Exception('Lany arity unexpected ' + repr(v))
```

Figure 10.9
Auxiliary functions for interpreting $\mathcal{L}_{\text{Any}}$.

True	⇒	Inject(True, BoolType())
e_1 + e_2	⇒	Inject(Project(e_1', IntType()) + Project(e_2', IntType()), IntType())
lambda x_1 ... : e	⇒	Inject(Lambda([(x_1,AnyType()),...], e') FunctionType([AnyType(),...], AnyType()))
$e_0(e_1 ... e_n)$	⇒	Call(Project(e_0', FunctionType([AnyType(),...], AnyType())), e_1', ...,e_n')
$e_1[e_2]$	⇒	Call(Name('any_tuple_load'), [e_1', Project(e_2', IntType())])

Figure 10.10
Cast insertion.

10.4 Cast Insertion: Compiling $\mathcal{L}_{Dyn}$ to $\mathcal{L}_{Any}$

The cast_insert pass compiles from $\mathcal{L}_{Dyn}$ to $\mathcal{L}_{Any}$. Figure 10.10 shows the compilation of many of the $\mathcal{L}_{Dyn}$ forms into $\mathcal{L}_{Any}$. An important invariant of this pass is that given any subexpression e in the $\mathcal{L}_{Dyn}$ program, the pass will produce an expression e' in $\mathcal{L}_{Any}$ that has type AnyType. For example, the first row in figure 10.10 shows the compilation of the Boolean True, which must be injected to produce an expression of type AnyType. The compilation of addition is shown in the second row of figure 10.10. The compilation of addition is representative of many primitive operations: the arguments have type AnyType and must be projected to IntType before the addition can be performed.

The compilation of lambda (third row of figure 10.10) shows what happens when we need to produce type annotations: we simply use AnyType.

10.5 Reveal Casts

In the reveal_casts pass, we recommend compiling Project into a conditional expression that checks whether the value's tag matches the target type; if it does, the value is converted to a value of the target type by removing the tag; if it does not, the program exits. To perform these actions we need two new AST classes: TagOf and ValueOf. The TagOf operation retrieves the type tag from a tagged value of type AnyType. The ValueOf operation retrieves the underlying value from a tagged value. The ValueOf operation includes the type for the underlying value that is used by the type checker.

If the target type of the projection is bool or int, then Project can be translated as follows:

```
Project(e, ftype)
⇒
Begin([Assign([tmp], e')],
      IfExp(Compare(TagOf(tmp),[Eq()],
                    [Constant(tagof(ftype))]),
            ValueOf(tmp, ftype)
            Call(Name('exit'), [])))
```

If the target type of the projection is a tuple or function type, then there is a bit more work to do. For tuples, check that the length of the tuple type matches the length of the tuple. For functions, check that the number of parameters in the function type matches the function's arity.

Regarding `Inject`, we recommend compiling it to a slightly lower-level primitive operation named `make_any`. This operation takes a tag instead of a type.

```
Inject(e, ftype)
⇒
Call(Name('make_any'), [e', Constant(tagof(ftype))])
```

The introduction of `make_any` makes it difficult to use bidirectional type checking because we no longer have an expected type to use for type checking the expression e'. Thus, we run into difficulty if e' is a `Lambda` expression. We recommend translating `Lambda` to a new AST class `AnnLambda` (for annotated lambda) that contains its return type and the types of its parameters.

The `any_tuple_load` operation combines the projection action with the load operation. Also, the load operation allows arbitrary expressions for the index, so the type checker for $\mathcal{L}_{\mathsf{Any}}$ (figure 10.7) cannot guarantee that the index is within bounds. Thus, we insert code to perform bounds checking at runtime. The translation for `any_tuple_load` is as follows.

```
Call(Name('any_tuple_load'), [e₁,e₂])
⇒
Block([Assign([t], e₁'), Assign([i], e₂')],
      IfExp(Compare(TagOf(t), [Eq()], [Constant(2)]),
            IfExp(Compare(i, [Lt()], [Call(Name('any_len'), [t])]),
                  Call(Name('any_tuple_load_unsafe'), [t, i]),
                  Call(Name('exit'), [])),
            Call(Name('exit'), [])))
```

10.6 Assignment Conversion

Update this pass to handle the `TagOf`, `ValueOf`, and `AnnLambda` AST classes.

10.7 Closure Conversion

Update this pass to handle the `TagOf`, `ValueOf`, and `AnnLambda` AST classes.

```
atm    ::=  Constant(int) | Name(var) | Constant(bool)
exp    ::=  atm | Call(Name('input_int'),[]) | UnaryOp(USub(),atm)
       |    BinOp(atm,Sub(),atm) | BinOp(atm,Add(),atm)
       |    Compare(atm,[cmp],[atm])
stmt   ::=  Expr(Call(Name('print'),[atm])) | Expr(exp)
       |    Assign([Name(var)], exp)
tail   ::=  Return(exp) | Goto(label)
       |    If(Compare(atm,[cmp],[atm]), [Goto(label)], [Goto(label)])
atm    ::=  GlobalValue(var)
exp    ::=  Subscript(atm,atm,Load()) | Allocate(int,type)
       |    Call(Name('len'),[atm])
stmt   ::=  Collect(int) | Assign([Subscript(atm,atm,Store())], atm)
exp    ::=  FunRef(label, int) | Call(atm, atm*)
tail   ::=  TailCall(atm, atm*)
params ::=  [(var,type), ...]
block  ::=  label:stmt* tail
def    ::=  FunctionDef(label, params, {block, ...}, None, type, None)
exp    ::=  Uninitialized(type) | AllocateClosure(len,type,arity)
       |    Call(Name('arity'), [atm]) | UncheckedCast(exp,type)
exp    ::=  Call(Name('make_any'), [atm,atm])
       |    TagOf(atm) | ValueOf(atm,ftype)
       |    Call(Name('any_tuple_load_unsafe'), [atm,atm])
       |    Call(Name('any_len'), [atm])
       |    Call(Name('exit'), [])
C_Any  ::=  CProgramDefs([def, ...])
```

Figure 10.11
The abstract syntax of $\mathcal{C}_{Any}$, extending $\mathcal{C}_{Clos}$ (figure 9.9).

10.8 Remove Complex Operands

The ValueOf and TagOf operations are both complex expressions. Their subexpressions must be atomic.

10.9 Explicate Control and $\mathcal{C}_{Any}$

The output of explicate_control is the $\mathcal{C}_{Any}$ language, whose syntax definition is shown in figure 10.11. Update the auxiliary functions explicate_tail, explicate_effect, and explicate_pred as appropriate to handle the new expressions in $\mathcal{C}_{Any}$.

10.10 Select Instructions

In the select_instructions pass, we translate the primitive operations on the AnyType type to x86 instructions that manipulate the three tag bits of the tagged value. In the following descriptions, given an atom e we use a primed variable e' to refer to the result of translating e into an x86 argument:

make_any We recommend compiling the **make_any** operation as follows if the tag is for **int** or **bool**. The **salq** instruction shifts the destination to the left by the number of bits specified by its source argument (in this case three, the length of the tag), and it preserves the sign of the integer. We use the **orq** instruction to combine the tag and the value to form the tagged value.

Assign([*lhs*], Call(Name('make_any'), [*e*, Constant(*tag*)]))
$\Rightarrow$
movq *e'*, *lhs'*
salq \$3, *lhs'*
orq \$*tag*, *lhs'*

The instruction selection for tuples and procedures is different because there is no need to shift them to the left. The rightmost 3 bits are already zeros, so we simply combine the value and the tag using **orq**.

Assign([*lhs*], Call(Name('make_any'), [*e*, Constant(*tag*)]))
$\Rightarrow$
movq *e'*, *lhs'*
orq \$*tag*, *lhs'*

TagOf Recall that the **TagOf** operation extracts the type tag from a value of type **AnyType**. The type tag is the bottom 3 bits, so we obtain the tag by taking the bitwise-and of the value with 111 (7 decimal).

Assign([*lhs*], TagOf(*e*))
$\Rightarrow$
movq *e'*, *lhs'*
andq \$7, *lhs'*

ValueOf The instructions for **ValueOf** also differ, depending on whether the type T is a pointer (tuple or function) or not (integer or Boolean). The following shows the instruction selection for integers and Booleans, in which we produce an untagged value by shifting it to the right by 3 bits:

Assign([*lhs*], ValueOf(*e*, *T*))
$\Rightarrow$
movq *e'*, *lhs'*
sarq \$3, *lhs'*

In the case for tuples and procedures, we zero out the rightmost 3 bits. We accomplish this by creating the bit pattern ... 0111 (7 decimal) and apply bitwise-not to obtain ... 11111000 (-8 decimal), which we **movq** into the destination *lhs'*. Finally, we apply **andq** with the tagged value to get the desired result.

Assign([*lhs*], ValueOf(*e*, *T*))
$\Rightarrow$
movq \$–8, *lhs'*

andq e', lhs'

any_len   The `any_len` operation combines the effect of `ValueOf` with accessing the
length of a tuple from the tag stored at the zero index of the tuple.

```
Assign([lhs], Call(Name('any_len'), [e₁]))
⟹
movq $-8, %r11
andq e₁', %r11
movq 0(%r11), %r11
andq $126, %r11
sarq $1, %r11
movq %r11, lhs'
```

any_tuple_load_unsafe   This operation combines the effect of `ValueOf` with reading an element of the tuple (see section 7.6). However, the index may be an arbitrary
atom, so instead of computing the offset at compile time, we must generate instructions to compute the offset at runtime as follows. Note the use of the new instruction
`imulq`.

```
Assign([lhs], Call(Name('any_tuple_load_unsafe'), [e₁,e₂]))
⟹
movq $-8, %r11
andq e₁', %r11
movq e₂', %rax
addq $1, %rax
imulq $8, %rax
addq %rax, %r11
movq 0(%r11) lhs'
```

10.11   Register Allocation for $\mathcal{L}_{\mathsf{Any}}$

There is an interesting interaction between tagged values and garbage collection
that has an impact on register allocation. A variable of type `AnyType` might refer
to a tuple, and therefore it might be a root that needs to be inspected and copied
during garbage collection. Thus, we need to treat variables of type `AnyType` in
a similar way to variables of tuple type for purposes of register allocation, with
particular attention to the following:

• If a variable of type `AnyType` is live during a function call, then it must be spilled.
  This can be accomplished by changing `build_interference` to mark all variables
  of type `AnyType` that are live after a `callq` to be interfering with all the registers.
• If a variable of type `AnyType` is spilled, it must be spilled to the root stack instead
  of the normal procedure call stack.

Another concern regarding the root stack is that the garbage collector needs to
differentiate among (1) plain old pointers to tuples, (2) a tagged value that points
to a tuple, and (3) a tagged value that is not a tuple. We enable this differentiation

by choosing not to use the tag 000 in the *tagof* function. Instead, that bit pattern is reserved for identifying plain old pointers to tuples. That way, if one of the first three bits is set, then we have a tagged value and inspecting the tag can differentiate between tuples (010) and the other kinds of values.

Exercise 10.1 Expand your compiler to handle $\mathcal{L}_{\mathsf{Dyn}}$ as outlined in this chapter. Create tests for $\mathcal{L}_{\mathsf{Dyn}}$ by adapting ten of your previous test programs by removing type annotations. Add five more test programs that specifically rely on the language being dynamically typed. That is, they should not be legal programs in a statically typed language, but nevertheless they should be valid $\mathcal{L}_{\mathsf{Dyn}}$ programs that run to completion without error.

Figure 10.12 gives an overview of the passes needed for the compilation of $\mathcal{L}_{\mathsf{Dyn}}$.

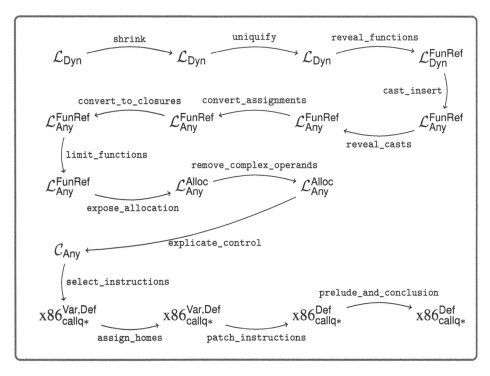

Figure 10.12
Diagram of the passes for $\mathcal{L}_{\mathsf{Dyn}}$, a dynamically typed language.

11 Gradual Typing

This chapter studies the language $\mathcal{L}_?$, in which the programmer can choose between static and dynamic type checking in different parts of a program, thereby mixing the statically typed $\mathcal{L}_\lambda$ language with the dynamically typed $\mathcal{L}_{\mathsf{Dyn}}$. There are several approaches to mixing static and dynamic typing, including multilanguage integration (Tobin-Hochstadt and Felleisen 2006; Matthews and Findler 2007) and hybrid type checking (Flanagan 2006; Gronski et al. 2006). In this chapter we focus on *gradual typing*, in which the programmer controls the amount of static versus dynamic checking by adding or removing type annotations on parameters and variables (Anderson and Drossopoulou 2003; Siek and Taha 2006).

The definition of the concrete syntax of $\mathcal{L}_?$ is shown in figure 11.1, and the definition of its abstract syntax is shown in figure 11.2. The main syntactic difference between $\mathcal{L}_\lambda$ and $\mathcal{L}_?$ is that type annotations are optional, which is specified in the grammar using the *prm* and *ret* nonterminals. In the abstract syntax, type annotations are not optional, but we use the **Any** type when a type annotation is absent. Both the type checker and the interpreter for $\mathcal{L}_?$ require some interesting changes to enable gradual typing, which we discuss in the next two sections.

11.1 Type Checking $\mathcal{L}_?$

We begin by discussing the type checking of a partially typed variant of the **map** example from chapter 8, shown in figure 11.3. The **map** function itself is statically typed, so there is nothing special happening there with respect to type checking. On the other hand, the **inc** function does not have type annotations, so the type checker assigns the type **Any** to parameter **x** and the return type. Now consider the + operator inside **inc**. It expects both arguments to have type **int**, but its first argument **x** has type **Any**. In a gradually typed language, such differences are allowed so long as the types are *consistent*; that is, they are equal except in places where there is an **Any** type. That is, the type **Any** is consistent with every other type. Figure 11.4 shows the definition of the **consistent** method. So the type checker allows the + operator to be applied to **x** because **Any** is consistent with **int**. Next consider the call to the **map** function shown in figure 11.3 with the arguments **inc** and a tuple. The **inc** function has type **Callable[[Any],Any]**, but parameter **f** of **map** has type **Callable[[int],int]**. The type checker for $\mathcal{L}_?$ accepts this call because the two types are consistent.

$$
\begin{array}{rcl}
exp & ::= & int \mid \text{input\_int()} \mid -exp \mid exp+exp \mid exp-exp \mid (exp) \\
stmt & ::= & \text{print}(exp) \mid exp \\
\hline
exp & ::= & var \\
stmt & ::= & var = exp \\
\hline
cmp & ::= & \text{==} \mid \text{!=} \mid \text{<} \mid \text{<=} \mid \text{>} \mid \text{>=} \\
exp & ::= & \text{True} \mid \text{False} \mid exp \text{ and } exp \mid exp \text{ or } exp \mid \text{not } exp \\
 & \mid & exp \; cmp \; exp \mid exp \text{ if } exp \text{ else } exp \\
stmt & ::= & \text{if } exp\text{: } stmt^{+} \text{ else: } stmt^{+} \\
\hline
stmt & ::= & \text{while } exp\text{: } stmt^{+} \\
\hline
cmp & ::= & \text{is} \\
exp & ::= & exp, \dots, exp \mid exp\,[int] \mid \text{len}(exp) \\
\hline
type & ::= & \text{Any} \mid \text{int} \mid \text{bool} \mid \text{tuple}[type, \dots] \mid \text{Callable}[[type, \dots], \; type] \\
exp & ::= & exp(exp, \dots) \mid \text{lambda } var, \; \dots : exp \mid \text{arity}(exp) \\
stmt & ::= & var : type = exp \mid \text{return } exp \\
prm & ::= & var \mid var\text{:}type \\
ret & ::= & \epsilon \mid \text{-> } type \\
def & ::= & \text{def } var(prm, \; \dots) \; ret\text{: } stmt^{+} \\
\mathcal{L}_{?} & ::= & def \dots stmt \dots
\end{array}
$$

Figure 11.1
The concrete syntax of $\mathcal{L}_{?}$, extending $\mathcal{L}_{\text{Tup}}$ (figure 7.1).

It is also helpful to consider how gradual typing handles programs with an error, such as applying map to a function that sometimes returns a Boolean, as shown in figure 11.5. The type checker for $\mathcal{L}_{?}$ accepts this program because the type of maybe_inc is consistent with the type of parameter f of map; that is, Callable[[Any],Any] is consistent with Callable[[int],int]. One might say that a gradual type checker is optimistic in that it accepts programs that might execute without a runtime type error. The definition of the type checker for $\mathcal{L}_{?}$ is shown in figures 11.7, 11.8, and 11.9.

Running this program with input 1 triggers an error when the maybe_inc function returns True. The $\mathcal{L}_{?}$ language performs checking at runtime to ensure the integrity of the static types, such as the Callable[[int],int] annotation on parameter f of map. Here we give a preview of how the runtime checking is accomplished; the following sections provide the details.

The runtime checking is carried out by a new Cast AST node that is generated in a new pass named cast_insert. The output of cast_insert is a program in the $\mathcal{L}_{\text{Cast}}$ language, which simply adds Cast and Any to $\mathcal{L}_{\lambda}$. Figure 11.6 shows the output of cast_insert for map and maybe_inc. The idea is that Cast is inserted every time the type checker encounters two types that are consistent but not equal. In the inc function, x is cast to int and the result of the + is cast to Any. In the call to map, the inc argument is cast from Callable[[Any], Any] to Callable[[int],int]. In the next section we see how to interpret the Cast node.

```
exp    ::=  Constant(int) | Call(Name('input_int'),[])
       |    UnaryOp(USub(),exp) | BinOp(exp,Add(),exp)
       |    BinOp(exp,Sub(),exp)
stmt   ::=  Expr(Call(Name('print'),[exp])) | Expr(exp)
exp    ::=  Name(var)
stmt   ::=  Assign([Name(var)], exp)
boolop ::=  And() | Or()
cmp    ::=  Eq() | NotEq() | Lt() | LtE() | Gt() | GtE()
bool   ::=  True | False
exp    ::=  Constant(bool) | BoolOp(boolop,[exp,exp])
       |    UnaryOp(Not(),exp) | Compare(exp,[cmp],[exp])
       |    IfExp(exp,exp,exp)
stmt   ::=  If(exp, stmt⁺, stmt⁺)
stmt   ::=  While(exp, stmt⁺, [])
cmp    ::=  Is()
exp    ::=  Tuple(exp⁺,Load()) | Subscript(exp,Constant(int),Load())
       |    Call(Name('len'),[exp])
type   ::=  AnyType() | IntType() | BoolType() | VoidType()
       |    TupleType(type*) | FunctionType(type*, type)
exp    ::=  Call(exp, exp*) | Lambda(var*, exp)
       |    Call(Name('arity'), [exp])
stmt   ::=  AnnAssign(var, type, exp, 0) | Return(exp)
prm    ::=  (var,type)
def    ::=  FunctionDef(var, prm*, stmt⁺, None, type, None)
L?     ::=  Module([def ... stmt ...])
```

Figure 11.2
The abstract syntax of $\mathcal{L}_?$, extending $\mathcal{L}_{\text{Tup}}$ (figure 7.2).

```
def map(f : Callable[[int], int], v : tuple[int,int]) -> tuple[int,int]:
  return f(v[0]), f(v[1])

def inc(x):
  return x + 1

t = map(inc, (0, 41))
print(t[1])
```

Figure 11.3
A partially typed version of the map example.

```
def consistent(self, t1, t2):
  match (t1, t2):
    case (AnyType(), _):
      return True
    case (_, AnyType()):
      return True
    case (FunctionType(ps1, rt1), FunctionType(ps2, rt2)):
      return all(map(self.consistent, ps1, ps2)) and consistent(rt1, rt2)
    case (TupleType(ts1), TupleType(ts2)):
      return all(map(self.consistent, ts1, ts2))
    case (_, _):
      return t1 == t2
```

Figure 11.4
The consistency method on types.

```
def map(f : Callable[[int], int], v : tuple[int,int]) -> tuple[int,int]:
  return f(v[0]), f(v[1])
def inc(x):
  return x + 1
def true():
  return True
def maybe_inc(x):
  return inc(x) if input_int() == 0 else true()

t = map(maybe_inc, (0, 41))
print(t[1])
```

Figure 11.5
A variant of the map example with an error.

```
def map(f : Callable[[int], int], v : tuple[int,int]) -> tuple[int,int]:
  return f(v[0]), f(v[1])
def inc(x : Any) -> Any:
  return Cast(Cast(x, Any, int) + 1, int, Any)
def true() -> Any:
  return Cast(True, bool, Any)
def maybe_inc(x : Any) -> Any:
  return inc(x) if input_int() == 0 else true()

t = map(Cast(maybe_inc, Callable[[Any], Any], Callable[[int], int]),
        (0, 41))
print(t[1])
```

Figure 11.6
Output of the cast_insert pass for the map and maybe_inc example.

```
class TypeCheckLgrad(TypeCheckLlambda):
  def type_check_exp(self, e, env) -> Type:
    match e:
      case Name(id):
        return env[id]
      case Constant(value) if isinstance(value, bool):
        return BoolType()
      case Constant(value) if isinstance(value, int):
        return IntType()
      case Call(Name('input_int'), []):
        return IntType()
      case BinOp(left, op, right):
        left_type = self.type_check_exp(left, env)
        self.check_consistent(left_type, IntType(), left)
        right_type = self.type_check_exp(right, env)
        self.check_consistent(right_type, IntType(), right)
        return IntType()
      case IfExp(test, body, orelse):
        test_t = self.type_check_exp(test, env)
        self.check_consistent(test_t, BoolType(), test)
        body_t = self.type_check_exp(body, env)
        orelse_t = self.type_check_exp(orelse, env)
        self.check_consistent(body_t, orelse_t, e)
        return self.join_types(body_t, orelse_t)
      case Call(func, args):
        func_t = self.type_check_exp(func, env)
        args_t = [self.type_check_exp(arg, env) for arg in args]
        match func_t:
          case FunctionType(params_t, return_t) \
                if len(params_t) == len(args_t):
            for (arg_t, param_t) in zip(args_t, params_t):
                self.check_consistent(param_t, arg_t, e)
            return return_t
          case AnyType():
            return AnyType()
          case _:
            raise Exception('type_check_exp: in call, unexpected '
                            + repr(func_t))
      ...
      case _:
        raise Exception('type_check_exp: unexpected ' + repr(e))
```

Figure 11.7
Type checking expressions in the $\mathcal{L}_?$ language.

```
def check_exp(self, e, expected_ty, env):
  match e:
    case Lambda(params, body):
      match expected_ty:
        case FunctionType(params_t, return_t):
          new_env = env.copy().update(zip(params, params_t))
          e.has_type = expected_ty
          body_ty = self.type_check_exp(body, new_env)
          self.check_consistent(body_ty, return_t)
        case AnyType():
          new_env = env.copy().update((p, AnyType()) for p in params)
          e.has_type = FunctionType([AnyType()for _ in params],AnyType())
          body_ty = self.type_check_exp(body, new_env)
        case _:
          raise Exception('lambda is not of type ' + str(expected_ty))
    case _:
      e_ty = self.type_check_exp(e, env)
      self.check_consistent(e_ty, expected_ty, e)
```

Figure 11.8
Checking expressions with respect to a type in the $\mathcal{L}_?$ language.

```
def type_check_stmt(self, s, env, return_type):
  match s:
    case Assign([Name(id)], value):
      value_ty = self.type_check_exp(value, env)
      if id in env:
        self.check_consistent(env[id], value_ty, value)
      else:
        env[id] = value_ty
    ...
    case _:
      raise Exception('type_check_stmts: unexpected ' + repr(ss))

def type_check_stmts(self, ss, env, return_type):
  for s in ss:
    self.type_check_stmt(s, env, return_type)
```

Figure 11.9
Type checking statements in the $\mathcal{L}_?$ language.

```
def join_types(self, t1, t2):
  match (t1, t2):
    case (AnyType(), _):
      return t2
    case (_, AnyType()):
      return t1
    case (FunctionType(ps1, rt1), FunctionType(ps2, rt2)):
      return FunctionType(list(map(self.join_types, ps1, ps2)),
                          self.join_types(rt1,rt2))
    case (TupleType(ts1), TupleType(ts2)):
      return TupleType(list(map(self.join_types, ts1, ts2)))
    case (_, _):
      return t1

def check_consistent(self, t1, t2, e):
  if not self.consistent(t1, t2):
    raise Exception('error: ' + repr(t1) + ' inconsistent with ' \
                    + repr(t2) + ' in ' + repr(e))
```

Figure 11.10
Auxiliary methods for type checking $\mathcal{L}_?$.

11.2   Interpreting $\mathcal{L}_{\text{Cast}}$

The runtime behavior of casts involving simple types such as int and bool is straightforward. For example, a cast from int to Any can be accomplished with the Inject operator of $\mathcal{L}_{\text{Any}}$, which puts the integer into a tagged value (figure 10.8). Similarly, a cast from Any to int is accomplished with the Project operator, by checking the value's tag and either retrieving the underlying integer or signaling an error if the tag is not the one for integers (figure 10.9). Things get more interesting with casts involving function, tuple, and array types.

Consider the cast of the function maybe_inc from Callable[[Any], Any] to Callable[[int], int] shown in figure 11.5. When the maybe_inc function flows through this cast at runtime, we don't know whether it will return an integer, because that depends on the input from the user. The $\mathcal{L}_{\text{Cast}}$ interpreter therefore delays the checking of the cast until the function is applied. To do so it wraps maybe_inc in a new function that casts its parameter from int to Any, applies maybe_inc, and then casts the return value from Any to int.

There are further complications regarding casts on mutable data, such as the list type introduced in the challenge assignment of section 7.9. Consider the example presented in figure 11.11 that defines a partially typed version of map whose parameter v has type list[Any] and that updates v in place instead of returning a new tuple. We name this function map_inplace. We apply map_inplace to an array of integers, so the type checker inserts a cast from list[int] to list[Any]. A naive way for the $\mathcal{L}_{\text{Cast}}$ interpreter to cast between array types would be to build

```
def map_inplace(f : Callable[[int], int], v : list[Any]) -> None:
  i = 0
  while i != len(v):
    v[i] = f(v[i])
    i = i + 1

def inc(x : int) -> int:
  return x + 1

v = [0, 41]
map_inplace(inc, v)
print(v[1])
```

Figure 11.11
An example involving casts on arrays.

a new array whose elements are the result of casting each of the original elements
to the target type. However, this approach is not valid for mutable data structures.
In the example of figure 11.11, if the cast created a new array, then the updates
inside **map_inplace** would happen to the new array and not the original one.

Instead the interpreter needs to create a new kind of value, a *proxy*, that intercepts
every array operation. On a read, the proxy reads from the underlying array and
then applies a cast to the resulting value. On a write, the proxy casts the argument
value and then performs the write to the underlying array. For the subscript v[i]
in f(v[i]) of **map_inplace**, the proxy casts the integer from int to Any. For the
subscript on the left of the assignment, the proxy casts the tagged value from Any
to int.

Finally we consider casts between the Any type and higher-order types such as
functions and lists. Figure 11.12 shows a variant of **map_inplace** in which parameter v does not have a type annotation, so it is given type Any. In the call to
map_inplace, the list has type list[int], so the type checker inserts a cast to
Any. A first thought is to use **Inject**, but that doesn't work because list[int] is
not a flat type. Instead, we must first cast to list[Any], which is flat, and then
inject to Any.

The $\mathcal{L}_{\mathsf{Cast}}$ interpreter uses an auxiliary function named **apply_cast** to cast a
value from a source type to a target type, shown in figure 11.13. You'll find that it
handles all the kinds of casts that we've discussed in this section. The definition of
the interpreter for $\mathcal{L}_{\mathsf{Cast}}$ is shown in figure 11.14, with the case for **Cast** dispatching
to **apply_cast**. Next we turn to the individual passes needed for compiling $\mathcal{L}_?$.

11.3 Overload Resolution

Recall that when we added support for arrays in section 7.9, the syntax for the array
operations were the same as for tuple operations (for example, accessing an element

```
def map_inplace(f : Callable[[Any], Any], v) -> None:
  i = 0
  while i != len(v):
    v[i] = f(v[i])
    i = i + 1

def inc(x):
    return x + 1

v = [0, 41]
map_inplace(inc, v)
print(v[1])
```

Figure 11.12
Casting an array to `Any`.

and getting the length). So we performed overload resolution, with a pass named `resolve`, to separate the array and tuple operations. In particular, we introduced the primitives `array_load`, `array_store`, and `array_len`.

For gradual typing, we further overload these operators to work on values of type `Any`. Thus, the `resolve` pass should be updated with new cases for the `Any` type, translating the element access and length operations to the primitives `any_load`, `any_store`, and `any_len`.

11.4 Cast Insertion

In our discussion of type checking of $\mathcal{L}_?$, we mentioned how the runtime aspect of type checking is carried out by the `Cast` AST node, which is added to the program by a new pass named `cast_insert`. The target of this pass is the $\mathcal{L}_{\mathsf{Cast}}$ language. We now discuss the details of this pass.

The `cast_insert` pass is closely related to the type checker for $\mathcal{L}_?$ (starting in figure 11.7). In particular, the type checker allows implicit casts between consistent types. The job of the `cast_insert` pass is to make those casts explicit. It does so by inserting `Cast` nodes into the AST. For the most part, the implicit casts occur in places where the type checker checks two types for consistency. Consider the case for binary operators in figure 11.7. The type checker requires that the type of the left operand is consistent with `int`. Thus, the `cast_insert` pass should insert a `Cast` around the left operand, converting from its type to `int`. The story is similar for the right operand. It is not always necessary to insert a cast, for example, if the left operand already has type `int` then there is no need for a `Cast`.

Some of the implicit casts are not as straightforward. One such case arises with the conditional expression. In figure 11.7 we see that the type checker requires that the two branches have consistent types and that type of the conditional expression is the meet of the branches' types. In the target language $\mathcal{L}_{\mathsf{Cast}}$, both branches

```
def apply_cast(self, value, src, tgt):
  match (src, tgt):
    case (AnyType(), FunctionType(ps2, rt2)):
      anyfun = FunctionType([AnyType() for p in ps2], AnyType())
      return self.apply_cast(self.apply_project(value, anyfun), anyfun, tgt)
    case (AnyType(), TupleType(ts2)):
      anytup = TupleType([AnyType() for t1 in ts2])
      return self.apply_cast(self.apply_project(value, anytup), anytup, tgt)
    case (AnyType(), ListType(t2)):
      anylist = ListType([AnyType() for t1 in ts2])
      return self.apply_cast(self.apply_project(value, anylist), anylist, tgt)
    case (AnyType(), AnyType()):
      return value
    case (AnyType(), _):
      return self.apply_project(value, tgt)
    case (FunctionType(ps1,rt1), AnyType()):
      anyfun = FunctionType([AnyType() for p in ps1], AnyType())
      return self.apply_inject(self.apply_cast(value, src, anyfun), anyfun)
    case (TupleType(ts1), AnyType()):
      anytup = TupleType([AnyType() for t1 in ts1])
      return self.apply_inject(self.apply_cast(value, src, anytup), anytup)
    case (ListType(t1), AnyType()):
      anylist = ListType(AnyType())
      return self.apply_inject(self.apply_cast(value,src,anylist), anylist)
    case (_, AnyType()):
      return self.apply_inject(value, src)
    case (FunctionType(ps1, rt1), FunctionType(ps2, rt2)):
      params = [generate_name('x') for p in ps2]
      args = [Cast(Name(x), t2, t1)
              for (x,t1,t2) in zip(params, ps1, ps2)]
      body = Cast(Call(ValueExp(value), args), rt1, rt2)
      return Function('cast', params, [Return(body)], {})
    case (TupleType(ts1), TupleType(ts2)):
      x = generate_name('x')
      reads = [Function('cast', [x], [Return(Cast(Name(x), t1, t2))], {})
               for (t1,t2) in zip(ts1,ts2)]
      return ProxiedTuple(value, reads)
    case (ListType(t1), ListType(t2)):
      x = generate_name('x')
      read = Function('cast', [x], [Return(Cast(Name(x), t1, t2))], {})
      write = Function('cast', [x], [Return(Cast(Name(x), t2, t1))], {})
      return ProxiedList(value, read, write)
    case (t1, t2) if t1 == t2:
      return value
    case (t1, t2):
      raise Exception('apply_cast unexpected ' + repr(src) + ' ' + repr(tgt))

def apply_inject(self, value, src):
  return Tagged(value, self.type_to_tag(src))

def apply_project(self, value, tgt):
    match value:
      case Tagged(val, tag) if self.type_to_tag(tgt) == tag:
        return val
      case _:
        raise Exception('apply_project, unexpected ' + repr(value))
```

Figure 11.13
The apply_cast auxiliary method.

```
class InterpLcast(InterpLany):
  def interp_exp(self, e, env):
    match e:
      case Cast(value, src, tgt):
        v = self.interp_exp(value, env)
        return self.apply_cast(v, src, tgt)
      case ValueExp(value):
        return value
      ...
      case _:
        return super().interp_exp(e, env)
```

Figure 11.14
The interpreter for $\mathcal{L}_{\mathsf{Cast}}$.

will need to have the same type, and that type will be the type of the conditional expression. Thus, each branch requires a `Cast` to convert from its type to the meet of the branches' types.

The case for the function call exhibits another interesting situation. If the function expression is of type `Any`, then it needs to be cast to a function type so that it can be used in a function call in $\mathcal{L}_{\mathsf{Cast}}$. Which function type should it be cast to? The parameter and return types are unknown, so we can simply use `Any` for all of them. Furthermore, in $\mathcal{L}_{\mathsf{Cast}}$ the argument types will need to exactly match the parameter types, so we must cast all the arguments to type `Any` (if they are not already of that type).

11.5   Lower Casts

The next step in the journey toward x86 is the `lower_casts` pass that translates the casts in $\mathcal{L}_{\mathsf{Cast}}$ to the lower-level `Inject` and `Project` operators and new operators for proxies, extending the $\mathcal{L}_{\lambda}$ language to $\mathcal{L}_{\mathsf{Proxy}}$. The $\mathcal{L}_{\mathsf{Proxy}}$ language can also be described as an extension of $\mathcal{L}_{\mathsf{Any}}$, with the addition of proxies. We recommend creating an auxiliary function named `lower_cast` that takes an expression (in $\mathcal{L}_{\mathsf{Cast}}$), a source type, and a target type and translates it to an expression in $\mathcal{L}_{\mathsf{Proxy}}$.

The `lower_cast` function can follow a code structure similar to the `apply_cast` function (figure 11.13) used in the interpreter for $\mathcal{L}_{\mathsf{Cast}}$, because it must handle the same cases as `apply_cast` and it needs to mimic the behavior of `apply_cast`. The most interesting cases concern the casts involving tuple, array, and function types.

As mentioned in section 11.2, a cast from one array type to another array type is accomplished by creating a proxy that intercepts the operations on the underlying array. Here we make the creation of the proxy explicit with the `ListProxy` AST node. It takes fives arguments: the first is an expression for the array, the second is a function for casting an element that is being read from the array, the third is a function for casting an element that is being written to the array, the fourth is the

```
def map_inplace(f : Callable[[int], int], v : list[Any]) -> void:
  i = 0
  while i != array_len(v):
    array_store(v, i, inject(f(project(array_load(v, i), int)), int))
    i = (i + 1)

def inc(x : int) -> int:
  return (x + 1)

def main() -> int:
  v = [0, 41]
  map_inplace(inc, array_proxy(v, list[int], list[Any]))
  print(array_load(v, 1))
  return 0
```

Figure 11.15
Output of `lower_casts` on the example shown in figure 11.11.

type of the underlying array, and the fifth is the type of the proxied array. You can
create the functions for reading and writing using lambda expressions.

A cast between two tuple types can be handled in a similar manner. We create a
proxy with the `TupleProxy` AST node. Tuples are immutable, so there is no need
for a function to cast the value during a write. Because there is a separate element
type for each slot in the tuple, we need more than one function for casting during
a read: we need a tuple of functions. Also, as we show in the next section, we need
to differentiate these tuples from the user-created ones, so we recommend using a
new AST node named `RawTuple` instead of `Tuple` to create the tuples of functions.
Figure 11.15 shows the output of `lower_casts` on the example given in figure 11.11
that involves casting an array of integers to an array of `Any`.

A cast from one function type to another function type is accomplished by generating a `lambda` whose parameter and return types match the target function type.
The body of the `lambda` should cast the parameters from the target type to the
source type. (Yes, backward! Functions are contravariant in the parameters.) After-
ward, call the underlying function and then cast the result from the source return
type to the target return type. Figure 11.16 shows the output of the `lower_casts`
pass on the `map` example given in figure 11.3. Note that the `inc` argument in the
call to `map` is wrapped in a `lambda`.

11.6   Differentiate Proxies

So far, the responsibility of differentiating tuples and tuple proxies has been the job
of the interpreter. In the `differentiate_proxies` pass we shift this responsibility
to the generated code.

We begin by designing the output language $\mathcal{L}_{POr}$. In $\mathcal{L}_?$ we used the type
`TupleType` for both real tuples and tuple proxies. Similarly, we use the type
`list` for both arrays and array proxies. In $\mathcal{L}_{POr}$ we return the `TupleType` type

```
def map(f : Callable[[int], int], v : tuple[int,int]) -> tuple[int,int]:
  return (f(v[0]), f(v[1]),)

def inc(x : any) -> any:
  return inject((project(x, int) + 1), int)

def main() -> int:
  t = map(lambda x: project(inc(inject(x, int)), int), (0, 41,))
  print(t[1])
  return 0
```

Figure 11.16
Output of `lower_casts` on the example shown in figure 11.3.

to its original meaning, as the type of just tuples, and we introduce a new type, `ProxyOrTupleType`, whose values can be either real tuples or tuple proxies. Likewise, we return the `ListType` type to its original meaning, as the type of arrays, and we introduce a new type, `ProxyOrListType`, whose values can be either arrays or array proxies. These new types come with a suite of new primitive operations.

A tuple proxy is represented by a tuple containing (1) the underlying tuple and (2) a tuple of functions for casting elements that are read from the tuple. The $\mathcal{L}_{POr}$ language includes the following AST classes and primitive functions.

InjectTuple
This AST node brands a tuple as a value of the `ProxyOrTupleType` type.

InjectTupleProxy
This AST node brands a tuple proxy as value of the `ProxyOrTupleType` type.

is_tuple_proxy
This primitive returns true if the value is a tuple proxy and false if it is a tuple.

project_tuple
Converts a tuple that is branded as `ProxyOrTupleType` back to a tuple.

proxy_tuple_len
Given a tuple proxy, returns the length of the underlying tuple.

proxy_tuple_load
Given a tuple proxy, returns the ith element of the underlying tuple.

An array proxy is represented by a tuple containing (1) the underlying array, (2) a function for casting elements that are read from the array, and (3) a function for casting elements that are written to the array. The $\mathcal{L}_{POr}$ language includes the following AST classes and primitive functions.

InjectList
This AST node brands an array as a value of the `ProxyOrListType` type.

InjectListProxy
This AST node brands an array proxy as a value of the `ProxyOrListType` type.

`is_array_proxy`
Returns true if the value is an array proxy and false if it is an array.

`project_array`
Converts an array that is branded as `ProxyOrListType` back to an array.

`proxy_array_len`
Given an array proxy, returns the length of the underlying array.

`proxy_array_load`
Given an array proxy, returns the ith element of the underlying array.

`proxy_array_store`
Given an array proxy, writes a value to the ith element of the underlying array.

Now we discuss the translation that differentiates tuples and arrays from proxies. First, every type annotation in the program is translated (recursively) to replace `TupleType` with `ProxyOrTupleType`. Next, we insert uses of `ProxyOrTupleType` operations in the appropriate places. For example, we wrap every tuple creation with an `InjectTuple`.

$\text{Tuple}(e_1, \ldots, e_n)$
$\Rightarrow$
$\text{InjectTuple}(\text{Tuple}(e'_1, \ldots, e'_n))$

The `RawTuple` AST node that we introduced in the previous section does not get injected.

$\text{RawTuple}(e_1, \ldots, e_n)$
$\Rightarrow$
$\text{Tuple}(e'_1, \ldots, e'_n)$

The `TupleProxy` AST translates as follows:

$\text{TupleProxy}(e_1, e_2, T_1, T_2)$
$\Rightarrow$
$\text{InjectTupleProxy}(\text{Tuple}(e'_1, e'_2, T'_1, T'_2))$

We translate the element access operations into conditional expressions that check whether the value is a proxy and then dispatch to either the appropriate proxy tuple operation or the regular tuple operation. Note that in the branch for a tuple, we must apply `project_tuple` before reading from the tuple.

The translation of array operations is similar to the ones for tuples.

11.7 Reveal Casts

Recall that the *tagof* function determines the bits used to identify values of different types, and it is used in the `reveal_casts` pass in the translation of `Project`. The `ProxyOrTupleType` and `ProxyOrListType` types can be mapped to 010 in binary (2 in decimal), just like the tuple and array types. Otherwise, the only other changes are adding cases that copy the new AST nodes.

11.8 Closure Conversion

The auxiliary function that translates type annotations needs to be updated to handle the `ProxyOrTupleType` and `ProxyOrListType` types. Otherwise, the only other changes are adding cases that copy the new AST nodes.

11.9 Select Instructions

Recall that the `select_instructions` pass is responsible for lowering the primitive operations into x86 instructions. So, we need to translate the new operations on `ProxyOrTupleType` and `ProxyOrListType` to x86. To do so, the first question we need to answer is how to differentiate between tuple and tuple proxies, and likewise for arrays and array proxies. We need just one bit to accomplish this; we use the bit in position 63 of the 64-bit tag at the front of every tuple (see figure 7.8) or array (section 7.9.1). So far, this bit has been set to 0, so for `InjectTuple` we leave it that way.

```
Assign([lhs], InjectTuple(e₁))
⇒
movq e₁′, lhs′
```

The translation for `InjectList` is also a move instruction. On the other hand, `InjectTupleProxy` sets bit 63 to 1.

```
Assign([lhs], InjectTupleProxy(e₁))
⇒
movq e₁′, %r11
movq (1 << 63), %rax
orq 0(%r11), %rax
movq %rax, 0(%r11)
movq %r11, lhs′
```

The translation for `InjectListProxy` should set bit 63 of the tag and also bit 62, to differentiate between arrays and tuples.

The `is_tuple_proxy` and `is_array_proxy` operations consume the information so carefully stashed away by the injections. It isolates bit 63 to tell whether the value is a proxy.

```
Assign([lhs], Call(Name('is_tuple_proxy'), [e₁]))
⇒
movq e₁′, %r11
movq 0(%r11), %rax
sarq $63, %rax
andq $1, %rax
movq %rax, lhs′
```

The `project_tuple` and `project_array` operations are straightforward to translate, so we leave that to the reader.

Regarding the element access operations for tuples and arrays, the runtime provides procedures that implement them (they are recursive functions!), so here we simply need to translate these tuple operations into the appropriate function call. For example, here is the translation for `proxy_tuple_load`.

```
Assign([lhs], Call(Name('proxy_tuple_load'), [e₁, e₂]))
⇒
movq e₁′, %rdi
movq e₂′, %rsi
callq proxy_vector_ref
movq %rax, lhs′
```

We translate `proxy_array_load` to `proxy_vecof_ref`, `proxy_array_store` to `proxy_vecof_set`, and `proxy_array_len` to `proxy_vecof_length`.

We have another batch of operations to deal with: those for the `Any` type. Recall that we generate an `any_load_unsafe` when there is a element access on something of type `Any`, and similarly for `any_store_unsafe` and `any_len`. In section 10.10 we selected instructions for these operations on the basis of the idea that the underlying value was a tuple or array. But in the current setting, the underlying value is of type `ProxyOrTupleType` or `ProxyOrListType`. We have added three runtime functions to deal with this: `proxy_vector_ref`, `proxy_vector_set`, and `proxy_vector_length` that inspect bit 62 of the tag to determine whether the value is a proxy, and then dispatches to the the appropriate code. So `any_load_unsafe` can be translated as follows. We begin by projecting the underlying value out of the tagged value and then call the `proxy_vector_ref` procedure in the runtime.

```
Assign([lhs], Call(Name('any_load_unsafe'), [e₁, e₂]))
⇒
movq ¬111, %rdi
andq e₁′, %rdi
movq e₂′, %rsi
callq proxy_vector_ref
movq %rax, lhs′
```

The `any_store_unsafe` and `any_len` operators are translated in a similar way. Alternatively, you could generate instructions to open-code the `proxy_vector_ref`, `proxy_vector_set`, and `proxy_vector_length` functions.

Exercise 11.1 Implement a compiler for the gradually typed $\mathcal{L}_?$ language by extending and adapting your compiler for $\mathcal{L}_\lambda$. Create ten new partially typed test programs. In addition to testing with these new programs, test your compiler on all the tests for $\mathcal{L}_\lambda$ and for $\mathcal{L}_{\text{Dyn}}$. Sometimes you may get a type-checking error on the $\mathcal{L}_{\text{Dyn}}$ programs, but you can adapt them by inserting a temporary variable of type `Any` that is initialized with the troublesome expression.

Figure 11.17 provides an overview of the passes needed for the compilation of $\mathcal{L}_?$.

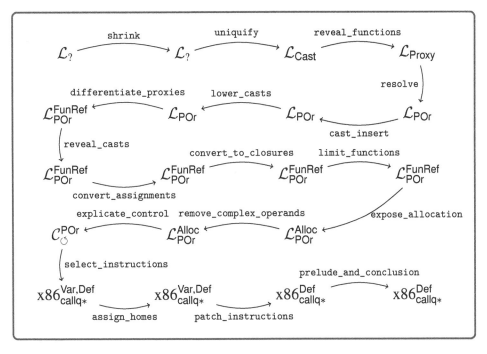

Figure 11.17
Diagram of the passes for $\mathcal{L}_?$ (gradual typing).

11.10 Further Reading

This chapter just scratches the surface of gradual typing. The basic approach described here is missing two key ingredients that one would want in an implementation of gradual typing: blame tracking (Tobin-Hochstadt and Felleisen 2006; Wadler and Findler 2009) and space-efficient casts (Herman, Tomb, and Flanagan 2007, 2010). The problem addressed by blame tracking is that when a cast on a higher-order value fails, it often does so at a point in the program that is far removed from the original cast. Blame tracking is a technique for propagating extra information through casts and proxies so that when a cast fails, the error message can point back to the original location of the cast in the source program.

The problem addressed by space-efficient casts also relates to higher-order casts. It turns out that in partially typed programs, a function or tuple can flow through a great many casts at runtime. With the approach described in this chapter, each cast adds another **lambda** wrapper or a tuple proxy. Not only does this take up considerable space, but it also makes the function calls and tuple operations slow. For example, a partially typed version of quicksort could, in the worst case, build a chain of proxies of length $O(n)$ around the tuple, changing the overall time complexity of the algorithm from $O(n^2)$ to $O(n^3)$! Herman, Tomb, and Flanagan (2007) suggested a solution to this problem by representing casts using the coercion calculus of Henglein (1994), which prevents the creation of long chains of proxies by compressing them into a concise normal form. Siek, Thiemann, and Wadler (2015) give an algorithm for compressing coercions, and Kuhlenschmidt, Almahallawi, and Siek (2019) show how to implement these ideas in the Grift compiler:

https://github.com/Gradual-Typing/Grift

There are also interesting interactions between gradual typing and other language features, such as generics, information-flow types, and type inference, to name a few. We recommend to the reader the online gradual typing bibliography for more material:

http://samth.github.io/gradual-typing-bib/

12 Generics

This chapter studies the compilation of generics (aka parametric polymorphism), compiling the $\mathcal{L}_{\mathsf{Gen}}$ subset of Python. Generics enable programmers to make code more reusable by parameterizing functions and data structures with respect to the types on which they operate. For example, figure 12.1 revisits the map example and this time gives it a more fitting type. This map function is parameterized with respect to the element type of the tuple. The type of map is the following generic type specified by the All type with parameter T:

```
All[[T], Callable[[Callable[[T],T], tuple[T,T]], tuple[T,T]]]
```

The idea is that map can be used at *all* choices of a type for parameter T. In the example shown in figure 12.1 we apply map to a tuple of integers, implicitly choosing int for T, but we could have just as well applied map to a tuple of Booleans. A *monomorphic* function is simply one that is not generic. We use the term *instantiation* for the process (within the language implementation) of turning a generic function into a monomorphic one, where the type parameters have been replaced by types.

In Python, when writing a generic function such as map, one does not explicitly write its generic type (using All). Instead, that the function is generic is implied by the use of type variables (such as T) in the type annotations of its parameters.

```
def map(f : Callable[[T],T], tup : tuple[T,T]) -> tuple[T,T]:
  return (f(tup[0]), f(tup[1]))

def add1(x : int) -> int:
  return x + 1

t = map(add1, (0, 41))
print(t[1])
```

Figure 12.1
A generic version of the map function.

exp	::=	*int* | input_int() | - *exp* | *exp* + *exp* | *exp* - *exp* | (*exp*)
stmt	::=	print(*exp*) | *exp*
exp	::=	*var*
stmt	::=	*var* = *exp*
cmp	::=	== | != | < | <= | > | >=
exp	::=	True | False | *exp* and *exp* | *exp* or *exp* | not *exp*
	|	*exp* *cmp* *exp* | *exp* if *exp* else *exp*
stmt	::=	if *exp*: *stmt*⁺ else: *stmt*⁺
stmt	::=	while *exp*: *stmt*⁺
cmp	::=	is
exp	::=	*exp*, ... , *exp* | *exp*[*int*] | len(*exp*)
type	::=	int | bool | void | tuple[*type*⁺] | Callable[[*type*, ...], *type*]
exp	::=	*exp*(*exp*, ...)
stmt	::=	return *exp*
def	::=	def *var*(*var*:*type*, ...) -> *type*: *stmt*⁺
exp	::=	lambda *var*, ... : *exp* | arity(*exp*)
stmt	::=	*var* : *type* = *exp*
type	::=	All[[*var* ...], *type*] | *var*
$\mathcal{L}_{\mathsf{Gen}}$	::=	*def* ... *stmt* ...

Figure 12.2
The concrete syntax of $\mathcal{L}_{\mathsf{Gen}}$, extending $\mathcal{L}_\lambda$ (figure 9.3).

Figure 12.2 presents the definition of the concrete syntax of $\mathcal{L}_{\mathsf{Gen}}$, and figure 12.3 shows the definition of the abstract syntax. The grammar for types is extended to include the type of a generic (All) and type variables (GenericVar in the abstract syntax).

By including the All type in the *type* nonterminal of the grammar we choose to make generics first class, which has interesting repercussions on the compiler.[1] Many languages with generics, such as C++ (Stroustrup 1988) and Standard ML (Milner, Tofte, and Harper 1990), support only second-class generics, so it may be helpful to see an example of first-class generics in action. In figure 12.4 we define a function apply_twice whose parameter is a generic function. Indeed, because the grammar for *type* includes the All type, a generic function may also be returned from a function or stored inside a tuple. The body of apply_twice applies the generic function f to a Boolean and also to an integer, which would not be possible if f were not generic.

The type checker for $\mathcal{L}_{\mathsf{Gen}}$ shown in figure 12.5 has several new responsibilities (compared to $\mathcal{L}_\lambda$) which we discuss in the following paragraphs.

Regarding function definitions, if the type annotations on its parameters contain generic variables, then the function is generic and therefore its type is an All type wrapped around a function type. Otherwise the function is monomorphic and its type is simply a function type.

---

1. The Python typing library does not include syntax for the All type. It is inferred for functions whose type annotations contain type variables.

$$
\begin{array}{rcl}
\textit{exp} & ::= & \texttt{Constant}(\textit{int}) \mid \texttt{Call(Name('input\_int'),[])} \\
& \mid & \texttt{UnaryOp(USub(),}\textit{exp}\texttt{)} \mid \texttt{BinOp(}\textit{exp}\texttt{,Add(),}\textit{exp}\texttt{)} \\
& \mid & \texttt{BinOp(}\textit{exp}\texttt{,Sub(),}\textit{exp}\texttt{)} \\
\textit{stmt} & ::= & \texttt{Expr(Call(Name('print'),[}\textit{exp}\texttt{]))} \mid \texttt{Expr(}\textit{exp}\texttt{)} \\
\hline
\textit{exp} & ::= & \texttt{Name(}\textit{var}\texttt{)} \\
\textit{stmt} & ::= & \texttt{Assign([Name(}\textit{var}\texttt{)],}\ \textit{exp}\texttt{)} \\
\hline
\textit{boolop} & ::= & \texttt{And()} \mid \texttt{Or()} \\
\textit{cmp} & ::= & \texttt{Eq()} \mid \texttt{NotEq()} \mid \texttt{Lt()} \mid \texttt{LtE()} \mid \texttt{Gt()} \mid \texttt{GtE()} \\
\textit{bool} & ::= & \texttt{True} \mid \texttt{False} \\
\textit{exp} & ::= & \texttt{Constant(}\textit{bool}\texttt{)} \mid \texttt{BoolOp(}\textit{boolop}\texttt{,[}\textit{exp}\texttt{,}\textit{exp}\texttt{])} \\
& \mid & \texttt{UnaryOp(Not(),}\textit{exp}\texttt{)} \mid \texttt{Compare(}\textit{exp}\texttt{,[}\textit{cmp}\texttt{],[}\textit{exp}\texttt{])} \\
& \mid & \texttt{IfExp(}\textit{exp}\texttt{,}\textit{exp}\texttt{,}\textit{exp}\texttt{)} \\
\textit{stmt} & ::= & \texttt{If(}\textit{exp}\texttt{, }\textit{stmt}^{+}\texttt{, }\textit{stmt}^{+}\texttt{)} \\
\hline
\textit{stmt} & ::= & \texttt{While(}\textit{exp}\texttt{, }\textit{stmt}^{+}\texttt{, [])} \\
\hline
\textit{cmp} & ::= & \texttt{Is()} \\
\textit{exp} & ::= & \texttt{Tuple(}\textit{exp}^{+}\texttt{,Load())} \mid \texttt{Subscript(}\textit{exp}\texttt{,Constant(}\textit{int}\texttt{),Load())} \\
& \mid & \texttt{Call(Name('len'),[}\textit{exp}\texttt{])} \\
\hline
\textit{type} & ::= & \texttt{IntType()} \mid \texttt{BoolType()} \mid \texttt{VoidType()} \mid \texttt{TupleType[}\textit{type}^{+}\texttt{]} \\
& \mid & \texttt{FunctionType(}\textit{type}^{*}\texttt{, }\textit{type}\texttt{)} \\
\textit{exp} & ::= & \texttt{Call(}\textit{exp}\texttt{, }\textit{exp}^{*}\texttt{)} \\
\textit{stmt} & ::= & \texttt{Return(}\textit{exp}\texttt{)} \\
\textit{params} & ::= & \texttt{(}\textit{var}\texttt{,}\textit{type}\texttt{)}^{*} \\
\textit{def} & ::= & \texttt{FunctionDef(}\textit{var}\texttt{, }\textit{params}\texttt{, }\textit{stmt}^{+}\texttt{, None, }\textit{type}\texttt{, None)} \\
\textit{exp} & ::= & \texttt{Lambda(}\textit{var}^{*}\texttt{, }\textit{exp}\texttt{)} \mid \texttt{Call(Name('arity'), [}\textit{exp}\texttt{])} \\
\textit{stmt} & ::= & \texttt{AnnAssign(}\textit{var}\texttt{, }\textit{type}\texttt{, }\textit{exp}\texttt{, 0)} \\
\hline
\textit{type} & ::= & \texttt{AllType([}\textit{var}\ldots\texttt{],}\textit{type}\texttt{)} \mid \texttt{GenericVar(}\textit{var}\texttt{)} \\
\mathcal{L}_{\textsf{Gen}} & ::= & \texttt{Module([}\textit{def}\ldots\textit{stmt}\ldots\texttt{])}
\end{array}
$$

Figure 12.3
The abstract syntax of $\mathcal{L}_{\textsf{Gen}}$, extending $\mathcal{L}_{\lambda}$ (figure 9.4).

```
def apply_twice(f : All[[U], Callable[[U],U]]) -> int:
  if f(True):
    return f(42)
  else:
    return f(777)

def id(x: T) -> T:
  return x

print(apply_twice(id))
```

Figure 12.4
An example illustrating first-class generics.

The type checking of a function application is extended to handle the case in which the operator expression is a generic function. In that case the type arguments are deduced by matching the types of the parameters with the types of the arguments. The `match_types` auxiliary function (figure 12.6) carries out this deduction by recursively descending through a parameter type `param_ty` and the corresponding argument type `arg_ty`, making sure that they are equal except when there is a type parameter in the parameter type. Upon encountering a type parameter for the first time, the algorithm deduces an association of the type parameter to the corresponding part of the argument type. If it is not the first time that the type parameter has been encountered, the algorithm looks up its deduced type and makes sure that it is equal to the corresponding part of the argument type. The return type of the application is the return type of the generic function with the type parameters replaced by the deduced type arguments, using the `substitute_type` auxiliary function, which is also listed in figure 12.6.

The type checker extends type equality to handle the `All` type. This is not quite as simple as for other types, such as function and tuple types, because two `All` types can be syntactically different even though they are equivalent. For example,

$$\text{All[[T], Callable[[T], T]]}$$

is equivalent to

$$\text{All[[U], Callable[[U], U]]}.$$

Two generic types are equal if they differ only in the choice of the names of the type parameters. The definition of type equality shown in figure 12.6 renames the type parameters in one type to match the type parameters of the other type.

```
def type_check_exp(self, e, env):
  match e:
    case Call(Name(f), args) if f in builtin_functions:
      return super().type_check_exp(e, env)
    case Call(func, args):
      func_t = self.type_check_exp(func, env)
      func.has_type = func_t
      match func_t:
        case AllType(ps, FunctionType(p_tys, rt)):
          for arg in args:
            arg.has_type = self.type_check_exp(arg, env)
          arg_tys = [arg.has_type for arg in args]
          deduced = {}
          for (p, a) in zip(p_tys, arg_tys):
            self.match_types(p, a, deduced, e)
          return self.substitute_type(rt, deduced)
        case _:
          return super().type_check_exp(e, env)
    case _:
      return super().type_check_exp(e, env)

def type_check(self, p):
  match p:
    case Module(body):
      env = {}
      for s in body:
        match s:
          case FunctionDef(name, params, bod, dl, returns, comment):
            params_t = [t for (x,t) in params]
            ty_params = set()
            for t in params_t:
              ty_params |= self.generic_variables(t)
            ty = FunctionType(params_t, returns)
            if len(ty_params) > 0:
              ty = AllType(list(ty_params), ty)
            env[name] = ty
      self.check_stmts(body, IntType(), env)
    case _:
      raise Exception('type_check: unexpected ' + repr(p))
```

Figure 12.5
Type checker for the $\mathcal{L}_{\text{Gen}}$ language.

```
def match_types(self, param_ty, arg_ty, deduced, e):
  match (param_ty, arg_ty):
    case (GenericVar(id), _):
      if id in deduced:
        self.check_type_equal(arg_ty, deduced[id], e)
      else:
        deduced[id] = arg_ty
    case (AllType(ps, ty), AllType(arg_ps, arg_ty)):
      rename = {ap:p for (ap,p) in zip(arg_ps, ps)}
      new_arg_ty = self.substitute_type(arg_ty, rename)
      self.match_types(ty, new_arg_ty, deduced, e)
    case (TupleType(ps), TupleType(ts)):
      for (p, a) in zip(ps, ts):
        self.match_types(p, a, deduced, e)
    case (ListType(p), ListType(a)):
      self.match_types(p, a, deduced, e)
    case (FunctionType(pps, prt), FunctionType(aps, art)):
      for (pp, ap) in zip(pps, aps):
        self.match_types(pp, ap, deduced, e)
      self.match_types(prt, art, deduced, e)
    case (IntType(), IntType()):
      pass
    case (BoolType(), BoolType()):
      pass
    case _:
      raise Exception('mismatch: ' + str(param_ty) + '\n!= ' + str(arg_ty))

def substitute_type(self, ty, var_map):
  match ty:
    case GenericVar(id):
      return var_map[id]
    case AllType(ps, ty):
      new_map = copy.deepcopy(var_map)
      for p in ps:
        new_map[p] = GenericVar(p)
      return AllType(ps, self.substitute_type(ty, new_map))
    case TupleType(ts):
      return TupleType([self.substitute_type(t, var_map) for t in ts])
    case ListType(ty):
      return ListType(self.substitute_type(ty, var_map))
    case FunctionType(pts, rt):
      return FunctionType([self.substitute_type(p, var_map) for p in pts],
                          self.substitute_type(rt, var_map))
    case IntType():
      return IntType()
    case BoolType():
      return BoolType()
    case _:
      raise Exception('substitute_type: unexpected ' + repr(ty))

def check_type_equal(self, t1, t2, e):
  match (t1, t2):
    case (AllType(ps1, ty1), AllType(ps2, ty2)):
      rename = {p2: GenericVar(p1) for (p1,p2) in zip(ps1,ps2)}
      return self.check_type_equal(ty1, self.substitute_type(ty2, rename), e)
    case (_, _):
      return super().check_type_equal(t1, t2, e)
```

Figure 12.6
Auxiliary functions for type checking $\mathcal{L}_{\mathsf{Gen}}$.

12.1 Compiling Generics

Broadly speaking, there are four approaches to compiling generics, as follows:

Monomorphization generates a different version of a generic function for each
set of type arguments with which it is used, producing type-specialized code.
This approach results in the most efficient code but requires whole-program
compilation (no separate compilation) and may increase code size. Unfortunately, monomorphization is incompatible with first-class generics because it is
not always possible to determine which generic functions are used with which
type arguments during compilation. (It can be done at runtime with just-in-time
compilation.) Monomorphization is used to compile C++ templates (Stroustrup
1988) and generic functions in NESL (Blelloch et al. 1993) and ML (Weeks 2006).

Uniform representation generates one version of each generic function and requires
all values to have a common *boxed* format, such as the tagged values of type Any
in $\mathcal{L}_{\mathsf{Any}}$. Both generic and monomorphic code is compiled similarly to code in
a dynamically typed language (like $\mathcal{L}_{\mathsf{Dyn}}$), in which primitive operators require
their arguments to be projected from Any and their results to be injected into Any.
(In object-oriented languages, the projection is accomplished via virtual method
dispatch.) The uniform representation approach is compatible with separate compilation and with first-class generics. However, it produces the least efficient code
because it introduces overhead in the entire program. This approach is used in
Java (Bracha et al. 1998), CLU (Liskov et al. 1979; Liskov 1993), and some
implementations of ML (Cardelli 1984; Appel and MacQueen 1987).

Mixed representation generates one version of each generic function, using a boxed
representation for type variables. However, monomorphic code is compiled as
usual (as in $\mathcal{L}_\lambda$), and conversions are performed at the boundaries between
monomorphic code and polymorphic code (for example, when a generic function
is instantiated and called). This approach is compatible with separate compilation and first-class generics and maintains efficiency in monomorphic code.
The trade-off is increased overhead at the boundary between monomorphic and
generic code. This approach is used in implementations of ML (Leroy 1992) and
Java, starting in Java 5 with the addition of autoboxing.

Type passing uses the unboxed representation in both monomorphic and generic
code. Each generic function is compiled to a single function with extra parameters
that describe the type arguments. The type information is used by the generated
code to determine how to access the unboxed values at runtime. This approach
is used in implementation of Napier88 (Morrison et al. 1991) and ML (Harper
and Morrisett 1995). Type passing is compatible with separate compilation and
first-class generics and maintains the efficiency for monomorphic code. There is
runtime overhead in polymorphic code from dispatching on type information.

In this chapter we use the mixed representation approach, partly because of its
favorable attributes and partly because it is straightforward to implement using the
tools that we have already built to support gradual typing. The work of compiling

generic functions is performed in two passes, `resolve` and `erase_types`, that we discuss next. The output of `erase_types` is $\mathcal{L}_{\mathsf{Cast}}$ (section 11.4), so the rest of the compilation is handled by the compiler of chapter 11.

12.2   Resolve Instantiation

Recall that the type checker for $\mathcal{L}_{\mathsf{Gen}}$ deduces the type arguments at call sites to a generic function. The purpose of the `resolve` pass is to turn this implicit instantiation into an explicit one, by adding `inst` nodes to the syntax of the intermediate language. An `inst` node records the mapping of type parameters to type arguments. The semantics of the `inst` node is to instantiate the result of its first argument, a generic function, to produce a monomorphic function. However, because the interpreter never analyzes type annotations, instantiation can be a no-op and simply return the generic function. The output language of the `resolve` pass is $\mathcal{L}_{\mathsf{Inst}}$, for which the definition is shown in figure 12.7.

The output of the `resolve` pass on the generic `map` example is listed in figure 12.8. Note that the use of `map` is wrapped in an `inst` node, with the parameter T chosen to be `int`.

12.3   Erase Generic Types

We use the `Any` type presented in chapter 10 to represent type variables. For example, figure 12.9 shows the output of the `erase_types` pass on the generic `map` (figure 12.1). The occurrences of type parameter T are replaced by `Any`, and the generic `All` types are removed from the type of `map`.

This process of type erasure creates a challenge at points of instantiation. For example, consider the instantiation of `map` shown in figure 12.8. The type of `map` is

`All[[T], Callable[[Callable[[T], T], tuple[T, T]], tuple[T, T]]]`

and it is instantiated to

`Callable[[Callable[[int], int], tuple[int, int]], tuple[int, int]]`

After erasure, the type of `map` is

`Callable[[Callable[[Any], Any], tuple[Any, Any]], tuple[Any, Any]]`

but we need to convert it to the instantiated type. This is easy to do in the language $\mathcal{L}_{\mathsf{Cast}}$ with a single `cast`. In the example shown in figure 12.9, the instantiation of `map` has been compiled to a `cast` from the type of `map` to the instantiated type. The source and the target type of a cast must be consistent (figure 11.4), which indeed is the case because both the source and target are obtained from the same generic type of `map`, replacing the type parameters with `Any` in the former and with the deduced type arguments in the latter. (Recall that the `Any` type is consistent with any type.)

$$
\begin{array}{rcl}
exp & ::= & \texttt{Constant}(\mathit{int}) \mid \texttt{Call(Name('input\_int'),[])} \\
& \mid & \texttt{UnaryOp(USub()},exp\texttt{)} \mid \texttt{BinOp(}exp\texttt{,Add()},exp\texttt{)} \\
& \mid & \texttt{BinOp(}exp\texttt{,Sub()},exp\texttt{)} \\
stmt & ::= & \texttt{Expr(Call(Name('print'),[}exp\texttt{]))} \mid \texttt{Expr(}exp\texttt{)} \\
\hline
exp & ::= & \texttt{Name(}var\texttt{)} \\
stmt & ::= & \texttt{Assign([Name(}var\texttt{)]}, exp\texttt{)} \\
\hline
boolop & ::= & \texttt{And()} \mid \texttt{Or()} \\
cmp & ::= & \texttt{Eq()} \mid \texttt{NotEq()} \mid \texttt{Lt()} \mid \texttt{LtE()} \mid \texttt{Gt()} \mid \texttt{GtE()} \\
bool & ::= & \texttt{True} \mid \texttt{False} \\
exp & ::= & \texttt{Constant(}bool\texttt{)} \mid \texttt{BoolOp(}boolop\texttt{,[}exp\texttt{,}exp\texttt{])} \\
& \mid & \texttt{UnaryOp(Not()},exp\texttt{)} \mid \texttt{Compare(}exp\texttt{,[}cmp\texttt{],[}exp\texttt{])} \\
& \mid & \texttt{IfExp(}exp\texttt{,}exp\texttt{,}exp\texttt{)} \\
stmt & ::= & \texttt{If(}exp,\ stmt^{+},\ stmt^{+}\texttt{)} \\
\hline
stmt & ::= & \texttt{While(}exp,\ stmt^{+},\ \texttt{[])} \\
\hline
cmp & ::= & \texttt{Is()} \\
exp & ::= & \texttt{Tuple(}exp^{+}\texttt{,Load())} \mid \texttt{Subscript(}exp\texttt{,Constant(}\mathit{int}\texttt{),Load())} \\
& \mid & \texttt{Call(Name('len'),[}exp\texttt{])} \\
\hline
type & ::= & \texttt{IntType()} \mid \texttt{BoolType()} \mid \texttt{VoidType()} \mid \texttt{TupleType[}type^{+}\texttt{]} \\
& \mid & \texttt{FunctionType(}type^{*},\ type\texttt{)} \\
exp & ::= & \texttt{Call(}exp,\ exp^{*}\texttt{)} \\
stmt & ::= & \texttt{Return(}exp\texttt{)} \\
params & ::= & (var,type)^{*} \\
def & ::= & \texttt{FunctionDef(}var,\ params,\ stmt^{+},\ \texttt{None},\ type,\ \texttt{None)} \\
\hline
exp & ::= & \texttt{Lambda(}var^{*},\ exp\texttt{)} \mid \texttt{Call(Name('arity'),[}exp\texttt{])} \\
stmt & ::= & \texttt{AnnAssign(}var,\ type,\ exp,\ 0\texttt{)} \\
\hline
type & ::= & \texttt{AllType([}var\dots\texttt{]},type\texttt{)} \mid var \\
exp & ::= & \texttt{Inst(}exp,\ \{var\texttt{:}type\dots\}\texttt{)} \\
\mathcal{L}_{\mathsf{Inst}} & ::= & \texttt{Module([}def\dots stmt\dots\texttt{])}
\end{array}
$$

Figure 12.7
The abstract syntax of $\mathcal{L}_{\mathsf{Inst}}$, extending $\mathcal{L}_\lambda$ (figure 9.4).

```
def map(f : Callable[[T],T], tup : tuple[T,T]) -> tuple[T,T]:
    return (f(tup[0]), f(tup[1]))

def add1(x : int) -> int:
    return x + 1

t = inst(map, {T: int})(add1, (0, 41))
print(t[1])
```

Figure 12.8
Output of the `resolve` pass on the `map` example.

```
def map(f : Callable[[Any],Any], tup : tuple[Any,Any])-> tuple[Any,Any]:
  return (f(tup[0]), f(tup[1]))

def add1(x : int) -> int:
  return (x + 1)

def main() -> int:
  t = cast(map, T₁, T₂)(add1, (0, 41))
  print(t[1])
  return 0

where
T₁ = Callable[[Callable[[Any], Any],tuple[Any,Any]], tuple[Any,Any]]
T₂ = Callable[[Callable[[int], int],tuple[int,int]], tuple[int,int]]
```

Figure 12.9
The generic map example after type erasure.

To implement the **erase_types** pass, we first recommend defining a recursive function that translates types, named **erase_type**. It replaces type variables with Any as follows.

GenericVar(T)
$\Rightarrow$
Any

The **erase_type** function also removes the generic All types.

AllType(xs, T_1)
$\Rightarrow$
T_1'

where T_1' is the result of applying **erase_type** to T_1. In this compiler pass, apply the **erase_type** function to all the type annotations in the program.

Regarding the translation of expressions, the case for **Inst** is the interesting one. We translate it into a **Cast**, as shown next. The type of the subexpression e is a generic type of the form AllType(xs, T). The source type of the cast is the erasure of T, the type T_s. The target type T_t is the result of substituting the deduced argument types d in T and then performing type erasure.

Inst(e, d)
$\Rightarrow$
Cast(e', T_s, T_t)

where T_t = erase_type(substitute_type(d, T)).

Finally, each generic function is translated to a regular function in which type erasure has been applied to all the type annotations and the body.

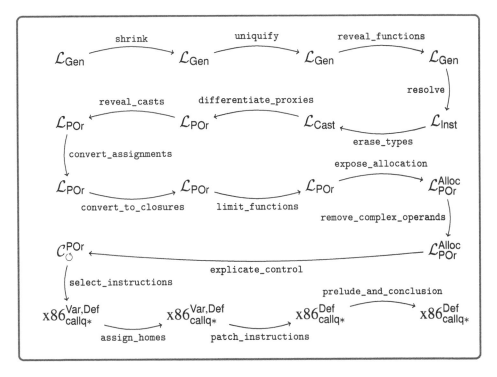

Figure 12.10
Diagram of the passes for $\mathcal{L}_{\mathsf{Gen}}$ (generics).

Exercise 12.1 Implement a compiler for the polymorphic language $\mathcal{L}_{\mathsf{Gen}}$ by extending and adapting your compiler for $\mathcal{L}_?$. Create six new test programs that use polymorphic functions. Some of them should make use of first-class generics.

Figure 12.10 provides an overview of the passes needed to compile $\mathcal{L}_{\mathsf{Gen}}$.

A Appendix

A.1 x86 Instruction Set Quick Reference

Table A.1 lists some x86 instructions and what they do. We write $A \rightarrow B$ to mean that the value of A is written into location B. Address offsets are given in bytes. The instruction arguments A, B, C can be immediate constants (such as $4), registers (such as %rax), or memory references (such as -4(%ebp)). Most x86 instructions allow at most one memory reference per instruction. Other operands must be immediates or registers.

Table A.1
Quick reference for the x86 instructions used in this book.

Instruction	Operation
addq A, B	$A + B \rightarrow B$
negq A	$-A \rightarrow A$
subq A, B	$B - A \rightarrow B$
imulq A, B	$A \times B \rightarrow B$ (B must be a register).
callq L	Pushes the return address and jumps to label L.
callq $*A$	Calls the function at the address A.
retq	Pops the return address and jumps to it.
popq A	$*\text{rsp} \rightarrow A$; $\text{rsp} + 8 \rightarrow \text{rsp}$
pushq A	$\text{rsp} - 8 \rightarrow \text{rsp}$; $A \rightarrow *\text{rsp}$
leaq A, B	$A \rightarrow B$ (B must be a register.)
cmpq A, B	Compare A and B and set the flag register (B must not be an immediate).
je L jl L jle L jg L jge L	Jump to label L if the flag register matches the condition code of the instruction; otherwise go to the next instructions. The condition codes are e for *equal*, l for *less*, le for *less or equal*, g for *greater*, and ge for *greater or equal*.
jmp L	Jump to label L.
movq A, B	$A \rightarrow B$
movzbq A, B	$A \rightarrow B$, where A is a single-byte register (e.g., al or cl), B is an 8-byte register, and the extra bytes of B are set to zero.
notq A	$\sim A \rightarrow A$ (bitwise complement)
orq A, B	$A \mid B \rightarrow B$ (bitwise-or)
andq A, B	$A \& B \rightarrow B$ (bitwise-and)
salq A, B	$B \ll A \rightarrow B$ (arithmetic shift left, where A is a constant)
sarq A, B	$B \gg A \rightarrow B$ (arithmetic shift right, where A is a constant)
sete A setl A setle A setg A setge A	If the flag matches the condition code, then $1 \rightarrow A$; else $0 \rightarrow A$. Refer to je for the description of the condition codes. A must be a single byte register (e.g., al or cl).

References

Abelson, Harold, and Gerald J. Sussman. 1996. *Structure and Interpretation of Computer Programs.* 2nd edition. MIT Press.

Aho, Alfred V., Monica S. Lam, Ravi Sethi, and Jeffrey D. Ullman. 2006. *Compilers: Principles, Techniques, and Tools.* 2nd edition. Addison-Wesley Longman.

Allen, Frances E. 1970. "Control Flow Analysis." In *Proceedings of a Symposium on Compiler Optimization,* 1–19. Association for Computing Machinery.

Anderson, Christopher, and Sophia Drossopoulou. 2003. "BabyJ: From Object Based to Class Based Programming via Types." *Electron. Notes Theor. Comput. Sci.* 82 (8): 53–81.

Anderson, T., J. Eve, and J. Horning. 1973. "Efficient LR(1) Parsers." *Acta Informatica* 2:2–39.

Appel, Andrew W. 1989. "Runtime Tags Aren't Necessary." *LISP and Symbolic Computation* 2 (2): 153–162.

Appel, Andrew W. 1990. "A Runtime System." *LISP and Symbolic Computation* 3 (4): 343–380.

Appel, Andrew W. 1991. *Compiling with Continuations.* Cambridge University Press.

Appel, Andrew W., and David B. MacQueen. 1987. "A Standard ML Compiler." In *Functional Programming Languages and Computer Architecture,* 301–324. Springer.

Appel, Andrew W., and Jens Palsberg. 2003. *Modern Compiler Implementation in Java.* Cambridge University Press.

Backus, J. W., F. L. Bauer, J. Green, C. Katz, J. McCarthy, A. J. Perlis, H. Rutishauser, et al. 1960. "Report on the Algorithmic Language ALGOL 60." Edited by Peter Naur. *Commun. ACM* 3 (5): 299–314.

Backus, John. 1978. "The History of Fortran I, II, and III." In *History of Programming Languages,* 25–74. Association for Computing Machinery.

Baker, J., A. Cunei, T. Kalibera, F. Pizlo, and J. Vitek. 2009. "Accurate Garbage Collection in Uncooperative Environments Revisited." *Concurr. Comput.: Pract. Exper.* 21 (12): 1572–1606.

Balakrishnan, V. K. 1996. *Introductory Discrete Mathematics.* Dover.

Barry, Paul. 2016. *Head First Python.* O'Reilly.

Blackburn, Stephen M., Perry Cheng, and Kathryn S. McKinley. 2004. "Myths and Realities: The Performance Impact of Garbage Collection." In *Proceedings of the Joint International Conference on Measurement and Modeling of Computer Systems, SIGMETRICS '04/Performance '04,* 25–36. Association for Computing Machinery.

Blelloch, Guy E., Jonathan C. Hardwick, Siddhartha Chatterjee, Jay Sipelstein, and Marco Zagha. 1993. "Implementation of a Portable Nested Data-Parallel Language." In *Proceedings of the Fourth ACM SIGPLAN Symposium on Principles and Practice of Parallel Programming, PPOPP '93,* 102–111. Association for Computing Machinery.

Bracha, Gilad, Martin Odersky, David Stoutamire, and Philip Wadler. 1998. "Making the Future Safe for the Past: Adding Genericity to the Java Programming Language." In *Proceedings of the 13th ACM SIGPLAN Conference on Object-Oriented Programming, Systems, Languages, and Applications, OOPSLA '98,* 183–200. Association for Computing Machinery.

Brélaz, Daniel. 1979. "New Methods to Color the Vertices of a Graph." *Commun. ACM* 22 (4): 251–256.

Briggs, Preston, Keith D. Cooper, and Linda Torczon. 1994. "Improvements to Graph Coloring Register Allocation." *ACM Trans. Program. Lang. Syst.* 16 (3): 428–455.

Bryant, Randal, and David O'Hallaron. 2005. *x86-64 Machine-Level Programming.* Carnegie Mellon University.

Bryant, Randal, and David O'Hallaron. 2010. *Computer Systems: A Programmer's Perspective.* 2nd edition. Addison-Wesley.

Cardelli, Luca. 1983. *The Functional Abstract Machine.* Technical report TR-107. AT&T Bell Laboratories.

Cardelli, Luca. 1984. "Compiling a Functional Language." In *ACM Symposium on LISP and Functional Programming, LFP '84,* 208–221. Association for Computing Machinery.

Cardelli, Luca, and Peter Wegner. 1985. "On Understanding Types, Data Abstraction, and Polymorphism." *ACM Comput. Surv.* 17 (4): 471–523.

Chaitin, G. J. 1982. "Register Allocation & Spilling via Graph Coloring." In *SIGPLAN '82: Proceedings of the 1982 SIGPLAN Symposium on Compiler Construction,* 98–105. Association for Computing Machinery.

Chaitin, Gregory J., Marc A. Auslander, Ashok K. Chandra, John Cocke, Martin E. Hopkins, and Peter W. Markstein. 1981. "Register Allocation via Coloring." *Computer Languages* 6:47–57.

Cheney, C. J. 1970. "A Nonrecursive List Compacting Algorithm." *Commun. of the ACM* 13 (11).

Chow, Frederick, and John Hennessy. 1984. "Register Allocation by Priority-Based Coloring." In *Proceedings of the 1984 SIGPLAN Symposium on Compiler Construction,* 222–232. Association for Computing Machinery.

Church, Alonzo. 1932. "A Set of Postulates for the Foundation of Logic." *Ann. Math.,* Second Series, 33 (2): 346–366.

Clarke, Keith. 1989. "One-Pass Code Generation Using Continuations." *Softw. Pract. Exper.* 19 (12): 1175–1192.

Collins, George E. 1960. "A Method for Overlapping and Erasure of Lists." *Commun. ACM* 3 (12): 655–657.

Cooper, Keith, and Linda Torczon. 2011. *Engineering a Compiler.* 2nd edition. Morgan Kaufmann.

Cooper, Keith D., and L. Taylor Simpson. 1998. "Live Range Splitting in a Graph Coloring Register Allocator." In *Compiler Construction: Proceedings of the 7th International Conference, CC '98, Held as Part of the Joint European Conferences on Theory and Practice of Software, ETAPS '98.* Lecture Notes in Computer Science 1383. Springer.

Cormen, Thomas H., Clifford Stein, Ronald L. Rivest, and Charles E. Leiserson. 2001. *Introduction to Algorithms.* McGraw-Hill Higher Education.

Cutler, Cody, and Robert Morris. 2015. "Reducing Pause Times with Clustered Collection." In *Proceedings of the 2015 International Symposium on Memory Management, ISMM '15,* 131–142. Association for Computing Machinery.

Danvy, Olivier. 1991. *Three Steps for the CPS Transformation.* Technical report CIS-92-02. Kansas State University.

Danvy, Olivier. 2003. "A New One-Pass Transformation into Monadic Normal Form." In *Compiler Construction: Proceedings of the 12th International Conference, CC '03, Held as Part of the Joint European Conferences on Theory and Practice of Software, ETAPS '03.* Lecture Notes in Computer Science 2622, 77–89. Springer.

DeRemer, Frank. 1969. "Practical Translators for LR(k) Languages." PhD diss., MIT.

Detlefs, David, Christine Flood, Steve Heller, and Tony Printezis. 2004. "Garbage-First Garbage Collection." In *Proceedings of the 4th International Symposium on Memory Management, ISMM '04,* 37–48. Association for Computing Machinery.

Dieckmann, Sylvia, and Urs Hölzle. 1999. "A Study of the Allocation Behavior of the SPECjvm98 Java Benchmark." In *Proceedings of the 13th European Conference on Object-Oriented Programming, ECOOP 1999,* Lecture Notes in Computer Science 1628, 92–115. Springer.

Dijkstra, E. W. 1982. *Why Numbering Should Start at Zero.* Technical report EWD831. University of Texas at Austin.

Diwan, Amer, Eliot Moss, and Richard Hudson. 1992. "Compiler Support for Garbage Collection in a Statically Typed Language." In *Proceedings of the ACM SIGPLAN 1992 Conference on Programming Language Design and Implementation, PLDI '92*, 273–282. Association for Computing Machinery.

Dunfield, Jana, and Neel Krishnaswami. 2021. "Bidirectional Typing." *ACM Comput. Surv.* 54 (5).

Dybvig, R. Kent. 1987a. *The Scheme Programming Language.* Prentice Hall.

Dybvig, R. Kent. 1987b. "Three Implementation Models for Scheme." PhD diss., University of North Carolina at Chapel Hill.

Dybvig, R. Kent. 2006. "The Development of Chez Scheme." In *Proceedings of the Eleventh ACM SIGPLAN International Conference on Functional Programming, ICFP '06*, 1–12. Association for Computing Machinery.

Dybvig, R. Kent, and Andrew Keep. 2010. *P523 Compiler Assignments.* Technical report. Indiana University.

Earley, Jay. 1970. "An efficient context-free parsing algorithm." *Commun. ACM* 13 (2): 94–102.

Felleisen, Matthias, M.D. Barski Conrad, David Van Horn, and Eight Students of Northeastern University. 2013. *Realm of Racket: Learn to Program, One Game at a Time!* No Starch Press.

Felleisen, Matthias, Robert Bruce Findler, Matthew Flatt, and Shriram Krishnamurthi. 2001. *How to Design Programs: An Introduction to Programming and Computing.* MIT Press.

Fischer, Michael J. 1972. "Lambda Calculus Schemata." In *Proceedings of ACM Conference on Proving Assertions about Programs*, 104–109. Association for Computing Machinery.

Flanagan, Cormac. 2006. "Hybrid Type Checking." In *Proceedings of the 33rd ACM SIGPLAN-SIGACT Symposium on Principles of Programming Languages, POPL '06*, 245–256. Association for Computing Machinery.

Flanagan, Cormac, Amr Sabry, Bruce F. Duba, and Matthias Felleisen. 1993. "The Essence of Compiling with Continuations." In *Proceedings of the ACM SIGPLAN 1993 Conference on Programming Language Design and Implementation, PLDI '93*, 502–514. Association for Computing Machinery.

Flatt, Matthew, Caner Derici, R. Kent Dybvig, Andrew W. Keep, Gustavo E. Massaccesi, Sarah Spall, Sam Tobin-Hochstadt, and Jon Zeppieri. 2019. "Rebuilding Racket on Chez Scheme (Experience Report)." *Proc. ACM Program. Lang., ICFP (August)* 3:1–15.

Flatt, Matthew, Robert Bruce Findler, and PLT. 2014. *The Racket Guide.* Technical report 6.0. PLT.

Flatt, Matthew, and PLT. 2014. *The Racket Reference 6.0.* Technical report. PLT. https://docs.racket-lang.org/reference/index.html.

Friedman, Daniel P., and Matthias Felleisen. 1996. *The Little Schemer.* 4th edition. MIT Press.

Friedman, Daniel P., Mitchell Wand, and Christopher T. Haynes. 2001. *Essentials of Programming Languages.* 2nd edition. MIT Press.

Friedman, Daniel P., and David S. Wise. 1976. *Cons Should Not Evaluate Its Arguments.* Technical report TR44. Indiana University.

Gamari, Ben, and Laura Dietz. 2020. "Alligator Collector: A Latency-Optimized Garbage Collector for Functional Programming Languages." In *Proceedings of the 2020 ACM SIGPLAN International Symposium on Memory Management, ISMM '20*, 87–99. Association for Computing Machinery.

George, Lal, and Andrew W. Appel. 1996. "Iterated Register Coalescing." *ACM Trans. Program. Lang. Syst.* 18 (3): 300–324.

Ghuloum, Abdulaziz. 2006. "An Incremental Approach to Compiler Construction." In *Scheme '06: Proceedings of the Workshop on Scheme and Functional Programming.* http://www.schemeworkshop.org/2006/.

Gilray, Thomas, Steven Lyde, Michael D. Adams, Matthew Might, and David Van Horn. 2016. "Pushdown Control-Flow Analysis for Free." In *Proceedings of the 43rd Annual ACM SIGPLAN-SIGACT Symposium on Principles of Programming Languages, POPL '16*, 691–704. Association for Computing Machinery.

Goldberg, Benjamin. 1991. "Tag-free Garbage Collection for Strongly Typed Programming Languages." In *Proceedings of the ACM SIGPLAN 1991 Conference on Programming Language Design and Implementation, PLDI '91,* 165–176. Association for Computing Machinery.

Gordon, M., R. Milner, L. Morris, M. Newey, and C. Wadsworth. 1978. "A Metalanguage for Interactive Proof in LCF." In *Proceedings of the 5th ACM SIGACT-SIGPLAN Symposium on Principles of Programming Languages, POPL '78,* 119–130. Association for Computing Machinery.

Gronski, Jessica, Kenneth Knowles, Aaron Tomb, Stephen N. Freund, and Cormac Flanagan. 2006. "Sage: Hybrid Checking for Flexible Specifications." In *Scheme '06: Proceedings of the Workshop on Scheme and Functional Programming,* 93–104. http://www.schemeworkshop.org/2006/.

Harper, Robert. 2016. *Practical Foundations for Programming Languages.* 2nd edition. Cambridge University Press.

Harper, Robert, and Greg Morrisett. 1995. "Compiling Polymorphism Using Intensional Type Analysis." In *Proceedings of the 22nd ACM SIGPLAN-SIGACT Symposium on Principles of Programming Languages, POPL '95,* 130–141. Association for Computing Machinery.

Hatcliff, John, and Olivier Danvy. 1994. "A Generic Account of Continuation-Passing Styles." In *Proceedings of the 21st ACM SIGPLAN-SIGACT Symposium on Principles of Programming Languages, POPL '94,* 458–471. Association for Computing Machinery.

Henderson, Fergus. 2002. "Accurate Garbage Collection in an Uncooperative Environment." In *Proceedings of the 3rd International Symposium on Memory Management, ISMM '02,* 150–156. Association for Computing Machinery.

Henglein, Fritz. 1994. "Dynamic Typing: Syntax and Proof Theory." *Science of Computer Programming* 22 (3): 197–230.

Herman, David, Aaron Tomb, and Cormac Flanagan. 2007. "Space-Efficient Gradual Typing." In *Trends in Functional Programming, TFP '07.*

Herman, David, Aaron Tomb, and Cormac Flanagan. 2010. "Space-Efficient Gradual Typing." *Higher-Order and Symbolic Computation* 23 (2): 167–189.

Hopcroft, John, Rajeev Motwani, and Jeffrey Ullman. 2006. *Introduction to Automata Theory, Languages, and Computation.* Pearson.

Horwitz, L. P., R. M. Karp, R. E. Miller, and S. Winograd. 1966. "Index Register Allocation." *J. ACM* 13 (1): 43–61.

Intel. 2015. *Intel 64 and IA-32 Architectures Software Developer's Manual Combined Volumes: 1, 2A, 2B, 2C, 3A, 3B, 3C and 3D.*

Jacek, Nicholas, and J. Eliot B. Moss. 2019. "Learning When to Garbage Collect with Random Forests." In *Proceedings of the 2019 ACM SIGPLAN International Symposium on Memory Management, ISMM '19,* 53–63. Association for Computing Machinery.

Johnson, Stephen C. 1979. "YACC: Yet Another Compiler-Compiler." In *UNIX Programmer's Manual,* 2:353–387. Holt, Rinehart, and Winston.

Jones, Neil D., Carsten K. Gomard, and Peter Sestoft. 1993. *Partial Evaluation and Automatic Program Generation.* Prentice Hall.

Jones, Richard, Antony Hosking, and Eliot Moss. 2011. *The Garbage Collection Handbook: The Art of Automatic Memory Management.* Chapman & Hall/CRC.

Jones, Richard, and Rafael Lins. 1996. *Garbage Collection: Algorithms for Automatic Dynamic Memory Management.* John Wiley & Sons.

Keep, Andrew W. 2012. "A Nanopass Framework for Commercial Compiler Development." PhD diss., Indiana University.

Keep, Andrew W., Alex Hearn, and R. Kent Dybvig. 2012. "Optimizing Closures in O(0)-time." In *Scheme '12: Proceedings of the Workshop on Scheme and Functional Programming.* Association for Computing Machinery.

Kelsey, R., W. Clinger, and J. Rees, eds. 1998. "Revised[5] Report on the Algorithmic Language Scheme." *Higher-Order and Symbolic Computation* 11 (1).

Kempe, A. B. 1879. "On the Geographical Problem of the Four Colours." *American Journal of Mathematics* 2 (3): 193–200.

Kernighan, Brian W., and Dennis M. Ritchie. 1988. *The C Programming Language*. Prentice Hall.

Kildall, Gary A. 1973. "A Unified Approach to Global Program Optimization." In *Proceedings of the 1st Annual ACM SIGACT-SIGPLAN Symposium on Principles of Programming Languages, POPL '73*, 194–206. Association for Computing Machinery.

Kleene, S. 1952. *Introduction to Metamathematics*. Van Nostrand.

Knuth, Donald E. 1964. "Backus Normal Form vs. Backus Naur Form." *Commun. ACM* 7 (12): 735–736.

Kuhlenschmidt, Andre, Deyaaeldeen Almahallawi, and Jeremy G. Siek. 2019. "Toward Efficient Gradual Typing for Structural Types via Coercions." In *Proceedings of the ACM SIGPLAN 2019 Conference on Programming Language Design and Implementation, PLDI '19*. Association for Computing Machinery.

Lawall, Julia L., and Olivier Danvy. 1993. "Separating Stages in the Continuation-Passing Style Transformation." In *Proceedings of the 20th ACM SIGPLAN-SIGACT Symposium on Principles of Programming Languages, POPL '93*, 124–136. Association for Computing Machinery.

Lehtosalo, Jukka. 2021. *MyPy Optional Type Checker for Python*. http://mypy-lang.org/.

Leroy, Xavier. 1992. "Unboxed Objects and Polymorphic Typing." In *Proceedings of the 19th ACM SIGPLAN-SIGACT Symposium on Principles of Programming Languages, POPL '92*, 177–188. Association for Computing Machinery.

Lesk, M. E., and E. Schmidt. 1975. *Lex - A Lexical Analyzer Generator*. Technical report. Bell Laboratories, July.

Lieberman, Henry, and Carl Hewitt. 1983. "A Real-Time Garbage Collector Based on the Lifetimes of Objects." *Commun. ACM* 26 (6): 419–429.

Liskov, Barbara. 1993. "A History of CLU." In *The Second ACM SIGPLAN Conference on History of Programming Languages, HOPL-II*, 133–147. Association for Computing Machinery.

Liskov, Barbara, Russ Atkinson, Toby Bloom, Eliot Moss, Craig Schaffert, Bob Scheifler, and Alan Snyder. 1979. *CLU Reference Manual*. Technical report LCS-TR-225. MIT.

Logothetis, George, and Prateek Mishra. 1981. "Compiling Short-Circuit Boolean Expressions in One Pass." *Software: Practice and Experience* 11 (11): 1197–1214.

Lutz, Mark. 2013. *Learning Python*. 5th edition. O'Reilly.

Matthes, Eric. 2019. *Python Crash Course*. 2nd edition. No Starch Press.

Matthews, Jacob, and Robert Bruce Findler. 2007. "Operational Semantics for Multi-Language Programs." In *Proceedings of the 34th ACM SIGPLAN-SIGACT Symposium on Principles of Programming Languages, POPL '07*. Association for Computing Machinery.

Matula, David W., George Marble, and Joel D. Isaacson. 1972. "Graph Coloring Algorithms." In *Graph Theory and Computing*, 109–122. Academic Press.

Matz, Michael, Jan Hubicka, Andreas Jaeger, and Mark Mitchell. 2013. *System V Application Binary Interface, AMD64 Architecture Processor Supplement*. Linux Foundation.

McCarthy, John. 1960. "Recursive Functions of Symbolic Expressions and their Computation by Machine, Part I." *Commun. ACM* 3 (4): 184–195.

Microsoft. 2018. *x64 Architecture*. https://docs.microsoft.com/en-us/windows-hardware/drivers/debugger/x64-architecture.

Microsoft. 2020. *x64 Calling Convention*. https://docs.microsoft.com/en-us/cpp/build/x64-calling-convention.

Milner, Robin, Mads Tofte, and Robert Harper. 1990. *The Definition of Standard ML*. MIT Press.

Minamide, Yasuhiko, Greg Morrisett, and Robert Harper. 1996. "Typed Closure Conversion." In *Proceedings of the 23rd ACM SIGPLAN-SIGACT Symposium on Principles of Programming Languages, POPL '96*, 271–283. Association for Computing Machinery.

Moggi, Eugenio. 1991. "Notions of Computation and Monads." *Inf. Comput.* 93 (1): 55–92.

Moore, E.F. 1959. "The Shortest Path Through a Maze." In *Proceedings of an International Symposium on the Theory of Switching*. Harvard University Press.

Morrison, R., A. Dearle, R. C. H. Connor, and A. L. Brown. 1991. "An Ad Hoc Approach to the Implementation of Polymorphism." *ACM Trans. Program. Lang. Syst.* 13 (3): 342–371.

Österlund, Erik, and Welf Löwe. 2016. "Block-Free Concurrent GC: Stack Scanning and Copying." In *Proceedings of the 2016 ACM SIGPLAN International Symposium on Memory Management, ISMM '16,* 1–12. Association for Computing Machinery.

Palsberg, Jens. 2007. "Register Allocation via Coloring of Chordal Graphs." In *Proceedings of the Thirteenth Australasian Symposium on Theory of Computing,* 3–3. Australian Computer Society.

Peyton Jones, Simon L., and André L. M. Santos. 1998. "A Transformation-Based Optimiser for Haskell." *Science of Computer Programming* 32 (1): 3–47.

Pierce, Benjamin C. 2002. *Types and Programming Languages.* MIT Press.

Pierce, Benjamin C., ed. 2004. *Advanced Topics in Types and Programming Languages.* MIT Press.

Pierce, Benjamin C., Arthur Azevedo de Amorim, Chris Casinghino, Marco Gaboardi, Michael Greenberg, Cătălin Hriţcu, Vilhelm Sjöberg, Andrew Tolmach, and Brent Yorgey. 2018. *Programming Language Foundations.* Vol. 2. Software Foundations. Electronic textbook. https://softwarefoundations.cis.upenn.edu/plf-current/index.html.

Pierce, Benjamin C., and David N. Turner. 2000. "Local Type Inference." *ACM Trans. Program. Lang. Syst.* 22 (1): 1–44.

Plotkin, G. D. 1975. "Call-by-Name, Call-by-Value and the Lambda-Calculus." *Theoretical Computer Science* 1 (2): 125–159.

Poletto, Massimiliano, and Vivek Sarkar. 1999. "Linear Scan Register Allocation." *ACM Trans. Program. Lang. Syst.* 21 (5): 895–913.

Python Software Foundation. 2021a. *Python GitHub Repository.* Python Software Foundation. https://github.com/python.

Python Software Foundation. 2021b. *The Python Language Reference.* Python Software Foundation.

Reynolds, John C. 1972. "Definitional Interpreters for Higher-Order Programming Languages." In *ACM '72: Proceedings of the ACM Annual Conference,* 717–740. Association for Computing Machinery.

Rosen, Kenneth H. 2002. *Discrete Mathematics and Its Applications.* McGraw-Hill Higher Education.

Russell, Stuart J., and Peter Norvig. 2003. *Artificial Intelligence: A Modern Approach.* 2nd ed. Pearson Education.

Sarkar, Dipanwita, Oscar Waddell, and R. Kent Dybvig. 2004. "A Nanopass Infrastructure for Compiler Education." In *Proceedings of the Ninth ACM SIGPLAN International Conference on Functional Programming, ICFP '04,* 201–212. Association for Computing Machinery.

Shahriyar, Rifat, Stephen M. Blackburn, Xi Yang, and Kathryn M. McKinley. 2013. "Taking Off the Gloves with Reference Counting Immix." In *Proceedings of the 24th ACM SIGPLAN Conference on Object Oriented Programming Systems Languages and Applications, OOPSLA '13.* Association for Computing Machinery.

Shidal, Jonathan, Ari J. Spilo, Paul T. Scheid, Ron K. Cytron, and Krishna M. Kavi. 2015. "Recycling Trash in Cache." In *Proceedings of the 2015 International Symposium on Memory Management, ISMM '15,* 118–130. Association for Computing Machinery.

Shinan, Erez. 2020. *Welcome to Lark's Documentation!* https://lark-parser.readthedocs.io/en/latest/index.html.

Shivers, O. 1988. "Control Flow Analysis in Scheme." In *Proceedings of the ACM SIGPLAN 1988 Conference on Programming Language Design and Implementation, PLDI '88,* 164–174. Association for Computing Machinery.

Siebert, Fridtjof. 2001. "Constant-Time Root Scanning for Deterministic Garbage Collection." In *Proceedings of Compiler Construction: 10th International Conference, CC 2001, Held as Part of the Joint European Conferences on Theory and Practice of Software, ETAPS '01,* edited by Reinhard Wilhelm, 304–318. Springer.

Siek, Jeremy G., and Walid Taha. 2006. "Gradual Typing for Functional Languages." In *Scheme '06: Proceedings of the Workshop on Scheme and Functional Programming,* 81–92. http://www.schemeworkshop.org/2006/.

Siek, Jeremy G., Peter Thiemann, and Philip Wadler. 2015. "Blame and Coercion: Together Again for the First Time." In *Proceedings of the ACM SIGPLAN 2015 Conference on Programming Language Design and Implementation, PLDI '15*. Association for Computing Machinery.

Sperber, Michael, R. Kent Dybvig, Matthew Flatt, Anton van Straaten, Robby Findler, and Jacob Matthews. 2009. "Revised[6] Report on the Algorithmic Language Scheme." *Journal of Functional Programming* 19:1–301.

Steele, Guy L. 1977. *Data Representations in PDP-10 MacLISP*. AI Memo 420. MIT Artificial Intelligence Lab.

Steele, Guy L. 1978. *Rabbit: A Compiler for Scheme*. Technical report. MIT.

Stroustrup, Bjarne. 1988. "Parameterized Types for C++." In *Proceedings of the USENIX C++ Conference*. USENIX.

Sweigart, Al. 2019. *Automate the Boring Stuff with Python*. No Starch Press.

Tene, Gil, Balaji Iyengar, and Michael Wolf. 2011. "C4: The Continuously Concurrent Compacting Collector." In *Proceedings of the International Symposium on Memory Management, ISMM '11*, 79–88. Association for Computing Machinery.

Tobin-Hochstadt, Sam, and Matthias Felleisen. 2006. "Interlanguage Migration: From Scripts to Programs." In *Companion to the 21st ACM SIGPLAN Conference on Object Oriented Programming Systems Languages and Applications (Dynamic Languages Symposium), DLS '06*. Association for Computing Machinery.

Tomita, Masaru. 1985. *Efficient Parsing for Natural Language: A Fast Algorithm for Practical Systems*. Kluwer Academic.

Ungar, David. 1984. "Generation Scavenging: A Non-Disruptive High Performance Storage Reclamation Algorithm." In *Proceedings of the First ACM SIGSOFT/SIGPLAN Software Engineering Symposium on Practical Software Development Environments, SDE 1*, 157–167. Association for Computing Machinery.

van Wijngaarden, Adriaan. 1966. "Recursive Definition of Syntax and Semantics." In *Formal Language Description Languages for Computer Programming*, edited by T. B. Steel Jr., 13–24. North-Holland.

Wadler, Philip, and Robert Bruce Findler. 2009. "Well-Typed Programs Can't Be Blamed." In *Proceedings of Programming Languages and Systems, 31st European Symposium on Programming, ESOP '09, Held as Part of the Joint European Conferences on Theory and Practice of Software, ETAPS '09*, edited by Giuseppe Castagna, 1–16. Springer.

Weeks, Stephen. 2006. "Whole-Program Compilation in MLton." In *Proceedings of the 2006 Workshop on ML '06*, 1. Association for Computing Machinery.

Wilson, Paul. 1992. "Uniprocessor Garbage Collection Techniques. Lecture Notes in Computer Science 637." In *Memory Management*, edited by Yves Bekkers and Jacques Cohen, 1–42. Springer.

Index